D1882433

INDIA'S TRADE WITH JAPAN

INDIA'S TRADE WITH JAPAN

CONSTRAINTS AND OPPORTUNITIES

A Study in Trade and Investment

ABRAHAM JOSEPH

GIAN PUBLISHING HOUSE
DELHI-110007

GIAN PUBLISHING HOUSE
29/6 SHAKTI NAGAR, DELHI-110 007

© 1988, DR. ABRAHAM JOSEPH

ISBN 81-212-0109-8

PRINTED IN INDIA

Published by Mrs. Gayatri Garg for Gian Publishing House, Delhi-110007 and Printed at Suman Printers, Delhi-110 053

Dedicated to

Dr. Saburo Okita

who inspired me most for working towards promotion of greater Indo-Japanese economic cooperation.

PREFACE

ECONOMIC growth of the Japanese economy in the post-war era has been an internal as well as external phenomenon. The external sector of the economy has played a pivotal role in the process. Low self-sufficiency in critical industrial inputs and consistent technology transfer has made the Japanese economic growth to be highly dependent on imports. Exports on the other hand have enabled the economy to build a productive capacity over domestic consumption to attain economies of scale.

The economic growth in Japan since the late 1950s accompanied a structural transformation in the economy. Resource and industrialisation efforts have been increasingly allocated to the heavy and chemical industrial sector than to the light industries. By 1980s, technology intensive sector has been given the utmost importance in industrial growth. The structural change in the economy has led to change in its pattern of trade with the world.

Newly industrialised countries (NICs) of Asia took this opportunity in diversifying and expanding exports to Japan. Their export drive to Japan has been often supported by technology transfer and direct investments from it. The volume and composition of these exports to Japan underwent drastic change.

However this was not the case for India. Though the value of India's trade with Japan increased over years, India's share in Japan's foreign trade declined. More significantly, the bulk of India's exports to Japan continued to be contributed by a few non-manufactures such as iron-ore, raw cotton and marine products. From the point of view of stabilization of export earnings in the long run and industrialisation through exports, it is only advisable to diversify the export structure by stepping up exports of manufactures.

Even though Japan's import of manufactures had provided opportunities for India's exports, certain unfavourable factors had militated against diversification. In this study, I will focus on those factors responsible for the low growth of manufactures to Japan. Internal barriers are identified as factors affecting India's manufactured exports to Japan. Unless these barriers are eliminated, it will be difficult for India to compete effectively in Japan, no matter how low levels of protection may be.

India's export constraints to Japan emanates from the fact that hitherto considerations of increasing exports on an enduring basis have not received adequate attention since the evolution of India's economic and industrial policies. The policies, no doubt, resulted in considerable expansion and diversification of industrial base but in the process consideration of cost and comparative efficiency have often been given inadequate attention.

I hope that the findings and conclusions of this study will be of some use to those who are keen watchers of the developments of India-Japan trade, technology transfer and investment co-operation. Also, I should be happy if this study were to inspire other researchers to proceed still further in an effort to deepen understanding of the whole gamut of India-Japan economic co-operation.

ACKNOWLEDGEMENTS

THIS publication is a revised and updated version of my Ph.D. thesis. Several of my teachers, colleagues and friends both in India and Japan contributed a lot in preparation and finalisation of the manuscript of this study.

First of all, with a deep sense of appreciation, I express my indebtedness to Dr. Saburo Okita, Chairman, Japan Economic Research Center, Tokyo for his advice and kind guidance. Despite his busy schedule he could spare time and made the most valuable suggestions which were of great use in building a theoritical framework in the study. My profound gratitute is also equally due to Prof. Sueo Sekiguchi, Osaka University, Osaka, for his constructive comments which were of immense use in the initial stages of the research.

I am beholden to Dr. Manmohan Singh, Deputy Chairman, Planning Commission for inspiration and support in pursuing my specialisation. I am extremely grateful to Prof. A.M. Khusro, former Vice-Chancellor of the Aligarh Muslim University and former Chairman of the Indo-Japan Study Committee in his capacity as Member of Indian Planning Commission and currently Chairman, National Institute of Public Finance and Policy, New Delhi, for giving useful comments and for continuous encouragement in undertaking this study. I am also grateful to Prof. Idris Qureshi, who provided helpful criticisms at various stages of the work. I am personally grateful to Mr. Gopal Behari, Director (Research), MRTP, Ministry of Industry, Government of India, for guidance in spearheading this publication.

I wish to record my deep gratitute to Mr. N.S. Choudhry, Executive Director, Indian Investment Centre (IIC), Mr. P.S. Bhatnagar, Secretary, IIC, Mr. P.G. Mankad, Joint Secretary (Investments), Ministry of Finance, Mr. V.N. Channa, Minister (Economic, Commercial and Investment), Embassy of India. Tokyo, Mr. K.P. Singh, Resident Director, IIC, London, Mr. Ashok Chawla, Deputy Secrctary (Investments), Ministry of Finance, Mrs. Veena Upadhyaya, Deputy Secretary, Ministry of Finance, Dr. V.G. Bhatia, Adviser, Planning Commission, and Mr. M.K. Ghoshal, Economic Adviser, IIC for their encourage ment in my research endeavour.

I acknowledge my friend Dr. Rahmatulla who devoted considerable time and energy going over my drafts that preceded the final version. My special debt to the assistance extended by Ms. Anjali V. Patil at United Nations Headquarters, New York. I am grateful to Mr. Attar Chand for arranging for its publication. Mr. L.D. Ajmani deserves my appreciation his care and efficiency in skilfully typing out this manuscript.

The Indian Council of Social Sciences Research, New Delhi and Japan Foundation, Tokyo, played a fundamental role by award of fellowships to undertake research both in India and Japan.

Last but not the least my thanks to criticisms and assistance given by my wife, Takako Hamaguchi, Indiana University, Bloomington, USA.

However, all final decisions of the manuscript were taken by me and thus any remaining errors or shortcomings are mine.

A word of appreciation to M/s. Gian Publishers, Delhi who took pains in bringing out the book in a short span of time.

CONTENTS

Preface *vii*

Acknowledgements *ix*

CHAPTER 1

Significance of India's Trade with Japan **1—12**

The Problem 1

Factors affecting India's Trade Growth to Japan 5

Methodology 7

Source of Data 10

Plan of Study 11

CHAPTER 2

International Trade and Economic Growth in India **13—27**

Trading in a Traditional Framework 13

Diversification with Manufactured Exports 18

Export Sector in India's Economic Growth 20

Trading in a New Framework 24

CHAPTER 3

Export of Non-Manufactures to Japan:
Some Issues During 1951-73 **28—68**

Retrospect of India-Japan Trade Development 28

Analysis of India's Non-Manufactured Exports 44

Iron-Ore Development and Export Trend to Japan 45
Export constraints to Japan 48
Policy on iron-ore export 50
Issues in iron-ore export development 51
Shrimp Fishery Development and Export Trend to Japan 53
Export constraints to Japan 57
Policy for shrimp export 59
Issues in shrimp export development 60
Barriers for Future Export Growth to Japan 61

CHAPTER 4

Effect of Cost Structure and Productivity Differentials on Japan's Propensity to Import Indian Sourced Manufactures 69—125

Cotton Textile Industry: Production and Export Trend 70
Handtools Industry: Production and Export Trend 74
Trend in Japan's Import of Manufactures 78
Japan's cotton textile industry and imports from India 78
Japan's handtools industry and imports from India 81
Competitiveness of India's Manufactures in Japan 84
Ganko keitai growth model 84
Ganko keitai growth in the international economy 87
Ganko keitai growth of cotton fabrics and handtools industries 90
Cost Structure and Productivity in Manufacturing Industries 97
Cost effectiveness in the cotton textile manufacturing industry 102
Cost effectiveness in handtools industry 110
Determinants for stimulating Trade-Growth to Japan 115

CHAPTER 5

Policy Directions of India and Japan towards Trade Growth 126—153

India's Export Policies for Manufactures 127
India's incentive scheme for manufactured exports 129
Policy direction for cotton textile export growth 131
Policy direction for handtools export growth 133
Japan's Trade Liberalisation Measures 134
Japan's GSP scheme for import from developing countries 138
Harmonisation of Trade Policies 142
Evolving Policies with Changing Environment 146

CHAPTER 6
Epilogue: Trade Growth and Manufactured Exports to Japan after 1973 **154—205**
Post-Oil Crisis and India's Comparative Advantage 156
Export Trend of Non-Manufactures 157
Iron ore industry and export trend 158
Development in frozen shrimp industry and export trend 161
Export Trend of Manufactures 164
Growth of cotton textile industry and export trend 164
Growth of handtools industry and export trend 169
Cost Structure and Productivity in Manufacturing Industries 173
Cost effectiveness in cotton textile manufacturing industry 175
Cost effectiveness in handtools manufacturing industry 184
Efficiency factor with respect to capital cost 187
Development in Policy Environment for India's Export to Japan 189
India's Trade and Industrial Policies fr Export Growth 189
Japan's Policies for import of Manufactures 194
Japan's Trade Policy Changes in 1980s 197

Technology Induction Policies for Manufacturing Industries 199

CHAPTER 7

Japan's Technology Transfer and Investment in India's Industrial and Foreign Trade Development **206—230**

Principal Findings 207

Widening India's Production Base for Manufactured Exports 209

Major Industrial Policy Changes in 1980s 210

Technology Transfer and Foreign Investment as Catalyst for Trade Development 213

Trade Linked Investment 215

Foreign Investment Policy of India 216

India-Japan Industrial Collaborations 219

Perspective of Trading in Technologies and Commodities 223

Bibliography 231

Index 243

1

SIGNIFICANCE OF INDIA'S TRADE WITH JAPAN

The Problem

INDIA'S constraint in foreign exchange reserves has become one of the major problems in its economic development especially since the Second Five Year Plan. There have been signs in the Indian economy of a foreign exchange crisis owing to the increasing burden of debt servicing. According to the estimate of the World Bank Report on India of 1985,[1] the debt servicing ratio standing at about 15.5 per cent in the fiscal year 1984-85, is to rise to over 20 per cent by 1987-88.

The prediction is based on the two important assumptions. Firstly, there will be a decline in growth of the flow of concessional loans which India has mainly relied on for its foreign assistance requirements. The net flow of such loans, which is considered to reach the peak in 1985-86, is expected to remain in the same level of Rs. 1.8 thousand million per annum in the subsequent years. The decline in availability of concessional loans is attributed to the prolonged economic protectionism in the aid-giving developed countries.

The Report also takes into account the flow of institutional non-concessional loans, such as project-linked lending, that is expected to grow at 16 per cent per annum during the period of next five years. However, the impact of the decline in the non-concessional loan flow is not likely to be neutralised by it. The share of non-concessional loans in the net transfer has decreased from about 60 per cent in 1982-83 to around 45 per cent by 1985. As for the uncovered gap in the requirements by foreign assistance of institutional loans, India has to go for borrowing on commercial terms.

Under such circumstances, commercial loans would be a more important content in India's foreign assistance flow to India. Increasing reliance on commercial loans, however, is not a desirable phenomenon to India's economy. To cope with the problem in its balance of payments and external debts, it is imperative for India to take measures to accumulate foreign exchange reserves in the short run, such as by export promotion along with the long run strategies to enhance the self-sufficiency in domestic financial resources by accelerating economic growth.[2]

Particularly in recent years, export promotion has become increasingly important to India's economic growth. It has been envisaged in the current Seventh Five Year Plan (1985-86 to 1990-91) that in order to sustain the GDP growth rate of 5 per cent per annum, the current account deficit in India's balance of payments will reach Rs. 220 billion over the plan period. This assumes that the export growth of 13-14 per cent per annum in value terms, which is considered to be higher compared to that achieved in the recent past. The rate of export growth per annum between 1977-78 and 1983-84 was 10.3 per cent. Based on these estimates on the current account, it is hoped to contain the debt-service ratio within a manageable 20 per cent during the plan period. In other words, failing to achieve the export growth envisaged, India's debt-servicing would be on 'the explosive path', as has been warned in the same Report by the World Bank.

Against this backdrop of the Indian economy, it has been observed that India's share in the world trade has declined over years (see Table 1.1). It indicates that India has not been able to keep up with the pace of expansion of the world trade. A similar trend has been seen in India's trade with Japan. Japan made steady inroads in India's foreign trade and has become one of its largest trade partners since the late 1960s among the countries like the U.S.A., the U.K. and the U.S.S.R. (see Table 1.2). On

TABLE 1.1

India's Share in World Trade (%)

Year	*Exports*	*Imports*
1950	2.06	2.00
1955	1.36	1.38
1960	1.04	1.72
1965	0.90	1.15
1970	0.73	0.75
1975	0.49	0.70
1980	0.41	0.68
1982	0.49	0.78

Source : United Nations, *International Trade Statistics Yearbook 1983*, Vol. 1 (New York, 1985).

the other hand, India has not been able to keep up with the rapid expansion of Japan's foreign trade and its share in Japan's trade has registered a decline (see Table 1.3).

It is reasonable to expect that as two of the major Asian economies, economic interaction through trade between India and Japan could have been at a much higher level. Japan, which had attained double-digit rates of economic growth in the 1960s, engaged in adjusting its industrial structure to make a smooth entry into the new era of industrialisation based on the knowledge-intensive technology. On other hand, India's economy which was based on agriculture, has undergone the process of industrialisation based on its resource endowments since the Second Five Year Plan (1956-57 to 1961-62). India, at the same time, has been facing a problem of raising adequate resources for investment to sustain the economic growth.

The central issue of the bilateral trade growth between India and Japan lies basically in India's capacity to promote exports to Japan.[3] As Japan's capacity to export is highly sensitive to the demand of the world market while its import demand being large and diversified, expansion of India-Japan trade is

TABLE 1.2

India's Trade with Major Countries

(% of total value)

Year	*Japan*		*U.S.A.*		*U.K.*		*U.S.S.R.*	
	Import	*Export*	*Import*	*Export*	*Import*	*Export*	*Import*	*Export*
1955	4.7	5.0	12.6	14.1	24.4	27.0	0.9	0.5
1960	5.5	5.5	19.6	15.7	20.1	26.4	1.4	4.5
1965	5.7	7.1	38.7	18.3	10.9	18.0	6.0	11.6
1970	12.8	13.9	28.6	13.5	6.3	11.6	7.8	13.4
1975	8.1	10.3	22.4	11.1	5.1	9.5	4.1	11.7
1980	5.0	9.7	11.5	11.3	5.3	6.1	4.0	16.8
1983	9.3	10.6	11.9	21.9	7.9	5.2	5.2	9.4

Source : United Nations, *Yearbook of International Trade Statistics* (New York), from various issues.

more or less upto India's initiative in increasing export and changing the structure of exports to Japan.

TABLE 1.3
India's Share in Japan's Trade
(% of total value)

Year	*India*		*India's Share in Japan's Trade with Asia*	
	Exports	*Imports*	*Exports*	*Imports*
1955	4.2	3.1	10.0	8.5
1960	2.7	2.8	7.5	9.2
1965	2.4	2.3	7.4	6.9
1970	0.5	2.1	1.6	7.1
1975	0.8	1.1	2.6	2.5
1980	0.7	0.7	1.8	1.3
1983	0.7	0.8	2.6	1.7

Source : Ministry of International Trade and Industry, *White Paper on International Trade* (Tokyo), from various issues.

Factors affecting India's Trade Growth to Japan

Non-manufactures are those which a developing economy can provide for exporting at the initial stage of development. It is often argued that a high content of non-manufactures in the export structure is an unfavourable factor to stabilisation and growth of the developing economy. Wide fluctuations in commodity prices make overall export earnings of the developing economy unstable. Moreover, the world demand for non-manufactures is bound to shrink owing to their low income-elasticities and the development of synthetic substitutes.

The diversification of exports by expanding manufactured exports, therefore, has been of importance, as it brings to a developing economy increasing benefits. The policy of export promotion of manufactures is usually kept in line with the programme for industrialisation in developing economies, since expansion of manufactured exports has favourable effects on economic growth. It is also useful vehicle in improving the resource allocation according to comparative advantage. The effects include the improvement of efficiency by the effective exploitation of economies of scale and the greater specialisation in production. In short manufacturing, sector today is considered as 'locomotive industry' for economic growth in developing countries.

An overview of the trend in the economies of India and Japan in the post-war period indicates various opportunities for expansion and diversification of their bilateral trade. The Indian economy, which has largely been based on agriculture, intensified the process of industrialisation after the introduction of Five Year Plans. In the course of time, the external sector has also become increasingly important. As a major part of the critical requirements for industrialisation, capital goods and technology have been imported consistently throughout the industrialisation. In turn, exports have been considered to be vital for financing such imports with their foreign exchange earnings.

On the other hand, Japan developed into one of the largest economies of the world in the post-war era, achieving high rates of economic growth. The traits of 'semi-backwardness' in the economy, such as abundant labour supply and the existence of the traditional sector, that survived the early stage of industrialisation in the pre-war period and the period subsequent to the war, contributed a great deal to the economic growth in the 1950s and 1960s, as comparative advantage.

Japan's economic growth has been an internal as well as external phenomenon. The external sector of the economy has been playing a vital role in the development. Low self-sufficiency in industrial materials and consistent updation of technology oriented the Japanese economy to be highly dependent on imports. The production expansion has not been planned only towards internal consumption, but also towards the world markets. Thus, as Japan's economic growth has been closely dependent on the international economic environment, so the growth has had a certain impact on the international economy.

One of the important impact of Japan's economic growth on the world economy has been the transmission of the structural changes in the Japanese economy, which has propagated the evolution of the international division of labour. Japan's economic growth has accompanied a drastic change in its economic structure, which resulted in the emphasis on the manufacturing sector. The manufacturing sector has become the most important sector in the economy with regard to its magnitude in terms of national income and the dynamic role played in the transformation of the economic structure. Accompanying the above change, the emphasis on growth within the manufacturing sector has shifted from the light labour-intensive sector to capital-intensive sector.

As the industrialisation made progress and the light manufacturing industries gave way to the heavy and chemical industries with regard to productivity and the level of the production, Japan enhanced imports of the light manufactures which were insignificant in volume until then. The expansion of Japan's imports of light manufactures stimulated the development of the industries of the developing countries in Far East and Southeast Asia. In these countries, with the policies directed to the growth of light manufactures and, in certain cases, with investment and technology transfer from Japan, the industries achieved high rates of growth in production and export. Compared to the growth and export performance of Far East and Southeast Asian countries to Japan, the light manufactured exports from India to Japan remained at a low level.

Although the level of the competing industries of India's and other developing countries were in the process of catching up for export expansion, certain differences were observed with regard to their respective export performance in the Japanese market. In this study, the differences are attempted to be explained by the variation in competitiveness in terms of the production efficiency existing between these industries of India and other exporting countries to Japan.

The problems in export growth of India's manufactures to Japan can be explained by the constraints in the industrial structure and the organisation of India's manufacturing sector as a whole. Like other developing countries, policies to facilitate and encourage investment and technology transfer to the manufacturing industries were necessary for stimulating higher export growth.

Methodology

The trend in the world economy since the 1960s may be

termed 'transitional growth',[4] that has been typically experienced in the newly industrialised countries which changed the traditional pattern of trade between primary-producing peripheral countries and industrial growth-center countries, into that among the continuous spectrum of countries, each in the process of catching-up and overtaking the other. The structure of comparative advantage in such a situation can only be explained by the composition of production and the 'quality' of productive factors. This version of comparative advantage is more useful in analysing the fierce competition emerging in the world markets.[5]

With the help of the concept of the Ganko Keitai Growth Model developed by K. Akamatsu, the level of industrialisation of the export industries of India, Japan and the competitors in the Japanese market are examined. The model formulates the process of the catching-up and overtaking in an industrial sector of a technologically less advanced country with advanced countries through trade. The entire growth process of the industry of the former is divided into four stages, that is, import stage, import substitution stage, export expansion stage and re-import stage. In the initial stage of import, the production technology is learned and the pressure of the domestic demand is created from imports, which will give an impetus for setting up the domestic production towards the next stage of import substitution.

If the industry succeeds to expand production over domestic consumption, it is ready for the third stage of the export promotion. Whether or not the industry reaches this stage from the earlier stage depends on how much the industry can expand production in excess to the consumption in domestic markets. The production expansion is feasible only when large investment is made to establish the economies of scale. On the other hand, the diminishing returns to scale start to operate, when the production exceeds the optimum scale and the production efficiency and eventually the level of production will be affected in this process. The last stage of the Ganko Keitai Growth, that of re-import, is reached when the product starts to be imported, so that the decline in the level of production is compensated for.

Dynamism of the Ganko Keitai Growth lies in the trend of

production efficiency implied in the scale of production. The improvement of competitiveness in the import substitution and the export expansion stages of the Ganko Keitai Growth is explained by an increase in production efficiency accompanying the production expansion, which in turn gives an incentive to further expansion of production and exports. Similarly, a decline in productivity arising when an industry passes the peak of expansion in the transit from the export expansion stage to the re-import stage, is supposed to a fall in competitiveness of the industry.

Difference in the performance of India's manufacturing industries and other economies that export to Japan can be interpreted as the difference in competitiveness of the industries among them, resulting alternatively from efficiency achieved in production by them. Improvement in competitiveness by reduction in cost can be realised by reducing factor prices such as wages and prices of raw materials and by increasing productivity with respect to various inputs such as output per worker and output-input ratio.

The production efficiency of an industry can be measured in a way by the cost of the product which the industry produces. However, measurement of the production efficiency by cost would not be practically possible since the specifications adopted for a single product item differ from product to product and the classifications of the manufacturing industry in the industrial statistics vary from country to country.

The study takes up the examination of the trend of major components of the efficiency of an industry, which enables to identify the sources of perceived phenomenon in the efficiency as well as to determine their overall effect that lead to a rise or fall in the cost on the whole. By disaggregating the production cost into three major components (short-run variable cost), that is, material input cost (n), wages (w) and depreciation cost (r), the efficiency is based on the three components of the cost, that is efficiency-material cost $\frac{n}{(O/R)}$, efficiency-wages $(\frac{w}{O/L})$ and efficiency-capital cost $(\frac{r}{O/K})$, which are obtained by deflating material input cost, wages and depreciation cost by output-input ratio (O/R), labour productivity (O/L) and output-capital ratio (O/K). A rise or fall in the production efficiency factors contributes to the changes in the overall efficiency of the production.

Taking up the case of the manufacturing industries of India, Japan, South Korea and the United States, the study examines: (1) the changes in wage cost and material cost per unit of product, (2) the changes in labour productivity and output-input ratio, and (3) the changes combined those in (1) and (2) by deflating the former by the latter, viz., the changes in the efficiency-wages and the efficiency-material cost.

Source of Data

The period under investigation of this study refers between 1951 and 1985, which is divided into two sub-periods. The first-sub period from 1951 to 1973 that is before the first oil crisis. During this period, the Japanese economy recovered from the setback in the World War II and achieved the average annual rate of the real GNP growth over 10 per cent in the 1960s. The Indian economy, on the other hand, was engaged in building foundation of industrialisation in this period.

The later sub-period of 1974 onwards is marked with the two oil crises in the international economy. Japan was the hardest-hit among OECD countries by the first crisis in 1973 and suffered from severe inflation and negative GNP growth in real terms. The adjustments that followed in the subsequent years oriented the economy more to stabilization of the growth, though export growth continued to be steady. India's annual rate of export volume growth averaged at 3.4 per cent in the 1960s rose to 7.8 per cent in 1971-72 to 1977-78, and reduced to 4.2 per cent in 1977-78 to 1983-84.

The data for this study have been collected from various sources and there were certain difficulty in adjustment on uniform basis. Some of the important sources consulted are listed below.[6] For the statistics regarding foreign trade, *Commodity Trade Statistics* and *Yearbook of International Trade* of the United Nations have been referred to, which are compiled under the Standard International Trade Classification (SITC). Some of the data pertaining to India's and Japan's trade were collected from *Monthly Statistics of Foreign Trade of India*, Department of Commercial Intelligence and Statistics, Government of India and *White Paper on International Trade*, Japan External Trade Organization, Ministry of International Trade and Industry of the Japanese Government, respectively.

For the industrial statistics of India and Japan, the publications consulted were *Annual Survey of Industries*, Central Statistical Organisations, Ministry of Planning, Government of India, and *Census of Manufacture—Report by Industries*, Ministry of International Trade and Industry of the Japanese Government. Some of India's sector-wise industrial statistics on iron ore, shrimps, cotton fabrics and handtools industries were collected respectively from *Indian Mineral Yearbook*, Indian Bureau of Mines, Ministry of Steel and Mines, Government of India; *Yearbook of Fishery Statistics*, Food and Agricultural Organization, United Nations; *Indian Textile Bulletin*, Textile Commissioner, Government of India; and *Handbook of Export Statistics*, Engineering Export Promotion Council of India.

Plan of Study

The study is divided into seven chapters. In chapter one, the constraints with respect to India's trade with Japan in post-war period are introduced. Chapter two presents the justification for India to diversify export structure particularly taking advantage of the manufacturing sector considered as 'locomotive industry' for trade and economic growth. Chapter three analysis India's trade growth with Japan and their composition of exports and imports. The extent of non-manufactured exports from India are examined and also some leading issues arising out of higher weightage from non-manufactured exports. Chapter four examines empirically the effect of cost structures and productivity differentials on Japan's prospensity to import Indian sourced manufactures during 1951 to 1973. Chapter five analyses the policy direction of India and Japan towards trade growth in this period. Chapter six focuses on India's trade growth and manufactured exports to Japan after 1973 and policy directions during 1973 to 1985. Chapter seven presents the findings and concluding remarks. Japanese technology transfer and investment to developing countries had played a crucial role in promoting trade growth with those countries. Here we examine the trend in Japanese technology transfer and investment to India and linkage with trade growth to Japan. Finally a likely scenario of trading in commodities and technologies is presented in the backdrop of Japan's yen appreciation and trade frictions with developed countries and also the restructuring of Japanese economy that had started in late 1980s.

The next chapter deals with the linkage of international trade and economic growth and specifically discusses on the role of foreign trade in the Indian economy. In this context, justification is presented for an economy like India to increasingly stress on diversification of its export structure with more dynamic economies like Japan. The experience of the past three decades has shown that the economic growth of developing countries is closely tied to the growth of their exports, especially of manufactured exports.[7]

REFERENCES

1. *Economic Times*, "Commercial Loan for Achieving 5 per cent GDP Growth" (New Delhi), 28 October 1985, p. 1.

2. The Economic Advisory Council, set up by the Prime Minister in February 1983, underlined in its first Report in May 1983 the importance of improvement in the tax administration to finance public investment under the existence of large external debts. See, *Mainstream*, "Indian Economy: Vital Urgent Issues" (New Delhi), Vol. 19, No. 41, June 1983, p. 9.

3. S. Okita, "Perspective of Indo-Japanese Relations", *Commerce* (Bombay), Vol. 123, No. 3161, December 1971, p. 14.

4. H.B. Chenery, "Transitional Growth and World Industrialisation", in B. Ohlin, ed., *The International Allocation of Economic Activity*. (London: Macmillan, 1977), pp. 3-5.

5. H.G. Johnson, "Technology and the Theory of International Trade", in R. Vernon, ed., *The Technology Factors in International Trade* (New York: National Bureau of Economic Research, 1970), pp. 9-21.

6. The complete list of the statistical references in this study is presented in Bibliography.

7. See William R. Cline, *Exports of Manufactures from Developing Countries* (Washington D.C.: Brookings Institution 1984).

2

INTERNATIONAL TRADE AND ECONOMIC GROWTH IN INDIA

INTERNATIONAL trade in a developing economy has become one of the important issues of economic growth since the end of the Second World War, when many of the developing countries achieved political independence and also became independent economic units. Since then the economists started to question the 'merits' of international trade elaborated in the traditional international trade theories in the context of developing economies. R. Prebisch, H.W. Singer and G. Myrdal were among those first to discuss it. Their opinions on the relationship between international trade and economic growth in a developing economy can be summed up as : ...not generally concede to the free trade doctrine its traditionally asserted status as the rational norm, in relation to which interferences have to be proved to be advantageous exceptions, applied to the severely unbalanced situation in which the underdeveloped countries find themselves as the result of history, such a pretence on the part of a non-interference policy has more obvious logical flaws...[1]

However, this argument has been gradually replaced by that of so-called 'trade optimists' who consider trade as 'engine of growth' and the economists who think that export is practically an effective measure to counter the balance of payments deficit in a short run caused by large import bills for the developmental requirements.

In recent years, economists view economic growth to take place by means of either factor accumulation or technical improvement. At constant relative prices of two commodities, a change in the supply of one of the productive factors changes the levels of output of the two goods. If the production effect of factor accumulation, at constant prices under constant terms of trade is combined with the consumption effect of the change at constant prices, the overall effect of factor accumulation on an economy's demand for imports in terms of its supply of exports at constant terms of trade is determined. The terms of trade of the economy improve if at constant prices the factor accumulation reduces the economy's demand for imports in terms of its supply of exports and vice-versa, if the factor accumulation increases the demand for imports.

In this chapter we will examine the problems of developing countries like India that is relying on trading in a traditional framework i.e. non-manufactures for manufactures with developed countries. Despite deterioration in their terms of trade, the developing countries have been highly dependent on foreign resources, which has been, in turn, apt to cause the balance of payments problem. By departing from the export structure with high concentration on non-manufactures and diversifying to manufactures, the developing countries could improve the balance of payments. In case if the manufacturing industries are not internationally competitive, it is significant to obtain technology from more dynamic industrial economies.

Trading in a Traditional Framework

Since the early 1950s, the terms of trade of developing countries have been deteriorating (see Table 1). The deterioration in the terms of trade for developing countries is considered to have arisen from the characteristics of their economies which in most cases 'specialise' in producting non-manufactures and supplying them to the industrial countries in exchange for manufactured goods. Table 2 shows a large proportion of exports from developing countries was non-manufactures though the share declined marginally.

TABLE 2.1

Terms of Trade Index Numbers* : Developed and Developing Countries
(1980=100)

	1954-56 (*average*)	*1960*	*1961*	*1962*	*1963*	*1964*	*1965*	*1966*	*1967*	*1968*	*1969*	*1970*	*1971*
Developed Market Economies	110	117	122	117	121	120	120	120	120	120	119	122	122
Major Oil Developing Exporters		22	22	22	22	21	20	20	19	19	19	19	22
Other Developing Economies		120	114	111	114	116	115	120	112	117	122	125	119
India												177	176
		1972	**1973**	**1974**	**1975**	**1976**	**1977**	**1978**	**1979**	**1981**	**1982**	**1983**	
Developed Market Economies		123	122	108	109	109	106	108	107	98	100	101	
Major Oil Developing Exporters		21	23	61	60	63	63	56	79	117	115	103	
Other Developing Economies		119	120	131	129	117	124	116	109	92	98	91	
India		125	120	107	111	137	146	143	130	91	91		

Note: *Unit value indcx of exports divided by unit value index of imports.

Source: United Nations Conference on Trade and Development (UNCTAD). *Handbook of the International Trade and Development Statistics*, New York, 1984.

The difficulties that developing economies may face due to the high content of non-manufactures in the export structure can be summarised as follows: (1) unstable export earnings caused by wide frequent fluctuations in prices of primary products; and (2) changes in the pattern of comparative advantage in the world economy after the Second World War that are not favourable for the primary-producing countries. According to the joint study by the International Monetary Fund and the International Bank for Reconstruction and Development,[3] fluctuations in export prices were two and a half to three times larger in developing countries than in industrial countries and fluctuations in export earnings were about twice as large in the former than in the latter between 1950 and 1965, owing to the high concentration of non-manufactures in the export structure of the former.

Though various factors are attributable, fluctuations in prices of the non-manufactures are usually led by business cycles in industrial countries. When the economy of the latter expands, the demand for non-manufactures increases and, if the supply side is not ready for the level of demand, their prices are forced to go up. A relatively small, temporary shortage often causes a sharp price increase. High prices for a brief period induce the investment for expansion of production. It goes to the extent of over-expansion in many cases, which is followed by prolonged period of low prices, since the short-run price elasticity of supply of non-manufactures are low and it takes time to adjust the production scale through withdrawal and under-investment to the level of demand.[4]

The difficulties caused by commodity export revenue fluctuations for the developing economies are well known.[5] An export revenue shortfall causes a balance of payments deficit. Unemployment problem is likely to arise when the balance of payments deficit exerts a damping effect on income. On the other hand, if a commodity boom causes a surplus in balance of payments, it will lead to inflationary pressures in the domestic economy. Export fluctuations also have a considerable impact on fiscal revenue and government spending in developing countries. High export revenue increases the tax base and the government fiscal revenue and it creates an incentive for govern-

Table 2.2

Composition of Exports of Industrial and Developing Countries

	1963	*1973*	*1981*[5]
A. *Industrial Countries*			
All commodities (billion US $)	99	391	1203
Composition (%)			
Primary Products[1]	26	22	18
Fuels	4	4	8
Manufactures of which—	67	73	73
Engineering[2]	36	41	43
Textiles[3]	7	6	3
B. *Oil-Exporting Developing Countries*[4]			
All commodities (billion US $)		42	271
Composition (%)			
Primary Products[1]		9	3
Fuels		89	94
Manufactures		2	2
C. *Other Developing Countries*			
All commodities (billion US $)	22	68	254
Composition (%)			
Primary Products[1]	76	56	38
Fuels	7	9	22
Manufactures of which—	14	34	39
Engineering[2]	2	9	14
Textiles[3]	6	12	5

Notes: 1. Excluding fuels.

2. SITC Section 7, Divisions 69 and 86 minus groups 862 and 868 subgroup 891.1.
3. SITC Divisions 65 and 84.
4. Including Algeria, Ecuador, Gabon, Indonesia, Iran, Iraq, Kuwait, Libya, Nigeria, Qatar, Saudi Arabia, the UAE and Venezuela.
5. Figures in 1980 for other developing countries.

Source : General Agreement on Tariffs and Trade, *International Trade 1981-1982* (Geneva, 1982).

ments to expand expenditure on infrastructure and social services with high recurrent costs that is difficult to be undertaken during times of low export revenue.

Another difficulty for developing countries in exporting non-manufactures is that they have been facing the secular downward trend in the terms of trade, especially since the Second World War. It is argued that the deterioration in the terms of trade for developing countries has been a result of a shift in comparative advantage in the world economy unfavourable for the economies with a high concentration of non-manufactures in their export structure.

The measures to stabilise the prices of non-manufactures can be classified into two groups, those to operate on the volume of transactions in relation to prices; and those to operate on prices to influence the volume of trade. The former includes buffer stocks and quotas, while the latter multinational contracts and national or conceivably international buffer funds.[5] In this regard, it should be noted that since the end of the Second World War, the United Nations Economic and Social Council (UNESC), the Food and Agricultural Organisation (FAO), the General Agreement on Tariffs and Trade (GATT) and since 1964 the United Nations Conference on Trade and Development (UNCTAD) have taken initiatives in discussing and taking actions on commodity problems and succeeded in concluding various international commodity agreements of wheat, sugar, tin, etc.[6]

Diversification with Manufactured Exports

In order to secure stable export earnings in the long run for developing countries, measures for diversification of the domestic production and export structure may be required. Diversification of exports, in this sense, means the various types of changes in the export structure in a developing economy which should provide basic solutions to their problems of trade and growth.

Conceptually, there are two types of diversification viz., horizontal and vertical diversification.[7] The former means simply an increase in the number of export products. In case the increase is made exclusively in the field of non-manufactures, risks will be spread over a wider range of the economy than before. Underlying this type of the structural change in exports is horizontal diversification of production, viz., a widening of the range of production possibilities within the primary producing sector. To the extent that the prices of many non-manufactures move sharply downward together in times of declining demand, the horizontal diversification of exports will provide a more limited insurance.

On the other hand, underlying the latter type of the change in the export structure is normally the sectoral shift in the structure of production. For a non-manufacturing exporting economy, diversification of exports particularly involves development of processing and manufacturing of domestically produced or imported raw materials and foodstuffs.

Manufactured exports from developing countries have increased the share from 14 per cent to 39 per cent between 1963 and 1981, indicating that the efforts of developing countries to diversify their export structure were effective. However, still, the share of developing countries manufactured exports in the total exports is much smaller than that of developed countries (see Table 2). Exports of manufactured goods, except those based on processing of local natural resources, are generally not feasible on any significant scale until the industrial development reaches a fairly advanced level.

Development of the manufacturing industry for exports usually starts in the labour-intensive sector, taking advantage of local natural resources, low wages and often undervalued exchange rate.[8] However, the competition is fierce in such area of industry and standards for the products are rigorous so that low wages must normally be combined with a disciplined, urbanised work force, sound infrastructural base and stable and efficient administration to preserve law and order to protect activities of private enterprise and to manage industrial relations. These conditions are not created quickly in a developing country. Moreover, manufactured exports, when first achieved, tend to involve small profit margins, even when accounting for local wages. Expenditure is to be high on the managerial, marketing know-how technology and design capabilities in the initial stage of industrialisation in developing economies, which are usually supplied by partners or collaborating firms from more advanced countries.

Apart from these difficulties, manufactured exports have practically more advantages than other exports. Like other exports, they are intrinsically desirable to help to pay for imports, provided they add to the supply of foreign exchange available. Also, expansion of manufactured exports has favourable effects on economic growth. Apart from the improvement in resource allocation according to comparative advantage which has been often argued, these effects are found to be effective in exploitation of economies of scale, reductions in product variety in individual plants (horizontal specialisation) and greater specialisation in the production of parts, components, and accessories (vertical specialisation) as well as in technological change that is stimulated by foreign competition.[9]

Particularly, where the manufactured exports are integrated with local industrial development, they are especially useful in freeing development from the constraints imposed by the small domestic market. It is also a beneficial factor for a developing economy that manufactured exports can usually be expanded over time based on the requirements of development.[10]

Export Sector in India's Economic Growth

India's foreign trade sector has grown over years despite foreign exchange constraints confronted by the economy and this aspect has been well documented in the Five Year Plan documents. The Second Five Year Plan which in fact laid the foundation of India's long term economic development had taken the closed economy assumption where transformation from trade is limited. The Plan states that 'this emphasis (on imports of capital goods)... is calculated in the long run to strengthen the country's external accounts as well as its investment potential',[11] implying that no specific measure was intended with respect to the balance of payments problem resulted from the utilisation of foreign resources.

It is only in the Third Five Year Plan that the foreign trade sector had entered as an independent entry in the planning model. In a paper prepared by the Planning Commission[12] in 1962, which is very close to the model for Third Five Year Plan, the objective of self-reliance was incorporated, that is, the requirement of foreign assistance to be zero toward the end of the Plan period. However the specification of import sector to be the residual of the debt servicing requirements provided a certain rate of exports exogeneously given to the system. The import and the export sectors specified under the self-reliance objective was incorporated as a component of the national product and the final demand, respectively. There was no guarantee that the export growth specified could be attained nor that the import specified would be sufficient to achieve the envisaged growth rate.

The Export Policy Resolution of 1970 clearly states the role of exports in the Indian economy:

> Government is of the view that expansion of export earnings is as crucial for financing the (Fourth Five Year Plan) as the mobilisation of domestic resources. To achieve national self-reliance and to reduce dependence on external assistance, export earnings need to be expanded at a high rate.. [13]

The 1970 Resolution advocated for the diversification of exports, besides the expansion of non-manufactured exports like tea, spices, raw cotton, jute and manufactured exports like cotton and jute textiles. The diversification of exports was supposed to be undertaken in every sector of the economy. For example, in the area of agriculture, the increase in exports of processed and finished goods based on agricultural products was emphasised. The Resolution also planned to diversify exports by expanding manufactured exports. It was, for example, intended to increase exports of iron and steel and other non-ferrous products rather than exporting unprocessed ores and pig iron products. The Resolution mentions that 'industrial products also constitute the most dynamic component of international trade' since 'the value added to the export product gives expanding opportunities for utilisation of our resources in skilled and unskilled labour.'[14]

The direction for diversification in manufactured exports itself was also mentioned in the 1970 Resolution. It was pointed out that in the case of textile products, the importance of 'expenditure on R and D to adopt traditional fibres to changing consumer preferences' as well as 'the improvements of its economic efficiency'. Expansion of engineering exports was also called for to reduce the concentration on few exports.

The Export Policy Resolution of 1970 intensified the export incentives that was existing until then such as cash assistance, import replenishments and duty drawbacks. Between 1970-71 and 1979-80, there was over a fivefold increase in the cash assistance provided to exporters from US $ 54.2 million to US $370.6 million. Major portion of the assistance were diverted to engineering exports which comprised more than 40 per cent on average during the period. The import replenishment licence issued also increased sixfold from US $ 194.1 million to US $ 1349.1 million by 1979-80. A bulk of import replenishment licence issued went for gems and jewellery industries, followed by engineering industries. The duty drawback extended to the exports in 1974-75 amounted to US $ 75.4 million which increased to US $94.8 million in 1975-76. Textiles and engineering goods received a drawback of one-fourth each of the total, followed by iron and steel industry given a drawback over 10 per cent of the total.

The trade deficit prompted the policy-makers to introduce a series of export incentive measures. The growth rate of exports in terms of volume was 3.4 per cent in 1960s which had increased to 7.8 per cent between 1971-72 and 1977-78. Later the growth declined to 4.2 per cent between 1977-78 to 1983-84.[15] The characteristics of export incentive scheme after mid-1970s is the liberalisation of industrial policies existing with respect to export activities.

A Technical Development Fund was set up in 1976 for exporters requiring imported capital goods, drawings and designs. In 1976-77 imports into Free Trade Zones were put on Open General Licence (OGL). In 1980, the 100 per cent Export Oriented Scheme was introduced and some more measures such as endorsement/recognition of capacity beyond restrictive trade regulations and reservations for small scale sector if in case of export production. The 1980 Industrial Policy Statement gave a further impetus to the export industry. In 1982, the units set up in Free Trade Zones as well as in the 100 per cent export-oriented scheme could now sell upto 25 per cent of the output to domestic tariff area.

The trade deficit took a new turn in 1980s. It reached an all time high of Rs. 50 billion in 1980-81 due to enlarged requirements for imports. One of the only solutions to the enlarged trade gap was to stimulate the export industry by further incentives. Moreover the past prescriptions by the various Committees[16] on Export-Import Policies and the targets by the E & C were presented to achieve substantial export growth. Government of India set up a Committee[17] on trade policies in 1984 to review the existing trade policies and to suggest the optimal policy mix of trade policies, industrial policies and fiscal policies so that it could bring out the maximum acceleration in economic growth. The Committee in its Report pointed out that the policies for export promotion should be more than a compensation for disadvantages faced by the exporters against the international markets on account of domestic economic policies.

Export promotion has become all the more important in India's development strategy during the Seventh Five Year Plan period. This is due to the fact that India's debt servicing ratio has been increasing due to the drawings from the IMF facility and larger reliance on commercial borrowings from international financial markets which has averaged US $1.2 billion a year in 1980s. This has pushed up the debt service ratio to 9 per cent in 1982-83 to 15.5 per cent in 1984-85. The requirements for borrowing from international financial market is estimated to be US $2 billion a year during the Seventh Plan since the funds from other sources such as international official assistance are expected to decline. This is considered to be necessary to finance the investment which would generate the GDP growth of 5 per cent. Since the Plan is expected to contain the debt servicing ratio within 20 per cent, it assumes an export growth of 13 to 14 per cent in volume terms which has been higher than to those achieved in earlier years. Failing this export target, the World Bank expects the current account deficit and debt service ratio would be in a serious situation.[18]

Trading in a New Framework

Over the last three and a half decades, Indian economy though grown to be of big size with diverse resources, its foreign trade sector accounts for only a small portion of the national product. There is little possibility of India to follow an export led growth model. On the other hand, growth led exports are the more likely scenario in India. As such an integrated view of the trade policy needs to be considered in consonance with the industrial policy.

A marked feature of the Indian economy since independence has been the low export growth. Between 1948 and 1970, World exports increased more than five times while India's exports rose by only 50 per cent. India's percentage of World export, dropped from 2.6 per cent to 0.72 per cent. Performance with regard to manufactured exports was especially weak. Between 1960 and 1978, manufactured exports from developing countries grew at 11.6 per cent per year. India's manufactured exports, however, grew at only 6.8 per cent.

A particular striking case is that of textiles. In 1953, India accounted for 38 per cent of all textile exports from developing countries. By 1970, India's share had fallen to 7 per cent. The absolute level of textile exports was about what it had been in 1953, while several other countries had made sensational progress. By 1970, South Korea's textile exports were 50 per cent above India's and Taiwan's exports were more than double. Meanwhile, Japan which had lost comparative advantage, entered the re-import stage. In addition to less dynamic policy, India invested little in textiles, failed to modernise antiquated plants and equipments and did not move quickly into synthetic fabrics as other countries were doing.[19]

In the 1980s, the issue of higher level of export growth has assumed all the more importance in the context of India's economic policies targetted for economic development. Imports of industrial materials, capital goods and technology are essential for India to accelerate economic growth. However, India's problem is to finance essential imports and suffers from the balance of payments deficit.

What is important for India is to move faster into a new

trading framework along with the progress achieved in industrialization. The diversification of exports by expanding manufactured exports, therefore, has been of importance, as it brings to a developing economy increasing benefits. Being a large size economy, India need to step into labour-intensive industrialisation and labour-intensive export orientation policies where its products could improve production efficiency by the effective exploitation of economies of scale and the greater specialisation in production.

The feature of the trade experience of developing countries since 1960s holds out the greatest optimism for the future extra-ordinary growth of manufactures. If export earnings of developing countries were to increase rapidly enough to permit them satisfactory rates of economic growth, this trend must be maintained. More and more developing countries have emerged on the scene as exporters of manufactures. In some developing countries including India, internal factors have militated against an expansion of exports of manufactures. Unless such internal barriers to manufactured exports are eliminated, it will be difficult to compete in foreign markets, no matter how low levels of protection may be.

In the next chapter we shall analyse India's trade with Japan during 1951 to 1973 to identify whether the nature of trade development corresponds with their economic development.

REFERENCES

1. G. Myrdal, *An International Economy* (New York: Harper and Brothers, 1956), p. 224.

2. International Monetary Fund and International Bank for Reconstruction and Development, *The Problem of Stabilization of Prices of Primary Products* (Washington D.C., 1969), pp. 33-60.

3. The example of coffee is the typical case. Brief periods of high prices in the late 1940s to the early 1950 led to over-expansion, which was followed by prolonged periods of low prices when withdrawal of investment and under-investment was undertaken. In many cases of primary commodities, structural disequilibria can be sometimes directly traced to price instability to which the term 'cobweb' is applied.

4. For example, see, E.M. Brook, E.R. Grilli and J. Waelbroock,

Commodity Price Stabilisation and Developing Countries—The Problem of Choice—World Bank Staff Working Paper No. 262 (Washington D.C., 1977), p. 3.

5. For detailed discussion on various measures for stabilisation of the prices of primary commodity exports, see International Monetary Fund and International Bank for Reconstruction and Development, *The Problem of Stabilisation of Prices of Primary Products*, *op. cit.*, pp. 61-102.

6. The measures related to trade in agricultural products embodied in the Yaounde Convention concluded between the EEC and 18 African countries may be separately viewed as an example of a multilateral—negotiated regional arrangement in which commodity arrangements were included as part of a more comprehensive economic association between these countries.

7. "The 'New Protectionism' and the International Economy", *Journal of World Trade Law* (Twickenham), Vol. 12, No. 5 September-October 1978, p. 136.

8. D.B. Keesing, "Trade Policy for Developing Countries", (World Bank Staff Working Paper No. 353) (Washington D.C., 1979), pp. 31-32.

9. B. Balassa, *World Trade and the International Economy—Trends, Prospects and Policies* (World Bank Staff Working Paper No. 282) (Washington D.C., 1978), p. 3.

10. Yamazawa designed a model which described the relation of expansion of foreign trade and process of industrial growth, taking an example of Japan's steel industry. The model states: (1) that industrial growth is initially motivated by the growth in the domestic demand through the increase in domestic income and the demonstration effect in the domestic market from imports; (2) that steady growth of domestic demand induces expansion of production, which accompanies the reduction of unit cost; (3) that the process (2) helps import substitution as well as stimulates the exports of which prices now are competitive against the world prices; and finally (4) that the stimulation to export induces further expansion of production in addition to the domestic demand. See, I. Yamazawa, "Industrial Growth and Foreign Trade", *Hitotshubashi Journal of Economics* (Tokyo), Vol. 12, No. 2, February 1972, pp. 41-59.

11. Planning Commission, Government of India (New Delhi), *Second Five Year Plan*, p. 101.

12. Perspective Planning Division (1962), "Perspectives of Development : 1961-76, Implications of Planning for Minimum Level of Living", in T.N. Srinivasan and P.K. Bardhan, eds., *Poverty and Income Distribution in India* (Calcutta : Statistical Publishing Society, 1974), pp. 9-38.

13. Ministry of Commerce, Government of India, *Report 1972-73* (New Delhi, 1973), p. 208.

14. *Ibid.*, p. 210.

15. M. Wolf, *India's Exports* (New York : Oxford University Press, 1982), pp. 79-112.

16. The Sondhi Committee on Engineering Exports 1974, The Tandon Committee 1976, The Alexander Committee 1978 and Abid Hussain Committee 1984.

17. Ministry of Commerce, Government of India, *Report on the Committee of Trade Policies 1984*, (New Delhi).

18. *The Economic Times*, "Commercial Loan for Achieving 5% GDP Growth" (New Delhi), 28 October 1985, p. 1.

19. Reynolds Lloyd, *Economic Growth in Third World Countries, 1950-1980* (New Haven and London : Yale University Press) 1985, p. 316.

3

EXPORT OF NON-MANUFACTURES TO JAPAN : SOME ISSUES DURING 1951-73

IT was discussed in Chapter two that a high concentration on non-manufactures in the export structure of a developing economy is not desirable. Instability in export earnings from non-manufactures is likely in the short run, while the rate of return from exporting them would decline in the long run.

In this chapter, we shall first analyse India's trade growth with Japan and their composition of exports and imports. Next we examine the extent to which non-manufacturing exports from India was dominating in Japan's foreign trade. Finally we assess some leading issues that arise out of higher weightage from non-manufacture exports to Japan.

Retrospect of India-Japan Trade Development

The traditional theory of international trade explains about the trade flow between the two countries that is determined by the difference in comparative advantage structure of their domestic economies. However, in practice, factors other than comparative advantage influence the trade flow. For example, according to the model constructed by I. Yamazawa,[1] the trade flow between the two countries, precisely, between an importing country and an exporting country, is a function of gravity of the two economies in terms of national income and trade intensity between them.

In terms of this model, the trade flow between India and Japan is expected to be high in relation to the factor concerning gravity of two economies. On the other hand, the influence on the trade flow between the two by the other factor, namely, the intensity of trade, depends on the structure of trade as well as economy of the two.

Japan has been playing an important role in India's foreign trade since the pre-war period. In 1938, Japan was the second largest importer of Indian products as well as the third largest exporter to India, which in value terms, constituted 8.9 per cent of India's total exports and 10.1 per cent of imports.[2] The outbreak of the Second World War temporarily hampered the trade flow between the two countries to the extent that Japan's share in India's foreign trade in 1951 declined to 2.7 per cent in the case of imports and 2.0 per cent in exports. Japan recovered its share in India's foreign trade to the pre-war level by 1973 (see Table 3.1), whereas India's share in Japan's foreign trade declined during the same period (see Table 3.2).

The value of Japan's total imports from India as well as that of its total exports to India increased considerably from US $52.4 million and US $51.7 million to US $676.8 million and US $338.7 million, respectively, during 1951-73. The growth, however, has not kept up with the overall growth in Japan's trade. India's share in Japan's total imports and exports declined from 3.6 per cent and 2.9 per cent to 1.5 per cent and 0.9 per cent respectively, over the same period. The growth of India's trade with Japan has been rather slow compared with the performance of Japan's trade with other developing countries in Asia (see Table 3.2). Among the developing countries in Asia, South Korea's trade with Japan achieved a rapid expansion since the 1960s, though prior to the 1960s South Korea's share in Japan's foreign trade was negligible.

The structure of trade between India and Japan over the period, explain that the trade between the two countries followed the traditional pattern of trade between a developing and a developed economies, viz., the former exporting non-manufactures to the latter in exchange for

TABLE 3.1

India's Trade with Major Trading Countries

(% of total value)

Year	Japan		U.S.A.		U.K.		U.S.S.R.		Total (Rs million)	
	Imports	Exports	Imports	Exports	Imports	Exports	Imports	Exports	Imports	Exports
1951-52	2.7	2.0	30.8	18.3	17.0	12.1	0.1	0.9	9793	7330
1955-56	4.7	5.0	12.7	14.2	24.5	27.2	1.8	0.5	6089	7744
1960-61	5.4	5.5	19.4	15.8	19.4	26.5	1.4	4.6	6429	11210
1965-66	5.6	7.1	38.0	18.4	10.7	18.1	5.9	11.6	8095	14085
1970	4.6	14.0	28.6	13.5	6.6	11.6	7.8	13.4	15933	15198
1973	9.0	13.8	17.5	13.8	10.0	10.1	3.7	13.3	24861	22656

Source: United Nations, *Yearbook of International Trade* (New York), from various issues of 1955 to 1975

TABLE 3.2

Japan's Trade with Developing Countries in Asia
(% of total value)

Year	*India*		*South Korea*		*Taiwan*		*Indonesia*		*Total (US $ million)*	
	Imports	*Exports*	*Imports*	*Exports*	*Imports*	*Exports*	*Imports*	*Exports*	*Imports*	*Exports*
1951	2.6	3.8	0.4	1.1	2.7	3.7	2.8	1.1	1995	1355
1955	3.2	4.2	0.4	2.0	3.3	3.2	3.3	3.2	2471	2011
1960	2.6	2.7	0.4	2.5	1.4	2.5	1.6	2.7	4491	4055
1965	2.2	2.4	0.5	2.1	1.9	2.6	2.2	2.5	8169	8452
1970	2.1	0.5	1.2	4.2	1.3	3.6	3.4	1.6	18881	19318
1973	1.5	0.9	3.1	4.8	2.3	4.4	4.7	2.4	38314	36930

Source: United Nations, *Yearbook of International Trade* (New York), from various issues of 1955 to 1975.

TABLE 3.3

Composition of Japan's Imports from India

(% of total value)

Year	*Primary Commodities and Products*						*Industrial Products*					*Total Imports (US $ 000)*
	Total	*Vegetable oil cakes*	*Shrimp frozen*	*Cotton*	*Iron ore*	*Manganese ore*	*Total*	*Leather and products*	*Textiles*	*Iron and Steel*	*Machinery and transport equipment*	
1955		n.a.	n.a.	28.4	23.6	5.2	n.a.	2.9	n.a.	n.a.	n.a.	77285
1960	93.2	n.a.	n.a.	12.9	40.7	4.1	n.a.	1 1	n.a.	1.5	n.a.	99474
1965	99.4	1.7	—	15.5	58.3	6.8	3.1	2.1	0.4	—	0.2	178969
1970	83.2	3.5	3.8	5.0	51.0	5.2	16.3	1.3	1.4	10.9	—	390061
1973	81.5	7.3	11.2	4.2	43.7	2.6	18.3	2.7	6.2	2.7	0.6	574900

Source: United Nations. *Commodity Trade Statistics* (New York) and Ministry of International Trade and Industry, Japan, *White Paper of International Trade*, (formerly, *Foreign Trade of Japan*) (Tokyo) from various issues of 1954 to 1974.

TABLE 3.4

Composition of Japan's Exports to India
(% of total value)

Year	*Primary Commodities and products*	*Industrial Products*							*Total Exports (US $ 000)*
			Light Industrial Products		*Heavy and Chemical Industrial Products*				
		Total	*Sub-total*	*Textiles*	*Sub-total*	*Chemicals*	*Metals and Products*	*Machinery and transport equipments*	
1956	1.1	n.a.	n.a.	9.2	n.a.	2.7	47.8	32.6	150297
1960	0.2	—	—	7.5	—	6.5	50.6	30.0	108714
1965	0.2	99.6	5.5	3.1	94.1	11.6	24.1	58.4	203549
1970	0.9	98.4	9.3	3.6	89.0	17.6	38.8	32.6	103118
1973	0.6	99.1	5.3	1.8	93.8	17.8	41.8	34.2	338726

Source: Ministry of International Trade and Industry, Japan, *White Paper on International Trade*, (Tokyo), from various issues of 1954 to 1974.

manufactured goods. The major portion of Japan's imports from India was constituted by non-manufacturs and their processed products, whereas industrial products constituted a dominantly large share of Japan's exports to India (see Tables 3.3 and 3.4).

Among India's export of non-manufacturs to Japan, iron ore was the most significant item during the 1951-73 especially from 1965 onwards, when its share increased to almost half of India's total exports to Japan. Raw cotton held the second position in terms of share in India's total exports next to iron ore until 1965. But when shrimps frozen and vegetable oil cakes expanded their shares after 1965, the share of raw cotton declined. Though changes in shares in the export composition were observed, the above items constituted a bulk in India's total exports to Japan over the period. Nevertheless, the gradual expansion of the share of industrial products against non-manufactures in India's exports to Japan is worth noting, which indicates that India's export structure to Japan underwent a certain change (see also Table 3.3).

In the composition of Japan's exports to India, industrial goods constituted more than 95 per cent between 1951-73. Yet a significant change was observed in the composition in which the share of exports of light industrial products declined over years, as Japan's export structure to the world underwent transformation in the same direction (see also Table 3.4). It is also notable that as the share of all the non-manufactures and their products declined slightly, the share of manufactures recorded a small increase.

In 1938, cotton was India's major export item to Japan constituting 65.7 per cent of India's total exports to Japan, while 56.1 per cent of India's total imports from Japan was textile products such as cotton yarns, rayon fabrics and silk fabrics.[3] The pattern of India's trade with Japan in the pre-war and post-war periods can be approximated to that of India's trade with the world in the pre-war period. In 1938, 68.5 per cent of its total exports to the world was unmanufactured crude materials, whereas manufactured and partly manufactured goods constituted 63.7 per cent of its total imports.[4] The pattern of trade was typical of the colonized

TABLE 3.5

Composition of India's Imports

(% of total value)

Year	*Food and other consumer goods*	*Raw Materials, fuels and other processed*	*Machinery and transport equipment*	*Total Imports (Rs. million)*
1951-52	31	47	17	9793
1952-53	29	43	20	7018
1953-54	20	48	20	6012
1954-55	25	50	20	6564
1955-56	12	46	25	7744
1956-57	9	51	28	9029
1957-58	13	48	30	10364

	Food	*Crude materials*	*Fuels*	*Manufactured materials*	*Machinery and transport equipment*	*Total Imports (Rs. million)*
1958-59	21	9	80	20	26	9036
1959-60	17	10	8	18	26	10710
1960-61	19	14	6	21	30	11210
1961-62	13	12	9	20	34	10916
1962-63	16	22	8	18	34	11315
1963-64	18	10	9	16	36	12229
1964-65	24	10	5	16	35	13490
1965-66	25	9	5	15	34	14085
1966-67				n.a.		
1967-68	30	10	4	13	25	19535
1968-69	21	10	7	13	27	19102
1969-70	20	11	9	15	25	15821
1970-71	17	12	8	21	24	16342
1971-72	11	12	11	24	26	18245
1972-73	9	10	11	25	30	18270
1973-74	21	7	21	20	24	26363

Source: Reserve Bank of India, *Reserve Bank of India Bulletin*, (Bombay), from various issues of 1952 to 1975.

TABLE 3.6

Composition of India's Export

Year	Primary Commodities and Products			Industrial Products			Total Exports (Rs. million)
	Total	Food	Raw Materials and Fuels	Total	Food	Machinery and transport equipment	
1951							
1952							
1953							
1954			n.a.				
1955							
1956							
1957							
1958	54.5	27.9	22.6	45.4	32.0	10.6	5850
1959	56.4	32.9	19.3	40.6	31.7	0.4	6139
1960-61	56.5	31,5	17.5	42.0	32.8	0.4	6429
1961-62	54.4	32.4	18.7	44.5	34.5	0.7	6620
1962-63	55.7	33.9	17.1	43.0	34.6	1.0	6937
1963-64	56.0	32.4	18.2	43.2	33.7	1.0	7669
1964-65	51.1	30.8	16.3	49.6	34.0	1.1	8384

(Contd.)

1965-66	50.9	29.8	17.8	47.9	34.2	1.4	8095
1966-67 (Ju-Mar)	52.0	31.4	18.9	47.2	31.3	1.4	9674
1967-68	49.8	30.2	16.2	50.5	29.3	1.8	11979
1968-69	46.6	26.8	16.5	52.8	26.2	3.3	13600
1969-70	44.2	24.4	17.0	55.2	25.6	4.0	14132
1970-71	45.9	26.9	16.5	52.9	22.8	5.4	15351
1971-72	45.5	26.3	15.8	54.1	27.2	4.6	15686
1972-73	45.8	26.6	14.6	53.9	23.3	4.4	19609
1973-74	45.9	26.8	15.0	53.8	22.6	4.7	24832

Source: Department of Commercial Intelligence and Statistics, Government of India, *Monthly Statistics of Foreign Trade of India* (Calcutta), from various issues of 1957 and 1974.

economies which were supposed to play a part of supplying raw materials to the ruling imperial countries and offering marketing opportunities for their manufactured products. The pattern of trade between India and Japan, however, was different from the pattern of India's trade with other economies. Though a high concentration on capital goods and industrial materials was observed in its import structure, more than half of India's exports to the world was processed and manufactured products (see Tables 3.5 and 3.6).

Of India's trade with the U.S.A., more than half of India's total exports to the U.S.A. was manufactured goods, while non-manufactures and their processed products constituted more than half of its total imports on average from 1965 onwards (see Table 3.7). Being an industrial economy with rich resource endowments, there was a larger share of non-manufactures in India's imports from the USA than its imports from Japan. On the other hand, it is notable that India was able to expand considerably the share of manufactured exports to the U.S.A.

A similar trend can be observed in the pattern of India's trade with the U.K. Since 1960s the composition of India's imports from the U.K., industrial products constituted a large share as in the case of its trade with Japan, while the share of manufactures gradually expanded to almost half of its exports to the U.K. by the 1970s (see Table 3.8). It can be said that significance of India as trade partner to these countries changed from a supplier of raw materials to that of a variety of commodities including manufactures. However, India's pattern of trade with Japan followed a traditional pattern.

The change in the pattern of India's trade with Japan was even at a slower pace when compared with that of trade between Japan and other developing countries in Asia such as South Korea and Taiwan. As for Japan's exports to these countries there was a small change in its composition. Exports of manufactures, especially heavy and chemical industrial products, constituted a dominant share (see Tables 3.9 and 3.10). A distinct change can be observed in the composition of Japan's imports from these countries. Until the early 1960s, Japan's imports from South Korea and Taiwan consisted mainly of

TABLE 3.7

Composition of India's Trade with U.S.A.

(% of total value)

Year	Exports					Imports					
		Industrial Goods					Industrial Goods				
	Primary commodities and products	*Total*	*Textiles*	*Iron and steel*	*Machinery and transport equipments*	*Primary commodities and products*	*Total*	*Textiles*	*Chemicals*	*Iron and steel*	*Machinery and transport equipment*
1962	38.6	60.9	n.a.	n.a.	0.2	51.6	48.0	n a.	6.0	0.9	24.9
1965	33.0	66.5	5.6	2.4	0.1	55.8	43.6	0.3	6.6	5.2	22.3
1970	37 8	61 8	4.6	3.3	0.3	56.3	43.1	0.3	16.6	7.9	15.7
1973	32 9	66.8	4.6	1.6	0.5	59.8	39.9	0.1	15.8	1.4	18.7

Source: United Nations, *Commodity Trade Statistics* (New York), from various issues of 1951 to 1973.

TABLE 3.8

Composition of India's Trade with the U.K. (% of total value)

Year	*Exports*					*Imports*					
		Industrial Goods					*Industrial Goods*				
	Primary Commodities and products	*Total*	*Textiles*	*Iron and steel*	*Machinery and transport equipments*	*Primary Commodities and products*	*Total*	*Textiles*	*Chemicals*	*Iron and steel*	*Machinery and transport equipments*
1962	73.5	26.3	18.1	n.a.	0.2	2.0	93.1	n.a.	11.6	2.9	58.7
1965	70.1	29.7	18.1	1.0	0.1	3.2	93.6	1.7	8.3	8.1	64.0
1970	67.9	31.6	13.7	1.3	1.2	5.1	92.1	1.1	10.7	14.7	50.0
1973	50.4	49.1	23.3	0.4	1.1	1.7	97.9	0.4	9.6	13.5	50.0

Source: United Nations, *Commodity Trade Statistics* (New York), from various issues of 1962 and 1975.

TABLE 3.9

Composition of Japan's Imports from Taiwan

(% of total value)

Year	*Primary Commodities and products*	*Industrial Products*			
		Total	*Textiles*	*Iron and steel*	*Machinery and transport equipments*
1960	96.5				
1965	96.7	2.6	0.3	0.2	n.a.
1970	64.8	34.2	6.2	0.5	7.2
1973	46.2	53.6	22.3	n.a.	7.3

Source: Calculated from United Nations, *Commodity Trade Statistics* (New York), from various issues between 1952 and 1975.

non-manufactures. Since then the share of these products in Japan's total imports had fallen gradually, while that of manufactures expanded. Both Taiwan and South Korea had experienced increase in the ratio of manufactures over that of non-manufactures in their exports to Japan in the early 1970s. From then these countries were able to increase exports of manufactures to a significant share in the Japanese market (see Tables 3.11 and 3.12).

TABLE 3.10

Composition of Japan's Imports from South Korea

(% of total value)

Year	*Primary Commodities and products*	*Industrial Products*			
		Total	*Textiles*	*Iron and steel*	*Machinery and transport equipments*
1960	83.0				
1965	88.2	10.6	5.7	0.9	0.3
1970	56.2	40.6	18.6	1.6	2.4
1973	32.2	65.9	19.1	0.7	6.5

Source: Calculated from United Nations, *Commodity Trade Statistics* (New York), from various issues between 1952 and 1975.

TABLE 3.11

Composition of Japan's Exports to Taiwan (% of total value)

Year	*Foodstuffs, raw materials and fuels*	*Industrial Goods*						
		Light Industrial Products			*Heavy & Chemical Industrial Products*			
		Total	*Sub-total*	*Textiles*	*Sub-total*	*Chemicals*	*Metals and metal products*	*Machinery and transport equipments*
1960	4.5	n.a.	n a.	6.3	n.a.	19 8	22.9	39.3
1965	3.0	96.6	14.6	11.1	82.0	15.0	23.7	43.2
1970	3.4	95.2	16.5	12 9	78.7	10.4	19.3	49.1
1973	4.0	95.1	17.3	13.5	77.8	12.4	20.8	44.6

Source: Calculated from United Nations, *Commodity Trade Statistics* (New York), from various issues between 1952 and 1975.

TABL 3.12

Composition of Japan's Exports to South Korea

(% of total value)

Year	Foodstuffs, raw materials and fuels	Industrial Products						
		Total	*Light Industrial Products*		*Heavy & Chemical Industrial Products*			
			Sub-total	*Textiles*	*Sub-total*	*Chemicals*	*Metal and metal products*	*Machinery and transport equipment*
1960	4.3	n.a.	n.a.	8.8	n.a.	33.3	6.8	36.8
1965	4.2	94.7	23.3	20.2	71.5	28.5	15.8	27.2
1970	17.1	81.4	22.2	18.4	59.2	10.8	12.2	36.2
1973	4.9	92.3	23.5	19.0	68.8	13.1	19.7	37.7

Source: Calculated from United Nations, *Commodity Trade Statistics* (New York), from various issues between 1951 and 1975.

Japan was initially the exporter of manufactures and the importer of non-manufactures (see Tables 3.13 and 3.14). Its import composition was characterised with concentration of imports on foodstuffs, raw materials and fuels. As observed in the previous chapter as well as in Table 3.14, the composition of imports underwent a change and there was an increase in the imports of manufactures. During this period import requirements had not only grown large but also diversified to a greater extent.

TABLE 3.13

Composition of Japan's Exports
(% of total value)

Year	*Food-stuffs*	*Crude materials and products*	*Industrial Products*			*Total Exports (US $ 000)*
			Total	*Light industrial products*[1]	*Heavy and chemical industrial products*[2]	
1951	5.2	2.8	90.1	n.a.	n.a.	1355
1955	6.3	3.3	90.1	n.a.	n.a.	2011
1960	6.3	2.2	91.0	46.7	44.4	4055
1965	4.1	1.5	93.9	31.9	62.0	8452
1970	3.4	1.0	94.8	22.4	72.4	19318
1973	2.3	0.9	95.7	16,3	79.4	36930

Note : (1) Including textiles, non-metallic mineral products, etc.
(2) Including chemicals, metal products, machinery and transport equipment.

Source: Ministry of International Trade and Industry, Japan. *White Paper on International Trade* (Tokyo), from various issues of 1952 to 1974.

Analysis of India's Non-Manufactured Exports

Among India's export items to Japan, non-manufactures like raw cotton and iron ore constituted more than half of India's total exports to Japan until the early 1960s. Towards the middle of the 1960s, the share of iron ore increased to more than half of the total exports while the share of raw cotton

TABLE 3.14
Composition of Japan's Imports by Commodity Groups
(% of total value)

Year	*Food-stuffs*	*Crude materials and fuels*	*Industrial Products*			*Total Exports* (US $ 000)
			Total	*Light industrial products*[1]	*Heavy and chemical industrial products*[2]	
1951	27.6	58.4	18.7	n.a.	n.a.	1995
1955	25.3	62.8	11.9	n.a.	n.a.	2471
1960	12.2	65.9	21.9	1.4	20.5	4491
1965	18.0	59.6	22.5	3.1	19.4	8169
1970	13.6	56.0	29.8	5.5	24.4	18881
1973	15.7	53.7	30.2	10.8	19.8	38314

Notes : (1) Including textiles, non-metallic mineral products, etc.
(2) Including chemicals, metals and metal products, machinery and transport equipment.

Source: Ministry of International Trade and Industry, Japan, *White Paper on International Trade* (Tokyo), from various issues of 1952 to 1974.

declined. At the same time, exports of vegetable oil cakes and frozen shrimps expanded the shares in India's exports to Japan. It can be said that the degree of concentration on non-manufactures in India's exports to Japan was extremely high, since a few items constituted a bulk in the total exports.

Below we will examine the development of India's iron ore and frozen shrimp industries and analyse the long-run potential of these industries for export to Japan.

Iron Ore Development and Export Trend to Japan

Imports of iron ore is a crucial factor to Japan's iron and steel industry, which is one of the basic industries in Japan, turning out 8.1 per cent of the total value of output by all the manufacturing industries in 1973.[5] Since iron ore deposits are inadequate to meet the demand for the domestic industry, the ratio of imports to the total supply in the domestic market of iron ore is extremely high in Japan. For example in 1973, the import-supply ratio in quantity terms was 99.5 per cent.[6] Japan had been the largest iron ore importer in the world since 1963. In 1973, Japan's imports of iron ore reached 135 millon tonnes, 35.3 per cent of the total iron ore traded as imports in the world.[7]

On the other hand, India's iron ore production was 22 thousand metric tonnes, comprising a share of 4.8 per cent of the total volume in the world iron ore production in 1973.[8] India was also one of the largest exporters of iron ore and its

TABLE 3.15

Direction of India's Exports of Iron Ore
(% of total quantity)

Year	*Japan*	*Rumania*	*GDR*	*Czechoslovakia*	*Total (tonnes 000)*
1955	70.2	—	6.1	11.9	1287
1960	57.6	1.7	2.7	23.5	3428
1965	69.9	5.0	5.5	5.5	11264
1970	81.8	7.4	1.2	3.2	21205
1973	80.5	—	—	2.9	21285

Source: Indian Bureau of Mines, Government of India, *Indian Minerals Yearbook* (Nagpur), from various issues of 1959 to 1974.

TABLE 3.16

Direction of Japan's Import's of Iron Ore
(% of total quantity)

Year	*India*[1]	*Australia*	*Chile*	*Peru*	*Malaysia*	*Total (tonnes M/T)*
1955	24.5	—	—	—	29.9	5459
1960	29.9	0.7	1.7	1.7	35.6	15036
1965	20.3	1.9	16.6	17.8	17.8	39018
1970	16.2	35.8	7.8	7.8	4.8	102090
1973	14.2	47.7	6.3	4.6	1.5	134724

Note: (1) Including exports from Goa, even before its repatriation to India.

Source: Ministry of International Trade and Industry, Japan, *White Paper on International Trade* (Tokyo), from various issues of 1957 to 1974.

share in the total quantity of the world exports of iron ore was 5.6 per cent, amounting to 21 million tonnes in 1973.[9] Table 3.15 shows that a major part of iron ore from India was exported to Japan.

However, the growth in India's exports of iron ore to Japan had been unable to keep up with the growth in demand in the Japanese market. India's share in Japan's total imports had declined considerably since the late 1960s. The expansion of iron ore exports to Japan by Australia, on the other hand, was remarkable compared with the performance of India and other exporters such as Malaysia, Peru and China (see Table 3.16), which had supplied to nearly half of Japan's import requirements by the 1970s. According to D. Nayyar the following three issues had posed as difficulties for India to rapidly expand exports of iron ore[10] to Japan during 1951-73 :

(1) Traditional iron ore mining industry in India has been conducted by manual operations.[11] For a rapid expansion of iron ore production, mining should be conducted on an efficient large-scale basis.[12]
(2) Most of the iron ore deposits are situated at a considerable distance away from the coast. Hence, there was a need not only for a better feeder and link roads from mines to loading stations, but also for adequate railway facilities.
(3) For iron ore exports, ports for shipping are supposed to accommodate ships of a large tonnage. It was necessary to mechanise the loading and unloading facilities at the ports in order to handle a larger quantity of exports.

Since the 1960s there have been some improvement in each of the above three areas. By 1976, out of 254 working iron ore mines, 22 were fully mechanised of which mining capacity amounted to 89 per cent of the total mining capacity in India. Most of the important loading points in the mines were connected to the ports by road and railway. For example, loading points of Bihar and Orissa mining area was connected by road and rail to the ports like Haldia and Paradip. The Bailadila mining area was connected by rail to Visakapatnam. The Bellery-Hospet mining area was connected by rail to the ports such as Madras, Mormugao, Karwar and Belikera.[13]

There was improvement also with respect to the port facilities in the 19 0s. The ports such as Haldia, Paradip, Visakapatnam, Madras, Mormugao and Mangalore have berths specially commissioned for iron ore loads. These ports were able to handle ore carriers of a large size. The carrier size (DWT) in tonnes of these ports are as follows: Haldia 30,000; Paradip 60,000; Visakapatnam, 120,000; Madras 80,000; and Mormugao 150,000.[14]

As a result, India's iron ore mining industry saw further expansion of production since the 1960s (see Table 3.17) Production of iron ore increased by about 270 per cent over a decade of the 1960s. Exports of iron ore increased faster than production, by about 460 per cent during the same period.

Export Constraints[15] to Japan

Japan began to import iron ore from India much before the Second World War. After the end of the war for a few years, the Allied Army occupying Japan had not allowed it to resume steel production fearing its rearmament. When the steel industry started production, the Philippines and Malaysia (Dungan) were the suppliers of iron ore to Japan. Ores supplied by these countries were of a very low quality. Especially ore from the Philippines contains phosphorus to a great extent and its use was restricted. In case of ore from Dungan, exports were possible only in fair seasons. Efforts had been made at the same time to find other sources of supply of ore.

In the course of time, Japan found Goa to be one of the most reliable source, taking into consideration the convenience for transporting ore from mines to the port Mormugao by inland water. Japan provided financial assistance for mechanising the Sisigao mine in 1951. This mechanised mine in Goa was commissioned in 1953. Negotiations continued on Kiriburu and Bailadila ore mines and Japan concluded an agreement with the Indian Government in 1958 for the ore produced from these mines to be shipped from Visakapatnam.

This agreement provided for the supply of 6 million tonnes

of iron ore a year from 1967 onwards. It was not until 1962 that orders were placed for installation of a mechanised plant that could handle 8 million tonnes of ore per annum. When the installation was completed, Japan found that the plant would not be in a position to handle 6 to 8 million tonnes of ore a year in a sustained manner. Moreover, India failed to develop the port Visakapatnam at a pace needed to materialise the agreement by the year specified.

Meanwhile, Japan concluded agreements with Australia for supply of iron ore and Japan's imports of iron ore from Australia started on a large scale in the late 1960s. Australia took the opportunity provided by the Japanese market to develop its iron ore deposits for exports to Japan. Fortunately, it had the backing of American mining interests which prompted the growth with heavy investment.[16]

Due to a spurt in India's ore exports since the 1960s which was greater than that in its production, the ratio of export to

TABLE 3.17

India's Iron Ore: Production, Exports,[1] Imports and Domestic Consumption[2]

(thousand tonnes)

Year	*Production*	*Export*	*Import*	*Consumption*	*Export output ratio (%)*	*Import consumption ratio (%)*
1955	4678	1287	n.a.	3087	27.5	n.a.
1960	10683	3428	960	n.a.	32.1	n a.
1965	17076	11264	108	9629	66.0	1.1
1970	31366	21205	153	11370	67.6	1.3
1973	35562	21285	175	12443	59.9	2.2

Notes: (1) Including those from Goa before repatriation.
(2) Only by the organised iron and steel mills.

Source: Indian Bureau of Mines, Ministry of Steel, Mines and Fuel, Government of India, *Mineral Production in India 1957* (New Delhi, 1957 upto 1956).

Indian Bureau of Mines, Ministry of Steel and Mines, Government of India, *Indian Minerals Yearbook* (Nagpur), of various issues from 1959 to 1974—1957 onwards.

output went up drastically until the middle of the 1960s. The pace of increase in exports dropped since then and the ratio was established to around 50 to 60 per cent towards the end of 1973 (see Table 3.17). The trend in the export-output ratio shows that the pressure of domestic demand did not cut into the potential exportable surplus. Thus it may be partly due to a constraint in India's iron ore supply capacity that India could not expand its share in Japan's imports of iron ore.[17]

The constraint in supply capacity is a reflection of the condition of operations of India's iron ore mining industry. Out of 254 working mines, only 22 have been mechanised by 1979. The rest are operated by manual labour which turns out only 11 per cent of India's total run of mine ores. At the same time, many of the iron ore mines in India are operated below their capacities. A study by the NCAER indicates that the total production of iron ore in 1974 was well below the installed capacities in the mechanised sector, which was equivalent to 53.1 per cent of the theoretical capacities.[18]

The problem apparently that inhibited India to expand its share of iron ore exports to Japan was that the price of India's iron ore was higher than that of its competitor countries such as Australia and Brazil. For example, in 1969 the c.i.f. price of Indian ore was US $2 per tonne which was more than that of Australian ore.[19] The higher freight rate for Indian ore was one of the factors which had priced India's ore higher than that of its competitors. The lower prices of iron ore from Australia and Brazil were mainly due to the lower costs of transportation, for larger freighters were used in transporting iron ore from them. For example, in 1971 the freighters of iron ore exports from Australia had capacities upto 150,000 tonnes, and those from Brazil 200,000 tonnes on average[20] against India's 35,000 tonne-capacity ships. India could utilise only the carriers of a smaller tonnage mainly because the ports in India were not fit to handle large ships.

Policy on Iron Ore Exports

India's policy for the export of iron ore has been sometimes shadowed by the opinions standing on the viewpoint of resource conservation. However, any policy aimed at conserving a mineral resource too far into future may turn a usable asset of today into a valueless one in future.[21] There is a high possibility for world consumption of iron ore to decline owing to the discovery of substitutes for steel, much before the reserves run out, even if considering the expected expansion in production.[22]

Very few incentives have been given for promotion of iron ore exports other than the formation of the Minerals and Metals Trading Corporation (MMTC) in 1963 to streamline the efforts in mining exports from India. To cope with the problems in exporting iron ore, large investment has to be made for development and improvement of mines, transporting and shipping facilities. The projection made by the NCAER[23] shows that only if Indian ports could be expanded to berth upto 100,000 to 150,000 tonnes carriers, a capacity equal to that of Australia, India was able to maintain the share of 12.5 per cent out of Japan's total imports of iron ore, which is estimated to be 13.50 million tonnes in 1985 and 13.90 million tonnes in 1990.

It was important for India's iron ore mining industry also to enter into long-term contracts, which Japan has usually adopted in purchasing iron ore from various supplying countries including Australia and Brazil. The strategy was to encourage new mining operations and guarantee them purchase contracts and fixed prices for a fixed period.[24] For example, the NCAER advised India's iron ore industry to enter into a ten year contract for exports of iron ore to Japan, which may provide the Japanese steel industry time to become interested enough to come forward with investment for development of mines and port facilities that can be financed by exports of iron ore.[25] During 1951-73, the MMTC had signed three long term arrangements for iron ore exports with Japan and Rumania.[26]

Issues in Iron-Ore Export Development

Long-term supply agreement, however, do not account for price hikes in the international market during the agreement period, while they will safeguard the price of the supplies under the agreement when prices are falling internationally. In 1973, for example, there was an increase in iron ore prices in the international market. MMTC tried to increase the prices agreed on a long-term basis, but was only able to secure two small increases enough to offset the devaluation of rupee against dollar in 1966.[27]

Besides the trend in prices of the world market, iron ore exports are vulnerable to the business cycle in the importing countries. For example, the recession in the world steel industry induced by the second oil crisis in 1978 hit the importing countries of Indian iron ore as well. The exports to Japan which comprises about three-fourths of the total exports of iron ore from India declined from 17.7 million tonnes to 14.2 million tonnes, resulting in a decline in export earnings worth of more than Rs. 300 million.

Decline in the demand for iron ore seems to be a long-term phenomenon. The growth in steel consumption in industrialized countries was found to be lower than that of their national product. It has been estimated that in the former part of the 1980s, the growth in steel consumption in industrial countries will grow at around 2.4 per cent per annum if the GDP growth would be around 3.8 per cent. Also, it has been observed that steel consumption by industrial countries declined considerably over years, from 5.5 per cent in 1970-73 to 2.4 per cent in 1978-85.[28] In addition to the recession following oil crises, an OECD study indicates a decline in steel intensity per national product over years, which must have contributed to a deceleration in steel consumption.[29]

The trend in the world steel industry would discourage India from exporting iron ore in a more processed form. In fact, a UNIDO study estimates that if developing countries processed all their current mineral output into more refined metal stage, their foreign sales of seven major ores, i,e., bauxite, copper, iron, lead, nickel, tin and zinc, would be increased more than five-fold, or from $10 billion in the late 1970s to $54 billion.[30] Though the value-addition in exports of refined metals from ores is tremendous, with the existing technology and production capacity in India, production over domestic consumption has never been achieved in India's iron and steel industry. The imports of iron and steel products comprised more than 60 per cent of India's total imports of metals in the early 1970s, reaching 1.2 million tonnes in 1974.

From the above analysis, the following issues are brought to focus :

—There was a sharp increase in demand for iron ore from Japan. Though initially India was selected as a supplier, it lost importance to other countries which are geographically much distant than India. These countries viz. Australia and Brazil had simultaneously improved their infrastructure facilities particularly port facilities for export.

—Australia and Brazil had entered into long term contract with Japan. Japanese preference for such arrangement was to secure an uninterrupted flow of iron-ore and also to secure a stable price. However, such long term arrangement has also demerits to developing countries like India. Any increase in price in the international market, may not give advantage to the exporting countries.

—Even though India had initially identified iron-ore as one of its lead exports for earning foreign exchange for paying its imports, India could not maintain its aggressiveness for exports to Japan.

Shrimp Fishery[31] Development and Export Trend to Japan

India has one of the largest landings of fishery catches in the world. It secured the share of 3.9 per cent in the total nominal catches of the world in 1957, though since then they declined to around 2.5 per cent by the early 1970s amounting to 1958 thousand metric tonnes.[32] Among India's marine catches, crustaceans consisting of shrimps, lobsters and crabs are by far the most important in terms of value. They form about 15 per cent of the total landed wet weight of India's marine catches, but their value exceeds 60 per cent of the value of the total catches.[33] In 1973, the nominal catches of marine shrimps by India were about 208 thousand metric tonnes, more than 10 per cent of the total catches of the item in the world.[34]

India has been also one of the world's major exporters of

fish and fish preparations. For example, in 1973 India's exports of fish and fish preparations amounted to US $96 million, which was equal to 2.3 per cent of the total value of the world's exports.[35] Table 3.18 indicates that since the early 1960s

TABLE 3.18

India's Exports of Fish and Fish Preparations

(million rupees)

Year	*Fish and fish preparations*	*Shrimps, chilled frozen or dried*	*Fish dried or salted*	*Share in fish and fish preparations of shrimps chilled frozen or dried*	*Share in fish and fish preparations of fish dried or salted*
1958	58.4	17.6	38.6	30.0	66.1
1965	65.6	47.3	8.3	72.2	12.6
1970	309.0	249.9	20.6	80.9	6,7
1973	745.7	650.2	8.3	87.2	1.1

Source: Food and Agricultural Organisation, *Yearbook of Fishery Statistics* (Rome), from various issues between 1960 and 1974.

shrimps chilled, frozen and dried had expanded the share in the total value of India's fishery exports to around 90 per cent by the early 1970s.

Since the early 1970s, India has become one of the largest exporters of shrimp products in the world. In 1973 India's exports of shrimps fresh, chilled or frozen was $ 84.1 million.[36] Table 3.19 shows the direction of India's exports of shrimps chilled or frozen during 1951-73. Until the early 1960s, India's exports of shrimps, chilled or frozen, was directed mostly to its neighbouring countries like Burma and Sri Lanka as well as to the U.S.A. By the middle of the 1960s, the exports to the neighbouring countries decreased to a negligible amount while those to the U.S.A. drastically increased. Meanwhile, India started to export the products also to Japan on a large scale and by 1973 Japan became the largest importer of India's chilled and frozen shrimps.

On the other hand, Japan started to liberalise imports of marine products since 1961. Since then the imports expanded

TABLE 3.19

Direction of India's Exports of Shrimps, Chilled or Frozen

(% of total quantity)

Year	*Japan*	*USA*	*Australia*	*Burma*	*Sri Lanka*	*Total (thousand M/T)*
1958	—	13.7	—	72.5	9.8	5.1
1963	1.4	51.4	2.9	24.3	4.3	7.0
1965	9.9	78.9	2.1	—	2.8	7.1
1970	63.3	3.0	3.3	—	—	21.5
1973	61.3	30.9	2.6	—	—	34.9

Source: Food and Agricultural Organisation, *Yearbook of Fishery Statistics* (Rome), from various issues of 1960 to 1974.

gradually and by 1973 the value of imports of fish and fish preparations was US $989 million, constituting 19.4 per cent in the world's import trade of the item.[37] Among various marine products imported by Japan, fresh, chilled and frozen shrimps constituted more than half of the total value of the fishery imports (see Table 3.20). At the same time, Japan's share in the world imports of crustaceans and mollusc traded as imports had increase from 10.0 per cent in 1964 to 35.4 per cent in 1973.[38]

TABLE 3.20

Japan's Imports of Fish and Fish Preparations

(million US $)

Year	*Fish and fish preparations*	*Shrimps fresh. chilled or frozen*[1]	*Share of shrimps fresh, chilled or frozen in fish and fish preparations (%)*
1960	4.3	n.a.	n.a.
1965	71.1	35.9	50.5
1970	261.7	137.0	52.4
1973	989.9	435.8	44.0

Note: (1) SITC Code No. 031-312.

Source: Japan Tariff Association, Ministry of Finance, Japan, *The Foreign Trade of Japan* (Tokyo), from various issues between 1965 and 1974.

Japan has been importing shrimps from various countries and the direction of imports has been diversified as the imports expanded. In 1975, Japan imported the products from 60 countries.[39] Table 3.21 shows that during 1951-73 though China was the first to enter exports of shrimps to the Japanese market, its share in Japan's total imports of the commodity declined gradually since the early 1960s as China was unable to meet the growing demand of the market as well as to ensure the stable supply. Meanwhile, Mexico and Thailand had increased the pace of exports, but the expansion proved to be short lived. Since the early 1970s, India became the largest exporter of shrimps to Japan (see Table 3.21).

TABLE 3.21

Direction of Japan's Imports of Shrimps—Fresh, Chilled or Frozen[1]

(% of total quantity)

Year	*India*	*Mexico*	*Thailand*	*China*	*Total (tonnes)*
1957	—	—	—	95.4	1542
1960	—	—	—	31.2	660
1965	4.0	24.8	9.4	28.0	21349
1970	11.2	12.6	10.5	—	57371
1973	18.6	7.5	8.5	3.8	117989

Note: (1) SITC 031-312.

Source: Japan Tariff Association, Ministry of Finance, Japan, *The Foreign Trade of Japan* (Tokyo), from various issues of 1965 to 1974.

The shrimps fishery industry[40] in India is mainly supported by littoral forms and they are distributed all along the 5,600 kms. coast line. Of the estimated 415,000 sq. kms. area of the continental shelf, only about 112,000 sq. kms. had been exploited by 1976. The existing shrimps fishery is restricted to the shoreward side of the continental shelf and the topographical diversity of the coastline probably gives rise to the existing pattern of distribution of shrimps fishery in general. Among the maritime states in India, Kerala produces one third of the total catches of crustacean in India, which is followed by Maharashtra.

The topographical diversity of the coastline also gives rise to the various species in particular. The catch of crustaceans in India can be broadly classified under three categories: (1) penaeid shrimps; (2) non-penaeid shrimps; and (3) other crustaceans. Among them, penaeid shrimps include large prawns are generally exported. From 1951 to 1974, the catch of penaeid shrimps increased by 282 per cent. The share of penaeid shrimps in the total catch of crustaceans also increased from 50 per cent to 64 per cent during 1951-73.

Export Constraints to Japan

Japan's imports of shrimps and their products have been on the rapid increase since the import liberalization on marine products was initiated. Moreover, the upgrading of diet accompanying a rise in income has accelerated the increase in demand for shrimps in Japan. Within the decade of 1960s, the annual per capita consumption of shrimps in Japan nearly doubled from 1.43 pounds to 3.06 pounds.[41]

The trend in Japan's import policy on marine products also supported the expansion in imports of the product. Since the initiation of import liberalisation in the early 1960s there has been a consistent move towards reduction of tariff barriers on marine products. Taking the above factors into account, Japan External Trade Organisation estimated that the imports of shrimps would be doubled from 177 thousand tonnes in 1973 to 230 thousand tonnes by 1985, and the domestic consumption would increase from 176 thousand tonnes in 1973 to 261 thousand tonnes in 1985, whereas the domestic catch would decline from 62 thousand tonnes to 35 thousand tonnes during the same period.[42]

Catches of shrimps by India can be increased substantially by mechanisation of the craft used in the capture fishery. Though no data is available, a considerable portion out of the total catch of shrimps was considered to be turned out by operations with the traditional, indigenously manufactured crafts[43] which numbered about 117,000 all over the country in

1976. These crafts have an operational range of 8 kms. from the shore. On the contrary, indigenously wooden-built and mechanised fishing vessels, while can operate upto 20 km. from the shore in the sea of about 50 metres in depth,[44] were negligible in number. The latter was estimated to be over 10,000 in number in 1976.[45]

The mechanisation of the fishing craft can be initiated in three areas as a first step.[46] To meet the requirements of fishing shrimps in creeks and shore waters, the traditional craft can be replaced with the small craft of a size between 5 metres and 6 metres in length with a outboard engine. To fish in water of a depth 50 metres, a mechanised vessel of 9.6 metres in length with a 40 brake horse power (BHP) engine is considered to be suitable. One of the essential needs of the shrimps fishery is the acquisition of necessary facility to fish in deeper regions of the continental shelf, without having a need to come to the shore everyday. This can be done only by the craft steel-built of more than 17 metres in length with necessary facilities.[47]

Appropriate processing facilities are essential for exporting shrimps. It has been already indicated that most of India's shrimp exports were in the form of chilled or frozen. By 1976, 48 freezing plants for marine products were installed with a processing capacity of about 60 thousand tonnes per annum. About 83 per cent of the total processing capacity for marine products in India is located in Kerala State. However, it has been reported that the utilisation of the capacity is usually only 30 per cent.[48] The over-capitalisation has arisen on account of the need to process large quantity during the short season of availability of the catch of shrimps. This fact might have affected relative profitability and competitiveness of India's exports of shrimp products. The idle capacities in times of non-availability of shrimps can be diverted for processing other export items like tuna or items for domestic consumption, to improve the profitability of marine products processing industry, which may in turn improve the competitiveness of the shrimp exports from India.

Improvement on the following two areas was necessary for India to offer competitive shrimp products to the Japanese market. One is the product development by improving freezing method. Instead of the block freezing method, the individually-quick-frozen form of processing has been adopted in the marine products processing industry since the early 1970s. However, owing to the limited supply of the machinery for such processing and a lack of initial technical know-how and investment, only a minor portion of exports were processed in this way.[49] The other point is that it has been often alleged that India's exports of marine products are black-listed by some of the importing countries from hygenic considerations, which has contributed to the sharp fall in prices especially in the U.S. market.[50] Measures to maintain quality control are needed to overcome such shortcomings for expanding the exports to the Japanese market.

In the longer perspective, efforts are necessary for the artificial culture of shrimps to enhance the catch above the estimated reserve. According to the Report by the National Commission on Agriculture (Ministry of Agriculture and Irrigation, Government of India), against the exploited crustacean resources of India about 183 thousand tonnes, a two-to-three-fold increase from the existing level of catch is considered to be justified, taking into account the rate of exploitation in different centres, the available area for expansion of fishery activity and the trends in the capture fishery.[51] By judicious development of capture fishery and by extension of the same into new fishing grounds, it would be possible to obtain an overall crustacean catch of 400 to 500 thousand tonnes a year, which was equal to twice of the catch in 1973.[52]

Taking into account the efforts in increasing production as well as in the product development, an unofficial estimate indicates that India's exports of frozen shrimps would increase to 81 thousand tonnes by 1985 from 34 thousand tonnes in 1973.[53]

Policy for Shrimp Export

In order to promote the exports of marine products, the Marine Products Export Promotion Council was set up under the Ministry of Commerce, Government of India in 1961. The Council was reconstituted in 1972 as the Marine Products Exports Development Authority (MPEDA) with considerable executive powers and autonomy in operation. The function of the MPEDA, as specified in the MPEDA Act 1972, is to promote marine products development, under the control of the Government of India, with special emphasis for exports.[54]

There were no specific policies meant for the promotion of shrimp exports from India until 1973 except for the establishment of the MPEDA. However, there were suggestions for introducing policies for export promotion of shrimp products at various points of time.[55]

With a view to ensuring the supply of shrimps on a sustained basis to meet the rising domestic demand, Japan has participated in joint ventures for the development of shrimps fishery mostly with developing countries such as Indonesia, Malaysia, Tanzania and Sri Lanka. By 1973, out of the 72 Japanese joint fishing ventures[56] in the world with a total investment of over $ 19 million, as many as 25 were those regarding shrimps fishery ventures.[57] These countries have developed their fisheries to a great extent by acquiring trawlers and techinal know-hows under joint collaboration arrangements with Japan. Joint ventures are advantageous for developing countries to cut short the time consuming process of development as well as to avoid the risk of investment. Also they were assured of disposing the catch in the market of their collaborators. By 1973 Japan had already concluded with Australia, Cuba and Mexico the agreements to secure a minimum quantity of shrimps annually.[58]

Issues in Shrimp Export Development

The liberalisation of import restrictions since 1961 and growing real disposable income leading to an increase in demand for quality seafoods constituted a strong demand in the Japanese import market of shrimps. However, the strong demand for shrimps continued through the 1960s and early 1970s more or less had slackened towards the mid-1970s. An FAO study[59] in which demand and prices are projected for 1982-87 shows clearly that the demand for shrimps in Japan became more responsive to changes in price than to those in income. In other words, in Japan shrimp competes directly with other animal protein foodstuffs.

The demand situation for shrimp in Japan since the mid-1970s characterised the market by short-term periods of growth followed by a decline. The fluctuations in prices became wide and ample in the Japanese market for shrimps, which further intensified the demand fluctuations. For example, in 1983, the price for a Indian white variety of shrimps fell as much as 20 to 30 per cent in eight months.[60] India's shrimp exports to Japan has to be prepared for such uncertainty in its import market.

From the above analysis, the following points stand out clearly :

—Demand for frozen shrimp has been rising and was faster after Japan introduced import liberalisation measures. There has also been closer relationship between demand and price.

—Supply from India has been rising. It was competitive both price and qualitywise.

—Infrastructure facilities for frozen shrimp exports were inadequate.

—India has no foreign collaborations in fishing industry.

—The question of relying in future on frozen shrimp as a lead export item for India arises from the problem of adequate reserves. In Chapter 6, we shall further analyse the production and export to Japan after 1973.

Barriers for Future Export Growth to Japan

From the overview of the India-Japan trade during 1951 to 1973 it could be observed that India was unable to achieve steady trade expansion and evolve a dynamic pattern of trade with Japan. India's pattern and diversification of trade presents a distinct contrast with that of other developing countries of Asia in Japanese market. These developing countries succeeded not only in expanding trade with Japan, but also in changing the pattern of trade.

The significant difference between the pattern of India's trade with Japan and that of the countries like South Korea and Taiwan was the increasing concentration of India's non-manufactures or primary exports to Japan. The degree of the export concentration on non-manufacturers in India's exports to Japan is found to be extremely high as only a few items of non-manufactures constituted a major portion of India's export earnings from Japan. Iron ore and shrimps were among India's export commodities to Japan, which were mainly responsible for the export concentration. It was also observed, that India's exports failed to keep up with the growing demand in the Japanese market as well as also to offer competitive prices.

It is evident from the discussion in this chapter that concentration of non-manufactures is not a desirable element for it tends to pose instability to the economy through fluctuations in export earnings, while also the expansion of non-manufactures does not promote economic development commensurate with the change and growth in the world economy. Diversification of exports by expanding manufactured exports is considered a suitable solution for the problems of developing economies in the export sector. Also, for a developing economy like India to intensify industrialisation, export diversification bears significant implications.

In the next chapter, the trends in India's export of manufactures to Japan is discussed. To shift to a new trading framework with Japan based on horizontal trade in manufactures, India will have to increase on a larger measure its weightage of manufactured exports.

REFERENCES

1. I. Yamazawa, "Intensity Analysis of World Trade Flow", *Hitotsubashi Journal of Economics* (Tokyo), Vol. 10, No. 2, February 1970, pp. 61-90.

2. Figures refer to the former British India including Pakistan, Bangladesh, etc. as well as to the former Japanese Empire including its territories and colonies in Korea, Taiwan, Saghalien, Kurile Islands, etc. United Nations, *Yearbook of International Trade, 1951* (New York, 1952), p. 29.

3. Bureau of Statistics, Prime Minister's Office, Japanese Government, *Japan Statistical Yearbook 1950* (Tokyo, 1950), pp. 216 and 222-31. In fact, the figures represent those of Japan's exports to and its imports from India. Also note that India's trade with the former territories of Japan, viz., South Saghalien and Kurile Islands was taken into account

in the figures, while India here refers to the former British India including Pakistan and Bangladesh.

4. Ministry of Commerce, Government of India, *Monthly Abstract of Statistics* (New Delhi), Vol. 1, No. 2 November 1948, pp. 2436. The figures exclude trade on Government account and include those of the territories of former British India, viz,, Pakistan and Bangladesh.

5. United Nations, *Yearbook of Industrial Statistics 1974*, Vol. 1 (New York, 1975), p. 75.

6. Bureau of Statistics, Prime Minister's Office, Japanese Government, *Statistical Yearbook of Japan 1275* (Tokyo, 1965), p. 275.

7. United Nations, *Yearbook of International Trade 1975, Vol. II* (New York, 1975), p. 1256.

8. United Nations, *Yearbook of Industrial Statistics 1976, Vol. II* (New York, 1976), p. 547.

9. United Nations, *Yearbook of International Trade 1975, op. cit.*, p. 1255.

10. D. Nayyar, *India's Export and Export Policies in the 1960s* (London: Cambridge University Press, 1976), p. 142. A study by National Council of Applied Economic Research (NCAER) suggested that in addition to the three points, India should adopt benefication of iron ore aimed particularly at: (1) size reduction; (2) improvement of chemical content; (3) utilisation of fines to compete in the international markets. It is well known that iron ore as industrial material should be as high a grade as possible. Experiments carried out in the USSR have shown that for an increaseo f 1 per of Fe the burden, the productivity increased by 2 per cent while the coke rate decreased by 3 per cent. Also. the studies carried out in Japan have shown that a 1 per cent decrease in the proportion of lumps larger than 35 mm in the burden corresponds to a decrease in the coke rate of approximately 2 kgs. per tonne and a 1 per cent decrease in fines of less than 6 mm base to a dccrease in the coke rate of 1 kg. per tonne. Changes in chemical content of iron ore are cssential, particularly for iron ore produced in India which contains alumina considerably. See for details, National Council of Applied Economic Research, *System Studies for Iron Ore Exports* (New Delhi, 1976), pp. 132-53.

11. In 1979, out of the total production of saleable iron ores, 12.7 per cent amounting to 8 million tonnes was turned out by manually-operated mines excluding fines generated in manual mines and separately. *Ibid.*, p. 153.

12. The same study by the NCAER shows that mechanised mining costs are much lower than in manual mining, since labour in manual mines operates through contractors on a piece-rate basis while in mechanised mines the operations are done departmentally, even taking into account the statutory minimum wages and other amenities like housing, medical facilities that the latter labourers are assured of. As a result, the average cost of mining in manual operations stands at Rs. 38.76

to Rs. 44.26 per tonne against Rs. 19.48 to Rs. 34.05 per tonne in mechanised operations. Moreover, in case of mechanised mines, their large throughout volume permits the provision of railway sidings close to the mines, while or from manual workings has to be transported to the nearest railway station by road and loaded into wagons there. As a result, the cost of transport to railway loading points and loading in case of mechanised mines stands at Rs. 1.50 to Rs. 250 per tonne against Rs. 8.50 to Rs. 10.50 per tonne in case of manual mines. See, *ibid.*, p. 159.

13. Unloading points in the Goa mining areas were connected with bargc to the port Mormugao. The Kudremukh mine which has a capacity of 22.5 million tons of run of mine ore is equlpped with a slurry pipeline to the port Mangalore in which magnetite concentrates in the forms of fincs can be transported along with the traditional means of transportation. See, *ibid.*, pp 167-.76.

14. *Ibid.*, pp. 177-86.

15. This section is based on V.D. Chowgule, "Japanese Market for Our Iron Ore", *Commerce* (Bombay), Vol. 123, No. 3161, December 1971, p. 41.

16. D. Nayyar attributes the competitiveness of Australian and Brazilian iron ore against Indian ore partly to the planned, large-scale operations which integrates mining with transportation and shipping for exports which were enabled only with large foreign investments. See D. Nayyar, *India's Export and Export Policies in the 1960s*, *op. cit.*, pp. 143-44.

17. *Ibid.*, p. 142.

18. National Council of Applied Economic Research, *System Study for Iron Ore Export*, *op. cit.*, p. 155.

19. National Council of Applied Economic Research, *Survey of India's Export Prospects to Japan* (New Delhi, 1970), pp. 167-68.

20. In addition, the price of iron ore exported from Brazil have been further reduced by the use of oil/ore carriers which permit carriage of oil for part of the return voyage from Middle East to West Europe or North America with a payload to distance ratio of 66 per cent. Owing to this factor, Brazil could reduce the price drastically despite its iong distance from Japan. See for details, National Council of Applied Economic Research, *System Study for Iron Ore Export*, *op. cit.*, p. 107.

21. *Ibid.*, pp. 129-31.

22. Assuming the annual exploitation rate of iron ore to be 127 million tonnes, given a hundred-year life for the reserves known (supposing no fresh discovery of reserves during the period) and the estimated requirements of ore for internal consumption, the exportable surplus would be 1953 million tonnes enough to sustain an export level of 45 million tonnes annually over 43 years, which is twice as high as the export level in 1973. See for details, *ibid.*, pp. 129-31.

23. *Ibid.*, pp. 107-8.

24. See, V.D. Chowgule, "Japanese Market for Our Iron Ore", *op. cit.*, p. 41.

25. National Council of Applied Economic Research, *Survey of India's Export Prospects in Japan, op. cit.*, p. 169. A. Halder supports India's exports of iron ore in the form of barter. His findings, based on the empirical data of India's iron ore exports in the 1960s, are as follows: (1) that India's iron ore was highly income-elastic in the world markets; (2) that, on the other hand, it showed insignificant elasticity for substitution; (3) that its price elasticity was insignificant particularly in the Japanese market. The first factor suggests that the growth of national income of those countries had a significant influence on iron ore exports from India. And the second and third factors were resulted from the characteristics of India's export agreements concluded with its customers, many of which took a form of barter. He mentions that price is not a crucial factor in India's exports of iron ore to Japan and it is more correlated with the economic growth of the importing countries. Also it is argued that the expansion of iron ore exports to Japan is highly dependent on the ability and strength of the MMTC to arrange favourable barter agreements with Japan. See for details, A. Halder, *India's Export Pattern—Analysis on Potential Diversification* (Calcutta: Minerva Associates, 1976), pp. 69-71.

26. The long-term agreements concluded by India's iron ore industry for exports were : (1) with Rumania to supply 23.4 million tonnes of iron ore between 1970 and 1980; (2) with eight Japanese steel mills to supply 71.5 million tonnes by 1979; (3) with some other Japanese mills to supply 61.3 million tonnes over 9 years. See, Ministry of Finance, Government of India, *Report on Currency and Finance* (Bombay), from the issues of 1969-70 and 1970-71, p. 79 and p. 98, respectively.

27. Prices of iron ore in the world market rose from US $ 9 per tonne in the late 1960s to US $ 12 per tonne in 1973-74 and to a higher price in the next year. D. Nayyar, *India's Export's and Export Policies in the 1960s, op. cit.*, p. 364.

28. OECD, *Steel in the 80s* (Paris, 1980), pp. 68-82.

29. *Ibid.*, p. 85. In North America, steel intensity per dollar of GDP fell from 0.20 kg. in the early 1950s to around 0.16 kg. in the early 1970s.

30. Quoted in J.C. Gandhi, "Export of Minerals", in Federation of Indian Mineral Industries, *Proceedings of National Mineral Convention* (New Delhi, 1981), pp. 519-22.

31. The long-tailed crustaceans consists of shrimp s(of a size upto 9 inches long), prawns (of a size from 9 inches to 2 feet long) and lobsters (of a size more than 2 feet long). In this section, shrimps are chosen to represent the crustaceans belonging to shrimps and prawns.

32. Food and Agricultural Organisation, *Yearbook of Fishery Statistics 1973* (Rome, 1974), Vol. 36, pp. 4 and 5.

33. Ministry of Agriculture and Irrigation, Government of India,

Report of the National Commission on Agriculture, Vol. VIII (New Delhi, 1976), p. 191.

34. Food and Agricultural Organisation. *Yearbook of Fishery Statistics, op. cit.*, pp. 472-77.

35. United Nations, *Yearbook of International Trade 1974, Vol. II* (New York, 1975), pp. 25 and 26.

36. Food and Agricultural Organisation, *Yearbook of Fishery Statistics* (Rome, 1974), Vol, 37, pp. 480 and 481.

37. *Ibid.*, pp. 25 and 26,

38. *Ibid.*, pp. 465 and 466.

39. Japan External Trade Organization, Ministry of International Trade and Industry, Japanese Government, *Access to Japan's Import Market—Frozen Shrimp* (Tokyo, 1980), p. 11.

40. This section is based on Ministry of Agriculture and Irrigation, Government of India, *Report of the National Commission on Agriculture, Vol. 8, op. cit.*, pp. 191-233.

41. K. Chidambaram, "Marine Products—Export Prospects", *Foreign Trade Review* (New Delhi), Voi. 9, No. 1, April-June 1974, p. 27.

42. Import quota imposed on fresh and chilled marine products including frozen shrimps was removed in October 1961. In place of it, import tariff was set out for fresh and frozen prawns in shell at 5 per cent and for pickled prawns at 4 per cent as preferential duty or at 6 per cent as temporary duty based on the c.i.f. value. At the Tokyo Round in July 1979, Japan agreed that the duty would be gradually reduced to 3 per cent in eight years from 1980. See, Japan External Trade Organisation, Ministry of International Trade and Industry, Japanese Government, *Access to Japan's Import Market—Frozen Shrimp, op. cit.*, p. 13.

43. Such traditional crafts can be basically classified as follows : (1) catemarans 6 m. x 0.7 m. to 7.6 m. x 1.4 m; (2) dug-outs 4m x 0.6m to 8m x 1,4m: (3) plank-built boat 6.6 m x 0.9 m to 14 m x 3.1 m. See for details Ministry of Agriculture and Irrigation, Government of India, *Report of the National Commission on Agriculture, Vol. VIII, op. cit.*, p. 197.

44. These crafts were introduced since the early 1950s. Most of them are of a size between 17m and 33m in length with a 10 to 60 BHP inboard engine' See, *Ibid.*, p. 197.

45. In addition, there were about 100 larger steel-built trawlers in use, of a size between 6.6 m and 12.5 m in length equipped with refrigerated fish holds, but their operations are only for the exploratory work by the government agencies and large business houses. From 1967 onwards, deepwater grounds between 150 m and 400 m, particularly lying on the continental slope off the southwest coast of India, were exploited for deepwater prawns by 4 to 5 modern exploratory trawlers owned by the government agencies. However, the catch of shrimps by them is only less than 100 tonnes annually, and moreover, deepwater shrimps carry a minor commercial value. See, *ibid.*, p. 192,

46. *Ibid.*, pp. 192-93.

47. It is also important for India's shrimps industry to be equipped with appropriate facilities for maintaining freshness of the highly perishable catch before processing. For example, facilities in harbour are critical for maintaining freshness of catch. However, because of the factors such as inadequacy in landing quays with provision for timely unloading, cleaning, sorting and display of catch for auction and cold storage facilities for preserving the catch till its disposal and transportation to the processing units, it often happens that the catch loses its freshness and its commercial value. Also transportation arrangements, refrigerated trucks and insulated vans for speedy movements of the catch have to be taken into account in case of the catch landed far away from the processing units. At the same time, the establishment of primary processing units in various landing areas is also suggested. See for details, Indian Institute of Foreign Trade, *Survey of India's Export Potential of Marine Products, Vol. 2* (New Delhi, 1970), pp. 84-117; Indian Institute of Foreign Trade, *Conclusions and Recommendations of a Seminar on Marine Products* (New Delhi, 1964), p. 32.

48. Ministry of Agriculture and Irrigation, Government of India, *Report of the National Commission on Agriculture, Vol. VIII, op. cit.* p. 228.

49. M.L. Varma, "Major Commodities in India's Exports-Marine Products", *Commerce* (Bombay), Vol. 123, No. 3165, Annual Number 1971, p. 54.

50. See for example, Federation of Indian Chambers of Commerce and Industry, *Export Plan For 1981-82* (New Delhi, 1981), p. 36. Also, the Marine Product Export Development Authority pointed out the high rate of rejections of Indian froglegs by the Food and Drug Administration of the US Government. See, Ministry of Agriculture and Irrigation, Government of India, *Report the National Commission on Agriculture, op. cit.*, p. 250. Many other factors besides the above seem to have contributed to a general fall in prices of Indian marine products in the world markets. The same Report indicates that sorting the products by species and sizes is not completely undertaken ln case of the exports from India and that it happens often that the products are not packed exactly according to the specified weight. See, for details, Indian Institute of Foreign Trade, *Conclusions and Recommendations of a Seminar on Marine Products Exports* (New Delhi, 1964). pp. 35-36.

51. Ministry of Agriculture and Irrigation, Government of India, *Report of the National Commission on Agriculture, Vol. VIII, op. cit.*, p. 201.

52. The Report also indicates that since the export species of shrimps available in India are suitable for cultivation in the brackishwater areas, there is a large scope for increasing production by cultivation. It is estimated that about 800 sq. km. of brackishwater available on the coastal regions can be brought under effective prawn cultivation. See, *ibid.*, pp. 203-4.

53. *Purchase* (Bombay), Vol. 5, No. 4, May 1982. p. 23.

54. Ministry of Agriculture and Irrigation, Government of India, *Report of the National Commission of Agriculture. op. cit.*, p. 248.

55. For example, the Federation of Indian Chambers of Commerce and Industry made the following suggestions for export promotion of the marine products :

(1) Marine products for exports should be exempted from purchase and sales taxes;

(2) Boats used for fishery for exports should be duty free, or a preferential treatment should be given in the price;

(3) Cost of diesel oil is one of the important factors which is preventing the prevalence of mechanisation of fishing boats. Therefore, fishing boats should be supplied diesel at concessional prices;

(4) Five per cent import entitlement has been given on exports of marine products, but this has not resulted in any assistance to the exporters. This needs to be replaced by cash compensatory support.

See, Federation of Indian Chambers of Commerce and Industry, *Export Plan for 1981-82, op. cit.*, pp. 36 and 37.

56. The types of joint ventures which the Japanese fishing industry has entered so far can be classified into four groups: joint management; charter establishment system; marketing contracts of fish catch; operating contracts of fishing bases and facilities. See, Indian Institute of Foreign Trade, *Survey of India's Export Potential of Marine Products, Vol. 38* (New Delhi, 1970), pp. 516-17.

57. K. Chidambaran, "Marine Products—Export Prospects", *op. cit.*, pp. 28-29.

58. *Ibid.*, pp. 28-29.

59. Quoted in International Trade Centre UNCTAD/GATT, *Shrimps: A Survey of the World Market* (Geneva, 1983), p. 207.

60. *Ibid.*, p. 261.

4

EFFECT OF COST STRUCTURE AND PRODUCTIVITY DIFFERENTIALS ON JAPAN'S PROPENSITY TO IMPORT INDIAN SOURCED MANUFACTURES

DIVERSIFICATION of exports by means of expansion of manufactured exports may be an ideal solution to the problems inherent in the export concentration of non-manufactures. Export expansion of manufactures brings to the economy such benefits as efficient allocation of resources through competition and a possibility of growth unconstrained by the domestic demand. Hence export diversification is often taken as one of the developmental strategies and kept in line with the programmes for industrialisation in the developing economies.

Though Japan's import structure has been originally oriented to its needs for industrial materials and fuels as observed in previous chapter, it has undergone significant changes. As Japan attained a higher level of industrialisation, new demand that was created in the process gave rise to new import requirements. One of the changes taken place in Japan's import structure was the increase of imports of manufactures accompanying the structural change in the economy. Developing countries such as South Korea and Taiwan have taken advantage of

Japan's import liberalisation policy for manufactures and succeeded in expanding their exports.

India's manufactured exports had made entry in the Japanese market since Japan's import liberalisation measures was introduced. However, manufactured exports did not grow and diversify to the desired extent.

In this chapter, we will first ascertain the level of industrialisation of the industry of India's, Japan's and some selected countries with the help of the Ganko Keitai Growth Model. Subsequently the industry's cost structure and differentials are examined to assess Japan's propensity to import Indian sourced manufactures. India's two vital manufacturing industries viz. cotton textiles and handtools are specifically selected as these two industries are widely recognised as good potential for India to be world leading producers and exporters.

Cotton Textile Industry: Production and Export Trend

The mechanisation of India's cotton textile industry started in the spinning sector in the 19th century. By 1825, handloom weavers began using mill-spun yarns. By the turn of the century, the mechanisation prevailed in the weaving sector. In 1900, there were 193 mills with 5 million spindles and 40,125 looms. The breakout of the Second World War contributed greatly to the growth of the cotton textile industry in India. The growth during the war was supported by the strong demand from the domestic market, which was attributed to the fact that the imports especially from the U.K. came to a standstill.[1]

The cotton textile industry in the post-war period continued to retain the traditional, decentralised sector which employ powerlooms and handlooms, along with the mechanised spinning and composite mills in the organised sector. The production of cotton fabrics turned out by both the sectors had been the highest in the world from 1968 on. In 1973, India's production of cotton fabrics constituted 21 per cent of the total production in the world.[2]

In 1951, 79 per cent of the total production of cotton fabrics in India was attributed to the mill sector. Since then, the decentralised sector increased the production after recovering from the post-war depression,[3] and the share of production by the mill sector declined to 54 per cent by 1973.[4] The mill sector of India's cotton textile industry constituted the largest single industrial segment in India's manufacturing sector in terms of value of output, value added and labour employed. In 1951, 34 per cent in the total value of output and 41 per cent in the total value added turned out by all the organised manufacturing industries were attributable to the cotton textile industry, while 39 per cent of labour engaged in the organised manufacturing belonged to the sector.[5]

However, the relative importance of the cotton textile industry in the manufacturing sector declined over years, partly because of the diversification of the manufacturing output and partly because of the stagnant growth of the industry itself. As a result, the share of the cotton textile industry in the total value of output, value added and labour employed by all the organized industries declined to 12 per cent, 13 per cent, 18 per cent, respectively by 1970.[6]

India's cotton textile industry has been facing two serious problems. One is the preponderance of the obsolete machinery and equipment. According to a survey by the working group appointed by the National Industrial Development Corporation (NIDC), about 60 per cent of the blow-rooms, 70 per cent of cards, 70 to 80 per cent of speed frames, 50 per cent of ring frames and 84 per cent of looms available in the cotton textile industry were used over years in 1960.[7] Even at the end of 1973, automatic looms constituted only 19 per cent of the total installed loomage in India.[8] It is widely known that productivity and quality of output of India's cotton textile industry has been affected by not improving the production technology.[9]

The second problem is that though India is one of the principal raw cotton producing countries, thep roduction has not kept pace with the demand of the cotton textile industry.[10] The yield per acre of Indian cotton is extremely low, which, for example, in the crop year 1972-73 stood at 134 bales, much below the world average of 257 bales.[11] It has been pointed out that inadequate inputs such as fertilisers and insecticides and the shortage of irrigated areas for cultivation[12] limited the production capacity.

Cotton textiles was one of India's dynamic exports soon

after the Second World War. Export growth was supported by the world-wide surge in demand during the reconstruction period and the domestic commercial policies such as devaluation.[13] However, as the increase in exports was not supported by the growth in production, the supply available for the domestic demand was badly affected.[14] As a result, the exports dropped from a record-high 1105 million metres to 350 million metres between 1950-51 and 1951-55.[15] The exports of cotton fabrics reached another peak in the early 1960s when the industry saw a drastic expansion in production. However, the exports remained at a low level in the following years mainly due to the devaluation of Rupee in 1966 and depression of the domestic economy in the late 1960s [16]

Cotton fabrics was one of the important exports not only in the textile group but also in all the export commodities and as Table 4.1 shows that cotton fabrics in value terms constituted a significant portion in the total and textile exports. Table 4.2

TABLE 4.1

Shares of Textiles and Cotton Fabrics in India's Total exports
(% of total value)

Year	*Textiles*	*Gotton Fabrics*	*Cotton Fabrics as of Textiles*
1955	n.a.	9.3	n.a.
1960	34.4	9.8	28.5
1965	34.2	7.0	20.5
1970	22.7	8.5	37.4
1973	22.6	10.7	47.3

Source: Calculated from United Nations, *Yearbook of International Trade*, from various issues between 1952 and 1975.

indicates the export-output ratio of cotton fabrics manufacturing industry. The ratio went up rapidly towards the early 1960s when the production expanded and vice-versa towards the late 1960s when the production declined.[17]

Regarding the direction of India's exports of cotton fabrics, significant changes could be noted between 1951 and 1973. In the 1950s, a considerable share in India's exports of cotton fabrics was directed to the markets in the developing countries. For example, in 1954, the exports to the former British East Africa such as Kenya, Tanganyika and Zanzibar, the former British West Africa such as Ghana and Nigeria, Sudan and

TABLE 4.2

India's Cotton Textile Industry: Export-Output and Import-Consumption Ratio (%)

Year	*Export-Output Ratio*		*Import-Consumption Ratio*
	All sectors	*Mill sector*	
1955	10.8	12.0	0.2
1960	10.0	12.3	0.1
1965	7.2	11.0	—
1970	5.1	8.9	—
1973	8.2	13.6	—

Source: Textile Commissioner, Government of India, *Indian Textile Bulletin* (Bombay) from various issues of 1960 to 1973.

Ethiopia constituted 31.1 per cent of India's total exports of cotton fabrics to the world in quantity terms, while 15.5 per cent was directed to India's neighbouring countries such as Burma, Sri Lanka, Pakistan, Afghanistan and Iran.[18] However, by 1973, the share of exports to all the developing countries declined to 29.6 per cent of India's total export value of cotton fabrics.[19] The less developed markets in Africa and Asia where India enjoyed substantial exports in the past developed their own textile industry and introduced trade and commercial policies to protect it from imports.[20] In the meantime, India's cotton fabrics exports increased to developed countries and centrally planned economies. In 1973, 58.0 per cent and 12.4 per cent of the total value of exports of cotton fabrics was directed to the former and the latter countries, respectively.[21] Table 4.3 shows the direction of India's exports of cotton fabrics to the major selected countries. It may be observed that U.S.A. and the U.K. were the largest importers of India's cotton fabrics. It was not until the late 1960s that India's cotton fabrics could make a significant entry to the Japanese market.

TABLE 4.3

Direction of India's Exports of Cotton Piece Goods[1]
(% of total quantity)

Year	*Japan*	*U.S.A.*	*U.K.*	*Nepal*	*Sri Lanka*	*Sudan*	*Total (million yards)*
1955	—	—	12.9	—	3.0	7.9	815.5
1960	—	4.8	27.5	—	3.4	8.9	723.7
1965	—	9.5	24.8	7.8	3.6	5.8	638.3
1969	—	13.5	25.5	13.1	—	5.7	532.8
1973	7.3	13.4	27.6	5.9	—	1.6	754.2

Note: (1) Including tire cord besides textiles; excluding handloom from 1966 on, except exports to Japan.

Source: International Cotton Advisory Committee, *Quarterly Bulletin of Cotton World Statistics* (Washington D.C.), from various issues of 1951 to 1973.

Handtools Industry : Production and Export Trends

Handtools which are produced in India can be broadly classified into six groups: (1) precision cutting tools, such as milling cutters, broaching tools, threading taps, dies, reamers, twist drills, diamond drill bits, etc.; (2) wood-working tools, such as saws, saw blades, augers, planes, bits and braces, chisels and punches, etc.; (3) forged handtools, such as spanners, wrenches, pliers, hammers, screw drivers, bolt and wire strand cutters, etc., (4) measuring tools, such as metal rules, scales and tapes, etc., (5) garden tools, such as spades, shovels, axes, rakes; and (6) other handtools, such as hacksaw frames, bearing pullers, hand drills, wire insulation strippers, etc.[22]

The complete data on the value of production by groups classified as above during 1951-73 are not available. But the value of production in 1974 by the major products by the large and small units registered with Directorate General of Technical Development, Government of India (DGTD), was as follows:[23] Forged handtools Rs. 128 million; hacksaw and band-saw blades Rs. 46 million; important tools such as grinding wheels, coasted abrasives, steel files Rs. 192 million; and other important tools such as twist drills, reamers, diamond drill bits, TC tipped tools, cemented carbide hard metal products Rs. 140 million.

Commercial production of handtools in India started only in the immediate post-war period. The industry for the first few years was confined to the small-scale sector. Production by the organised sector began in the early 1950s.[24] The handtools industry continued to retain the cottage and the small-scale sectors, along with the large scale organised sector.

The cottage units, with their limited production capacity, primarily cater to the demand emanating from the nearby regions where they are situated.[25] According to the survey conducted by the Small Industrial Service Institutes (SISI) in Delhi, Madras, Calcutta and Bombay, there were 1349 units in 1956-57 in the cottage sector of the handtools industry in India.[26] On the other hand, the small units have a relatively larger geographical marketing range and some of the progressive units, apart from the domestic market, have also acquired markets abroad. According to the survey by the Development Commissioner for Small Scale Industries (DCSSI), there were 161 units under this category in 1966.[27]

The production of handtools by large units commenced in the early 1950s. In the beginning, only steel files were manufactured. Production of other items of handtools in the sector began around 1961, including carpenters' tools like adzes, cramps, augers and tools for smithy. By 1978, 88 organised units were set up, all of which were registered with the DGTD.[28]

Raw materials[29] and technical tools required for the production of the tools have been mostly imported under the import replenishment scheme. The equipment and machinery required for forging, casting and machining was made available by the domestic production by the late 1970s. The technical know-hows have been developed over years from the technology which was initially imported.[30]

The exports of handtools started to be promoted in an organised way by the Engineering Export Promotion Council (EEPC) in the mid-1950s, along with the other engineering products.[31] Handtools increased its share in the total value of the engineering exports (see Table 4.4).[32]

TABLE 4.4

Shares of Engineering Goods and Handtools in India's Total Exports

(% of total value)

Year	*Engineering goods*	*Handtools*	*Handtools as of Engineering goods*
1960	1.6	—	0.6
1965	3.6	0.1	2.7
1970	7.5	0.3	3.8
1973	7.8	0.4	4.7

Source: Calculated from Engineering Export Promotion Council, *Handbook of Export Statistics 1974-75* (Calcutta, 1975).

Exports are essential for the handtools industry since a large portion of raw materials for production are to be imported. Despite the strong demand in the domestic market for the product, the export-output ratio of the industry had been higher than the average of all engineering products and increased rapidly after 1970 (see Table 4.5). A guidance and plan for

TABLE 4.5

India's Engineering, Metal Products and Handtools Industries: Export-Output Ratio and Import-Consumption Ratio (%)

Year	*Export-Output Ratio*			*Import-Consumption Ratio*	
	Engineering[1] products	*Metal products*	*Hand tools*	*Engineering[1] products*	*Metal products*
1957-58	0.7	2.4	—	42.4	40.5
1960-61	0.9	1.8	2.4	36.5	18.2
1965-66	1.0	1.8	4.3	25 6	6.9
1970-71	5.2	7.7	18.8	17.3	2.7

Note: (1) Excluding miscellaneous engineering products which account for approximately 1 per cent of total production, exports, imports and consumption.

Source: A.G. Majumdar, *The Indian Engineering Industry—Trends and Prospects* (New Delhi, 1972), etc.

India's handtools industry suggests that the net saving for foreign exchange in the sector should exceed 60 per cent of the f.o.b. value of exports.[33]

With the level of technology India had during 1951-73, it was not able to manufacture the entire range of handtools which were in demand in world markets.[34] Exports of handtools from India were more or less concentrated on the following items: spanners; wrenches; pliers; pincers: interchangeable tools for machine tools, etc.; files and rasps; other items such as handtools for agriculture and forestry, handsaws and various saw blades, metal working handtools, interchangeable tools for handtools, dies, drilling bits, taps, tungstein carbide tips, tipped tools.[35] The break up of exports of handtools by major commodities in 1972-73 were as follows: spanners 33.9 per cent; pipe wrenches 17.7 per cent; pliers 4.1 per cent; steel files 9.6 per cent; and twist drills 11.9 pcr cent.[36]

India's exports of handtools had increasingly concentrated on the markets of developed countries, though in earlier years a considerable portion was directed to the developing and centrally planned economies. In 1965, India's exports of handtools to the former and the latter comprised 30.0 per cent and 34.2 per cent of its total exports of handtools,[37] which declined to 22.3 per cent and 18.6 per cent, respectively, by 1973.[38]

At the same time, the exports to developed countries consi-

TABLE 4.6

Direction of India's Exports of Handtools
(% of total value)

Year	*Japan*	*U.S.A.*	*U.K.*	*West Germany*	*Czechoslovakia*	*Total (thousand rupees)*
1960-61	—	0.3	—	0.2	—	636
1965-66	—	19.2	5.8	2.6	43.8	8062
1970-71	5.4	18.4	7.9	7.4	7.6	43784
1973-74	2.4	16.7	9.9	8.5	9.1	90536

Source: Department of Commercial Intelligence & Statistics, Government of India, *Monthly Statistics of the Foreign Trade of India* (Calcutta), from various March issues of 1966 to 1974.

derably increased. In particular, the exports of handtools to three developed countries, the U.S.A., the U.K. and West Germany, constituted almost one third of India's total exports of handtools (see also Table 4.6). India's exports of handtools to the developed countries are mainly of low or non-professional handtools where India's products have competitiveness[39]

India's exports of handtools to the Japanese market started on a large scale only in 1969. India has been facing fierce competition, as similar products exported from the countries like South Korea and Taiwan have been proved to be more competitive, achieving higher unit value realisation.[40]

TREND IN JAPAN'S IMPORTS OF MANUFACTURES

Japan's Cotton Textile Industry and Imports from India

Japan's cotton textile industry,[41] has been one of the important industries tn the manufacturing sector since the pre-war period. In 1938, the output by the cotton textile industry constituted 11 per cent of the total value of output by the entire manufacturing sector. Cotton textiles were also one of the major exports of Japan. In 1934, cotton facrics displaced raw silk as Japan's largest exports. Japan's cotton fabrics exports was the largest in the world from 1933 on until the out-break of the Second World War.

The industry suffered a great deal during the war and its production plummeted to the one-fourth of the pre-war level. In rebuilding the industry after the war, the latest technology was introduced. As a result, the industry recovered to the pre-war level of production within two years from the end of the war. Until the late 1950s, Japan's cotton textile industry continued to be the largest component of the textile industry. The labour engagad in cotton manufacturing equalled to 6.2 per cent of all manufacturing workers in establishments of four or more employees and generated one-twentieth of the total value added by the manufacturing sector in 1956. The industry also recovered the position as the world's largest exporter in 1954.

Progressive industralisation from the late 1950s to the early 1960s brought about the structural change in the Japanese economy, in which the heavy and chemical industry became the leading sector in the economy. Also, accompanying by the change there was a relative decline in the importance of the light industrial sector including textiles against the heavy and chemical industry. By 1973, the share of the cotton textile industry in the total value of production by all the manufacturing industries as well as in the total labour engaged in manufacturing declined, and the absolute level of production also started to fall from the early 1960 onwards (see Figure 4.1).

FIGURE 4.1

Cotton Fabrics—Japan : Production, Exports and Imports

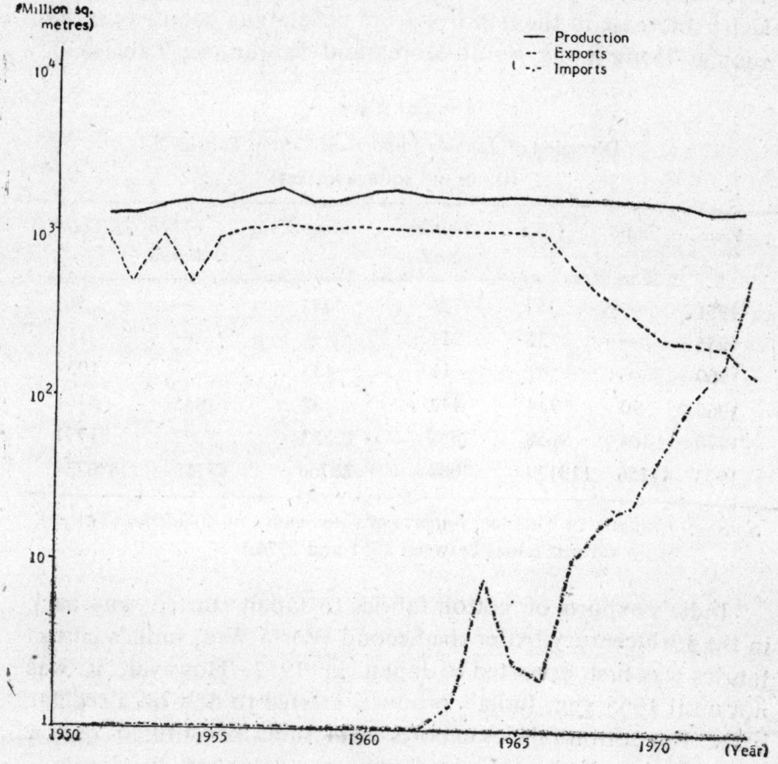

Source: United Nations, *Growth of World Industry* (Vol. II), (New York), from various issues—Production; Ministry of International Trade and Industry, Japan, *White Paper on International Trade*, (Tokyo), from various issues—exports and imports.

The trend in exports of cotton fabrics followed the trend in production. The growth in the exports levelled off in the early 1960s when the level of production reached the ceiling before the exports began to fall with the decline in production. On the other hand, the imports of cotton fabrics, which was negligible until then, started to expand as exports and production declined (see also Figure 4.1). Increase in imports of cotton fabrics was made possible with the import liberalisation measures timely adopted since 1964. In the early stages of the liberalisation, Japan had mainly enlarged the imports from developed countries under the trade pacts on import quotas. The imported items were mainly high quality products.[42] After 1967, there was a sharp increase in the imports from developing countries in Asia such as Hong Kong, South Korea and Taiwan (see Table 4.7).

TABLE 4.7

Direction of Japan's Imports of Cotton Fabrics

(thousand square metres)

Year	*India*	*USA*	*Switzer-land*	*Hong Kong*	*South Korea*	*Total*
1951	—	357	26	111	—	560
1955	—	32	11	—	—	132
1960	—	87	11	133	—	1059
1965	90	734	442	32	1845	4461
1970	484	9658	1899	13353	7377	71771
1973	47756	118129	3088	26766	87718	686734

Source: Ministry of Finance, *Imports of Commodity by Countries* (Tokyo), from various issues between 1951 and 1974.

India's exports of cotton fabrics to Japan started way back in the 19th century. After the Second World War, India's cotton fabrics was first exported to Japan in 1952. However, it was not until 1965 that India's products started to flow on a regular basis. But cotton fabrics exports from India constituted only a small protion of Japan's total imports. Some of the developing countries in Asia which were unknown to Japan's cotton fabrics import market until the early 1960s achieved rapid export growth, while India's export remained at a low level.

Japan's Handtools Industry and Imports from India

Most of the handtools manufacturers in Japan belong to the small-scale industry with 2 to 4 types of handtools as their complete product range.[43] However, there are also large-scale manufacturers, though small in number, which turn out half of the total value of production of the whole sector. The latter produce a variety of tools with wide range of specifications in each item in a mechanised process with numerically controlled equipments.[44] Japan has been one of the largest producers and exporters of handtools in the world. Among Japan's handtools export items, cutting tools and drop forged tools have been traditionally competitive in the world markets.

Rapid growth of Japan's engineering industry since the early 1960s have had a distinct impact on its domestic demand for handtools. The upsurge in the demand for handtools had accompanied the commencement of the imports of handtools on a large scale in the late 1960s (see Figure 4.2).

The handtools import market in Japan consists of two large segments.[45] One is for industrial end-use market and the other is the do-it-yourself (DIY) market. According to the All Japanese Machinist Handtool Manufacturers' Association, about 60 to 65 per cent of the imports of handtools were directed to the former in 1978. The imports of the industrial end-use market included certain tools, especially some of the small and cutting tools, which Japan had to import from the developed countries such as the U.S.A., West Germany, the U.K., Sweden and Switzerland owing to Japan's lower technological sophistication and functional perfection of the tools than that of these countries (see Table 4.8).

The DIY market has emerged because of the necessity for maintaining a household by its members themselves owing to the rise in labour cost. The demand in the DIY market was initially catered by the local small-scale manufacturers. Since the late 1960s, the developing countries in Asia such as Taiwan, South Korea and China started to supply the products for Japan's DIY market for handtools. Taiwan and South Korea have had certain edge over other foreign suppliers to the market, since in many cases they have taken an advantage of joint ventures in which Japan provided know-how as well as investment. The handtools exported from China have been also in the DIY market, as a result of its efforts in finding outlet for their products as a part of its vigorous exports promotion policy. The handtools exports from India to Japan were mainly directed to the DIY market.[46]

FIGURE 4.2

Handtools—Japan : Production, Exports and Imports

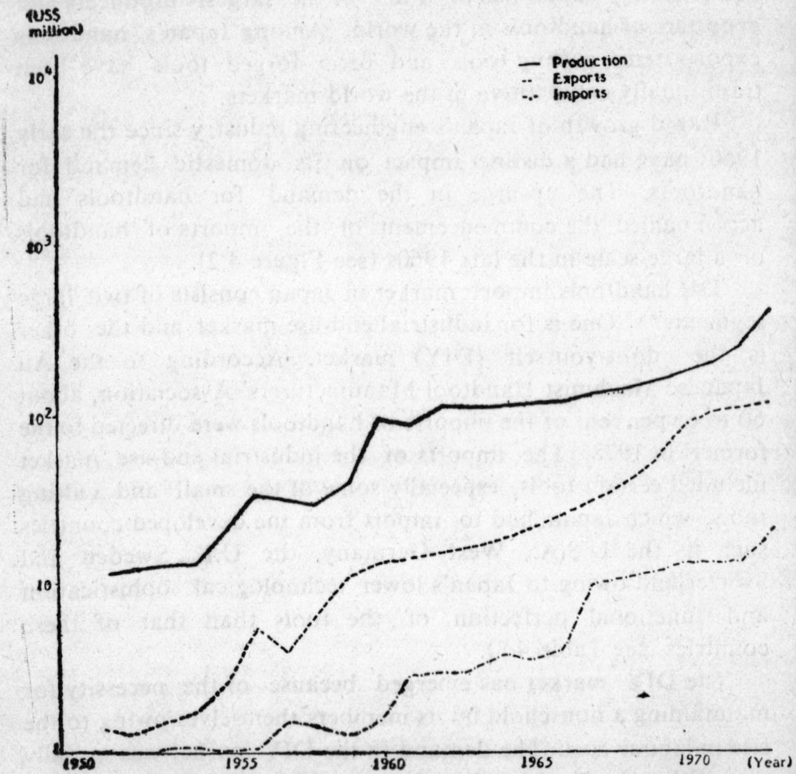

Source: Ministry of International Trade and Industry, Japan, *Census of Manufactures—Report by Industries* (Tokyo), from various issues —Production; Ministry of International Trade and Industry, Japan, *White Paper on International Trade* (Tokyo), from various issues—exports and imports.

TABLE 48

Direction of Japan's Imports of Handtools
(thousand yen)

Year	*India*	*U.S.A.*	*West Germany*	*South Korea*	*Taiwan*	*China*	*Total (thousand yen)*
1955				n.a.			404306
1960				n.a.			947899
1965		1301144	792766	—	—	—	2118838
1970	89120	3795809	1109650	2883	29270	2514	7409013
1973	136517	4174882	1539513	64745	142550	58531	10468675

Source: Ministry of Finance, Japan, *Imports of Commodity by Countries* (Tokyo), from various December issues between 1965 and 1974.

Competitiveness of India's Manufactured Exports

A majority of the manufactured exports from developing countries usually are labour-intensive, technologically stable products produced usually depending on their advantage of low wages as well as foreign buyers for marketing and product design.[47] A less advanced country, before establishing its own manufacture of a product (usually a consumer good) has to accumulate knowledge and experience for the production through a learning effect from the imports of the product from an advanced country for a certain period. Steady growth in domestic demand for the product, which is as well important in starting the domestic production, also depends on the learning effect from the imports.

At the time when a developing economy establishes domestic production of a product that has not existed before, the domestic market for the product is presumably fairly dominated by imports. As the production expands, the imports in the market are gradually substituted for the goods domestically produced. In some cases, the domestic industry of the product succeeds in securing a major share in the domestic market. If the production further expands beyond domestic consumption, the country may go for exporting the product to other countries, including the economies from which the less advanced country initially imported the product.

Assuming that India's export industry has more or less followed the process of development as above, India's manufactured exports to Japan represent an example of the growth of an industry in a developing economy catching up and overtaking the same industry in an industrial country. The success in catching up and overtaking of an industry of a developing economy largely depends on the pace and the extent of the growth achieved by the industry. We shall empirically analyse below India's and Japan's cotton fabrics and handtools industries in terms of the Ganko Keitai Growth model and compare it also with some selected countires.

Ganko Keitai Growth Model

K. Akamatsu formulated the process of catching-up and overtaking[48] an advanced economy by a product of a less advanced economy and termed it as Ganko Keitai Growth ('Wild-Geese-Flying' Pattern of Growth)'[49] which is divided into four stages: (1) import stage; (2) import substitution stage; (3) export expansion stage; and (4) re-import stage.[50] In the initial stage of import, a product, usually a consumer good which is not domestically produced in a less advanced economy, is provided by the advanced economy. Imports of the product by the less advanced economy stimulate its domestic demand for the product as well as provide a chance to acquire the technology for the production.

The less advanced economy derives an impetus for setting up domestic production for the product from the pressure of the domestic demand and the accumulation of knowledege and experience for the production derived and acquired from imports. Commencement of domestic production of the product indicates the beginning of the second stage of import substitution. The degree of success which would be achieved by the industry in acquiring the share in the domestic market in this stage, competing with the imports dominant in the market in the previous stage, basically depends upon the pace of expansion in domestic production. In case the domestic demand for the product fairly exceeds the level of domestic production, imports may continue to constitute a significant share in the domestic market. With the beginning of the imports substitution stage of the consumer goods industry, the import stage of capital goods commences as they are required at the time of establishing the domestic production.[51]

The industry of the product in the less advanced country enters the third stage of export expansion when it is able to expand the production to the extent to create a surplus over the domestic consumption. The industry is developed to be an export industry when more and more surplus over consumption is produced and exported. At the same time, domestic demand for capital goods makes steady growth as the production of the consumer product expands. Also by then the technology for the production of capital goods may be accumulated through the imports to a certain extent. Under such circumstances, it is most likely that domestic production of the capital goods starts and that the capital goods industry reaches the beginning of the import substitution stage.

Akamatsu concluded from the experience of Japan's cotton textile industry that the industry in the less advanced country may further enter the reimport stage after passing through the export expansion stage. The least advanced countries which have been importing the product establish domestic production when it is backed sufficiently by the growth in domestic demand and the learning effect. Also, it is noted that when the industry in the export expansion stage reaches the peak of expansion, it usually faces the slower growth in productivity compared to the sharp increase in wages.

The declining productivity will have an adverse repercussion on the export competitiveness of the industry in question which is at the stage of export expansion. This has actually happened to Japan's cotton fabrics industry in the mid-1960s when there was a larger increase in wages compared to that in productivity, which affected the cost structure of exports. Exports declined as they were not able to compete with those from later-comers where the productivity increased rapidly accompanying expansion at the catching-up stage. As exports of the industry declined, the production registered an absolute decrease. One of the reasons behind this phenomenon would be that the industry were unable to sustain the optimal capacity due to the lack in export demand.

The absolute decline in production in the industry of the less advanced country which has been at the export expansion stage opens up a possibility for imports to sustain the level of domestic consumption from the least advanced countries at the export expansion stage which is in the process catching-up the former. Thus, the industry in question enters the import stage, that is, the final stage in the Ganko Keitai Growth.[52]

The Ganko Keitai Growth in the model formulated based on the empirical data. Yamazawa has attempted to explain the dynamic property of the Ganko Keitai Growth.[53] He maintains that an industry is given an impetus for export expansion originally by the growth in domestic demand. Steady growth in domestic demand, often assisted by the demonstration effect in the domestic market, induces expansion in production. Growth in production usually accompanies a reduction in production cost which makes domestic price of the product close to or lower than the import price. The lower domestic price of the product encourages import substitution and, in case the domestic price is lower than the import price, the industry is prepared to launch into export expansion, as it is able to provide the product to the world markets at a competitive price. Once the industry makes entry to the world markets, exports may be stepped depending on the price which the industry offers as well as on the growth in income of the world, which will stimulate further expansion in production.[54]

The important characteristics of Yamazawa's model is that a reduction in the production cost accompanied by the production expansion is dealt as dynamic force of the model.[55] Terming it as 'the long-run decreasing cost curve in the international economics',[56] he attributed causes of the phenomenon to the following factors : (1) Firstly, the cost reduction is accompanied by expansion in the productive capacities which allows the operation at the optimal capacity; (2) besides the effect as (1), it also relates to the improvement of productivity by the learning effects from the imports on technology, management and skill of workers of the industry.

Ganko Keitai Growth in the International Economy

Another important version of Ganko Keitai Growth on which Akamatsu formulates is in the setting of the international economy.[57] He contends that various economies in the world, each in the different stage of the Ganko Keitai Growth, are presenting various degrees of 'complementaries' to each other. Complementarity in this sense determines the nature of interaction among the economies which are at the different stages of development. For example, when the two economies chosen are in the same or similar stage of development, the complementarity which exists among them is not supposed to be significant. On the other hand, when the two economies are at different developmental stages, there exists a great deal of complementarity. The larger the difference in the level of development, the greater will be the complementarity of the two economies. Taking the particular example of the economic relations between

European and Asian countries from the late 18th century to the early 20th century, the former which were in the much advanced stage of industrialisation than the latter experienced the various degree of complementary with the latter in the course of their interaction. The handloom industry of the Asian countries was marginalised by being dominated in the domestic markets by the exports of manufactured textiles from the European countries which often enforced customs duty preferences for them and imposed excise duties on the domestic products in the Asian countries to protect their exports.

However, on achieving independence from the colonial rule after the Second World War, the Asian countries launched industrialisation and set up their own domestic production in many areas. As the industry of the Asian countries expanded production, the imports of manufactures from the European countries gradually declined in the former's domestic market. The process was in particular helped by the imposition of tariff and non-tariff barriers by the former nations. On the other hand, as the domestic production expanded in the Asian countries, there was a great increase in demand for capital products. It induced imports from European countries in these areas to Asian countries.

The entire process of interaction through trade between a less advanced country and an advanced country, in which the former is in the process of catching up and overtaking the latter, can be characterised by the sequence of the stages of 'heterogeneisation' and 'homogeneisation' of the levels of economic development of the two economies. When the levels of industrial development of the less advanced country and the advanced country are heterogeneous, viz., when there exists a gap in the industrial levels between the two economies, there will be harmonious relations in terms of economic relations between them.

As the industry of the less advanced country expands production and tries to catch up with the industry of the advanced country, the difference that existed in the levels of development narrows. When the level of the industry of the former reached the level similar to the industry of the latter, there will be conflicting relations between the two.

The sequence of the stages of heterogeneisation and homogeneisation of the industrial levels of the less advanced and the advanced economies appears, for example, in the following manner. In the first stage of import, a great deal of heterogeneity presumably exists between the levels of development in an industrial sector, usually a consumer goods industry, between the less advanced economy and the advanced economy since the level of the domestic production in the less advanced economy is very low (or the production may be yet to be established), compared with the level of production of the advanced country which is at the higher stage of development. When the industry of the less advanced country starts to expand the production, the gap in the heterogeneous levels of development of the industry between the two begins to narrow. On the other hand, there exists a great deal of heterogeneity in the levels of development in the capital goods industrial sector, when the less advanced economy starts to import the capital goods from the advanced economy as the former expands production of the consumer goods.

Production of the consumer goods industry of the less advanced economy may possibly expand to such an extent that the domestically produced goods eliminate the imports from its domestic market. The direction in the flow of goods may change into that from the less advanced economy to the world depending on the surplus produced by the former beyond its domestic consumption. Also by the time the level of production in the industry of the advanced economy tends to stagnate after the peak of expansion. Under such circumstances, there is all possibility that the less advanced economy is able to step up the exports to the advanced economy.

When the former increases exports to the latter, the process of homogeneisation of the levels in the consumer goods industry between the two is under way resulting in emergence of their non-harmonious relations. On the other hand, the less advanced country is prepared to set up the production of capital goods after a certain period of accumulation of pressure from the domestic demand as well as of knowledge and experience in production through imports from the advanced country. Thus there comes a stage of homogeneisation of the levels of development in the capital goods industry between the less advanced and the advanced economies.

Ganko Keitai Growth of the Cotton Fabrics and the Handtools Industries

Akamatsu symbolically represents the Ganko Keitai Growth of an industry in the three time-series curves in a diagram, each denoting the levels of its production, exports and imports (see Chart 4.1). The curves based on the empirical data of production, exports and imports of an industrial product usually have the shape of inverse V like the wild geese flying in formation, after which the pattern of the industrial growth is termed.

CHART 4.1

Pattern of Ganko Keitai Growth of an Industry

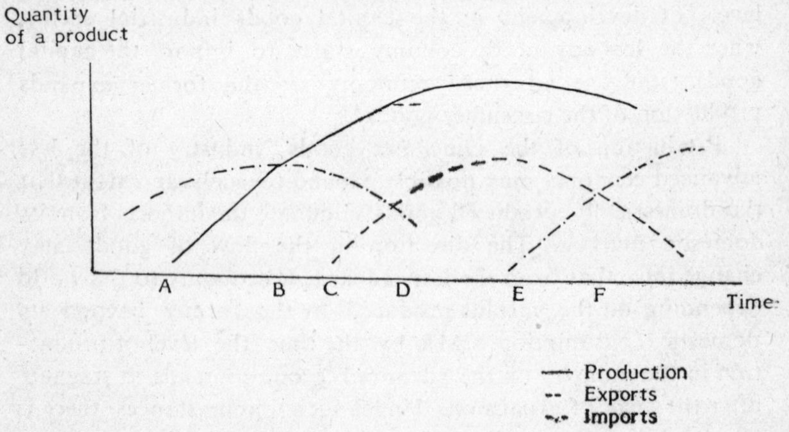

In Chart 4.1, the import curve starts prior to the other two curves when the domestic production of the product has not been commenced in the initial stage in the growth. The point A in the Chart indicates the beginning of the import substitution and the point C shows the start of export stage.[58] However, since initial level of the domestic production in a less advanced country is too small to be called as the beginning of the import substitution stage and the low level of production sometimes continues over a long period, the intersection B of the falling imports and the rising production curves is identified as the beginning of the import substitution stage. Similarly, the intersection D of the rising export and the falling import curves is indicated as the beginning of the export expansion stage,[59] while the intersection F of the rising import and the falling export curves as the re-import stage.

In Figures 4.1, 4.3 and 4.4, 4.5. the time-series data of production and exports of the cotton fabrics (weaving) industry and imports of cotton fabrics respectively, of Japan, India and South Korea and the U.S.A. are graphically presented.

The cases of the industry in South Korea and the U.S.A. are taken here for comparison. They enable us to compare the performance of the industry in India in the former case and that in Japan in the latter.

It is clear from Figure 4.1 that Japan's cotton fabrics industry entered the re-import stage of the Ganko Keitai Growth towards 1973 at which the rising import curve intersects with the falling export curve. The trend of the cotton fabrics industry of the U.S.A. is characterised with the absolute fall in production since the mid-1960s. Although the exports were also rising, the decline in the domestic availability of cotton fabrics gave rise to the increase in imports. Thus growth of the industry in the U.S.A. is considered to have reached the re-import stage in the mid-1960s, nearly a decade ahead of the industry in Japan (see Figure 4.3). On the other hand, the growth stage of the cotton fabrics industry of India and South Korea can be identified as the export expansion stage when the production and the exports were rising (see Figures 4.4 and 4.5). If we interpret these trends in terms of the Ganko Keitai Growth, it is argued that the difference in the levels of development that existed from 1951 to 1973 in the cotton fabrics industry between Japan, on one hand, and India and South Korea, on the other, would have brought opportunities for India and South Korea to establish the export footing in the Japanese market.

Figures 4.2, 4.6, 4.7 and 4.8 show the trends in production, exports and imports of the handtools industry,[60] respectively of Japan, India, South Korea and the U.S.A. It is important to note that India emerged as a net exporter of handtools towards the late 1960s. In case of the industry in South Korea, the

FIGURE 4.3

Cotton Fabrics—India: Production, Exports and Imports

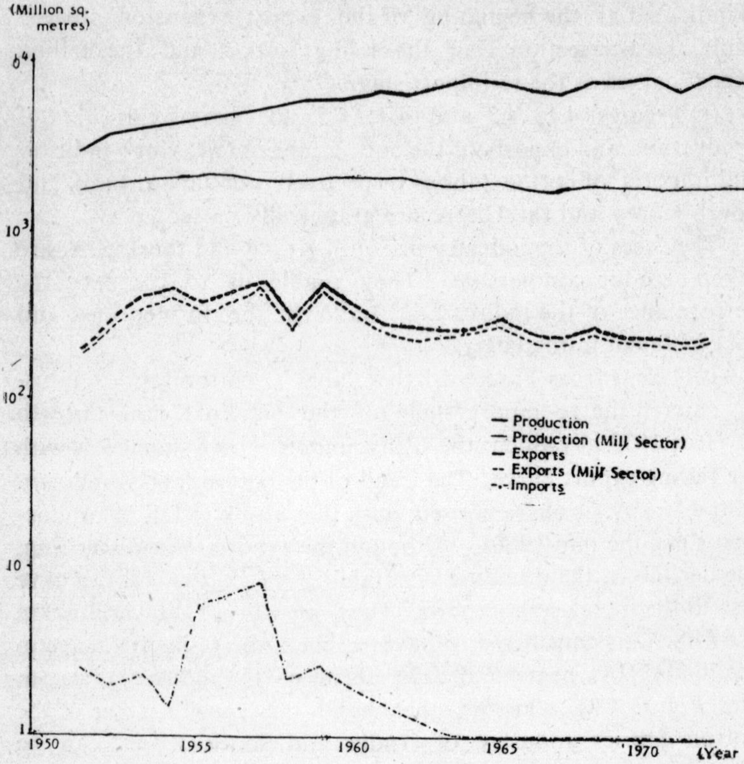

Source: Textile Commissioner, Government of India, *Indian Textile Bulletin* (Bombay), from various issues.

FIGURE 4.4

Cotton Fabrics—South Korea: Production, Exports and Imports

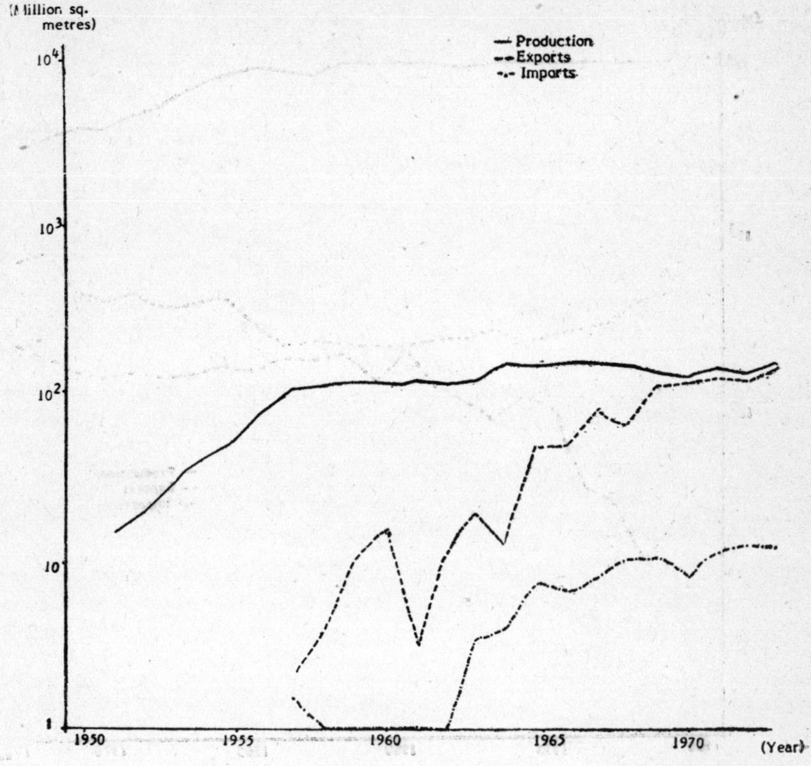

Source: The Bank of Korea, *Economic Statistics Yearbook* (Seoul), from various issues.

FIGURE 4.5

Cotton Fabrics—The U.S.A.: Production, Exports and Imports

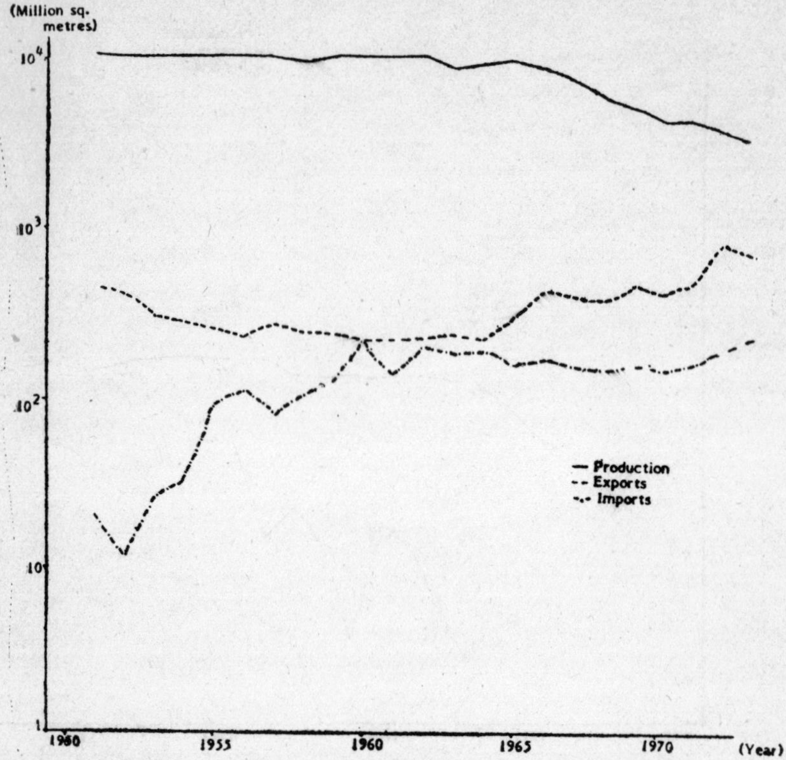

Source: United Nations, *Growth of World Industry* (Vol. II), (New York), from various issues—Production; United Nations *Yearbook of International Trade Statistics* (Vol. I) (New York), from various issues-Exports and Imports.

FIGURE 4.6

Handtools—India: Production, Exports and Imports

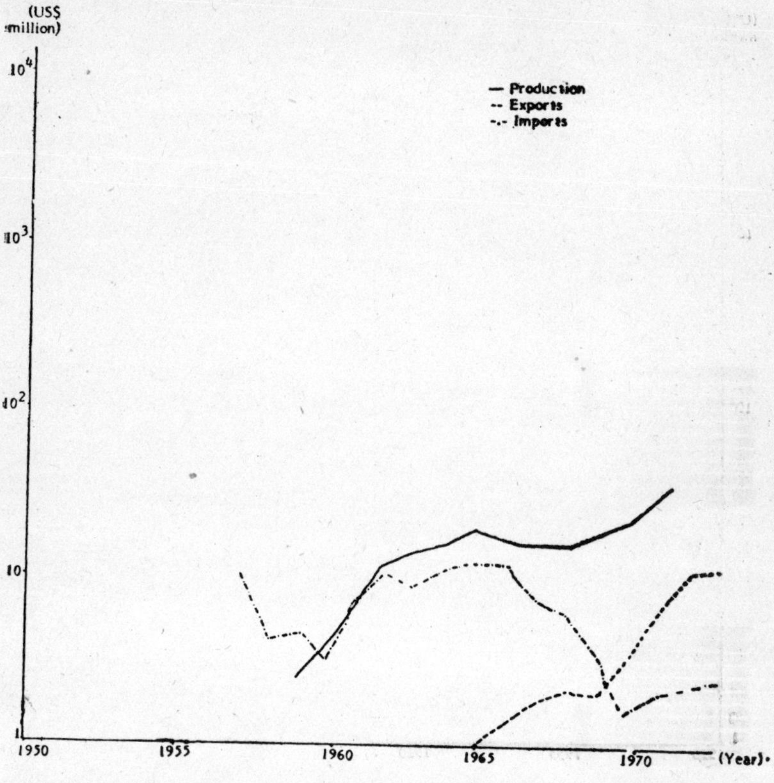

Source: Central Statistical Organisation, Government of India, *Annual Survey of Industries* (New Delhi), from various issues—Production; United Nations, *Commodity Trade Statistics* (New York), from various issues.

FIGURE 4.7

Handtools—South Korea: Production, Exports and Imports

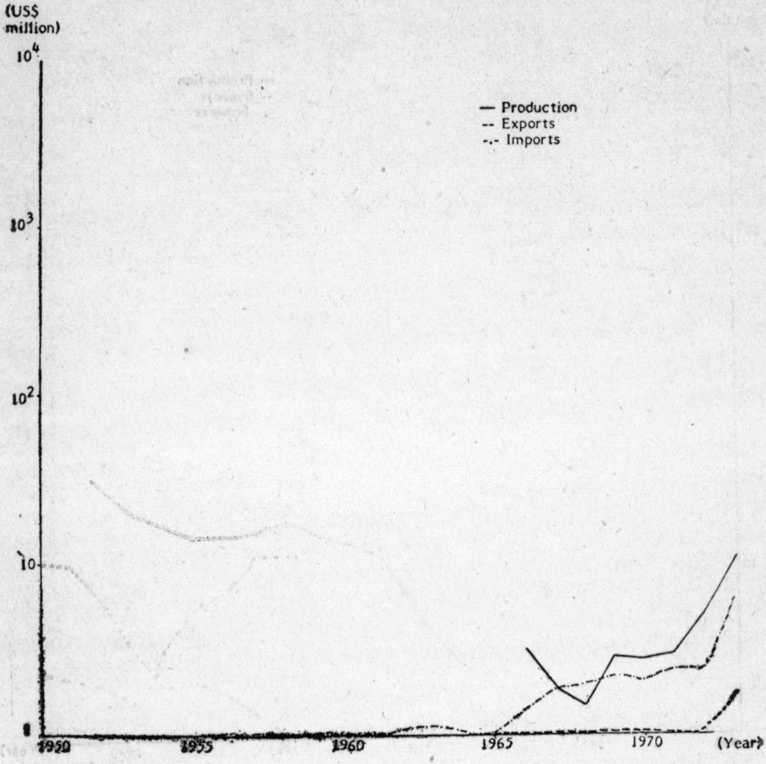

Source: The Bank of Korea, *Economic Statistics Yearbook* (Seoul), from various issues.

production also surpassed the imports. On the other hand, the industry in Japan seems to have reached the re-import stage in the early 1970s when the imports exceeded exports and accompanied by the stagnant growth in production. There was no significant structural change in the handtools industry in the U.S.A. in terms of the Ganko Keitai Growth.

Cost Structure and Productivity of Manufacturing Industries

It has been discussed that improvement in productivity accompanying the production expansion in an industry leads to the enhancement of the competitive position of the industry in the international market in the Ganko Keitai Growth. An ideal indicator for the trend in productivity of an industry is the price of the product which the industry produces. However, various specifications embodied in products and classifications adopted in trade and industrial statistics by countries make the country-to-country comparison extremely difficult. Table 4.9 shows the trend in prices of cotton fabrics of Japan and the major exporting countries of the product to Japan. The comparison of the prices of cotton fabrics among the countries in the Table gives us only a rough idea about the competitive position of the cotton fabrics industry of the countries, as the specifications of the product are not exactly the same for all the countries.

One of the alternative ways of indicating the productivity of an industry is to examine its cost structure. It is assumed here that changes in the cost structure lead to improvement or deterioration in the production efficiency. The major components of the cost of an industrial product can be identified in the following way.[61] Since the total value of cost for the given level of output turned out in an industry consists mainly of three factors, viz., cost of labour required for the production, cost of depreciation in capital employed in the production and cost of material inputs required for the production, which can be expressed as

$$Oc = wL + rK + nR \ldots\ldots\ldots\ldots (1)$$

where O is the given level of output in quantity terms of the industry; c the cost required per unit of product; w the wage

FIGURE 4.8

Handtools—the U.S.A.: Production, Exports and Imports

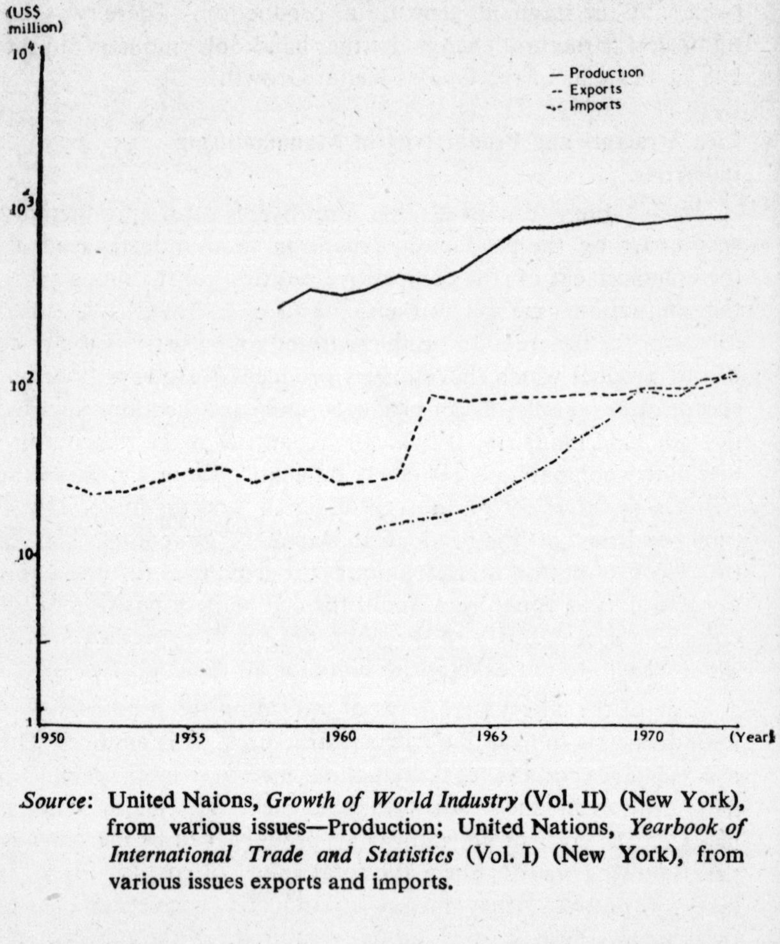

Source: United Naions, *Growth of World Industry* (Vol. II) (New York), from various issues—Production; United Nations, *Yearbook of International Trade and Statistics* (Vol. I) (New York), from various issues exports and imports.

TABLE 4.9

Cotton Fabrics Prices
(US cent per lb.)

Year	*Japan*		*India (Shirting grey)*	*Hong-Kong (Golden peak)*	*Taiwan (Similar to SITC 2003)*		*Mainland China (Similar to SITC 2003)*	*U.S.A. (Printed cloth)*	*U.K. (Cambric)*
	Domestic	*Export*			*Domestic*	*Export*			
1958	12.2	10.9	13.0	14.6	n.a.	n.a.	n.a.	16.3	17.9
1959	14.2	13.9	13.0	15.5	n.a.	n.a.	n.a.	16.8	16.1
1960	14.6	14.6	14.9	16.3	n.a.	n.a.	n.a.	17.3	19-1
1961	12.9	13.4	15.9	13.2	17.5	13.0	12.3	15.7	20.7
1962	10.9	11.6	15.9	12.4	16 3	12.2	11.1	17.5	18.4
1963*	13.0	14.2	15.9	13 0	17.9	12 7	11.8	18.7	18.9
1964*	12.8	13.8	15.9	12 7	n.a.	n.a.	n.a.	17.5	n.a.

*Price in December

Source: Japan Economic Research Centre, *Measures for Trade Expansion and Developing Countries—Report of a Japan Economic Research Centre International Conference* (Japan Economic Research Centre Paper No. 5), (Tokyo), 1965, pp. 184 and 185.

cost per worker; L the total labour employed for the production; r the rate of depreciation cost per unit of (physical) capital; K the amount of capital employed in the production in physical terms; n the cost of material inputs per unit; R the total volume of inputs required for the production. Therefore, the cost per product can be expressed as

$$c=\frac{w}{O/L}+\frac{r}{O/K}+\frac{n}{O/R} \qquad \ldots\ldots(2)$$

O/L, O/K and O/R in the equation (2) can be called as labour productivity, output-capital ratio and output-input ratio, respectively. (2) indicates that the production cost of a product is an increasing function with respect to w, r and n, while it is also a decreasing function with respect to O/L, O/K and O/R. In other words, the production cost of an industrial product consists of three factors $\frac{w}{O/L}$, $\frac{r}{O/K}$, $\frac{n}{O/R}$ which can be called an efficiency-wages, efficiency-capital and efficiency-material cost, respectively.

Based on the above factors, the trend in the cost structure of cotton fabrics and handtools industries, respectively of India, Japan, South Korea and the U.S.A. is examined in order to find out the production of the industries of the three countries. Among the three major components in the cost, viz., efficiency-wages, efficiency-material cost, and efficiency-capital cost the former two are crucial in determining the overall cost of production. To support this contention, as Table 4.10 shows, wages and material costs constitute a dominant portion of the total production cost.

The dominance of wages and material costs in the cost structure of a product implies that the changes in wages and material cost are more likely to affect the overall production cost structure. Hence the levels in efficiency-wages and efficiency-material cost are crucial to the determination of productivity of the industry. Assuming the above, the trends in efficiency-wages and efficiency-material cost of the cotton fabrics and the handtools industries respectively of India, Japan, South Korea and the U.S.A. are examined.

TABLE 4.10

Composition of Product Cost of India's Cotton Textile Industry[1] (%)

Year	*Wages*[2]	*Material inputs*[3]	*Depreciation*
1951	19.5	67.6	0.0
1952	22.7	71.2	0.0
1953	24.9	66.3	0.0
1954	23.7	66.4	0.0
1955	23.4	63.7	0.0
1956	24.1	64.5	0.0
1957	25.0	68.8	0.0
1958	24.9	67.7	0.0
1959	25.7	66.3	0.0
1960	24.0	65.6	0.0
1961	22.9	65 3	0.1
1962	24.0	67.5	0.1
1963	23.2	69.0	0.1
1964	23.4	69.4	0.0
1965	24.9	70.4	0.1
1966	24.7	70.5	0.1
1967	23.2	72.2	0.1
1968	23.2	73.6	0.1
1969	21.9	72.2	0.1
1970	20.8	73.9	0.1
1971	19.5	74.2	0.1

1. As defined in the footnote 62 of this chapter.
2. Wages paid to the total employees, including benefits, salaries and contributions.
3. Including fuels, electricity etc , taxes and duties, service charges and materials like stationery.

Source: Calculated from Central Statistical Organization, Government of India, *Census of Indian Manufactures* (Calcutta), from various issues between 1951 and 1958 and Central Statistical Organisation, Government of India, *Annual Survey of Industries* (Calcutta), from various issues between 1959 and 1971.

Cost Effectiveness in the Cotton Fabrics Manufacturing Industry[62]

To examine the trend in efficiency-wages and efficiency-material cost in the cost structure of the cotton fabrics manufacturing sector, it is useful to disaggregate the former into wages and labour productivity and the latter into material cost and output-input ratio. Figure 4.9 indicates the trend in per worker wages (w)[63] of the cotton fabrics industry (of cotton textile industry) of Japan,[64] India,[65] South Korea[66] and the U.S.A.[67] The figures indicate that the wages in the cotton fabrics industry of the U.S.A. was higher than the industry of the other three. The wages in the industry of the U.S.A. experienced a sharp increase until the mid-1960s, which was followed by a period of stabilisation of the increase. On the other hand, the wages in the industry in Japan registered a rapid increase after the mid-1960s, while in terms of the absolute level they were much below those in the U.S.A. The wages in South Korea and India remained relatively stable, compared to the other two, though the wages in the former country was on an increase since the late 1960s.

Figure 4.10 indicates the changes in output per worker (or employee), (O/L) of the industry of the four countries.[67] It is noted that the output per worker in the cotton fabrics industry in Japan experienced a steady but slower increase after the late 1950s following a large decline in the years prior to then, while that in India remained at a low level throughout the period. The output per worker of the cotton fabrics industry in the U.S.A. stayed at a much higher level compared with the other three and increased over years but with a few cycles. A similar variety of cycles were observed in the industry of South Korea, though remained at a low level.

Combining the movements of the wages and the labour productivity curve, the efficiency-wages $\frac{w}{O/L}$ curve is obtained as in Figure 4.11. The efficiency-wages in Japan's cotton fabrics industry registered a rapid increase over years and caught up the level of the efficiency wages of the U.S.A. in the early 1970s. In case of India, after experiencing a large increase in the mid-1960s, the efficiency wages declined, but still above the level

FIGURE 4.9
Cotton Fabrics: Wages (w)

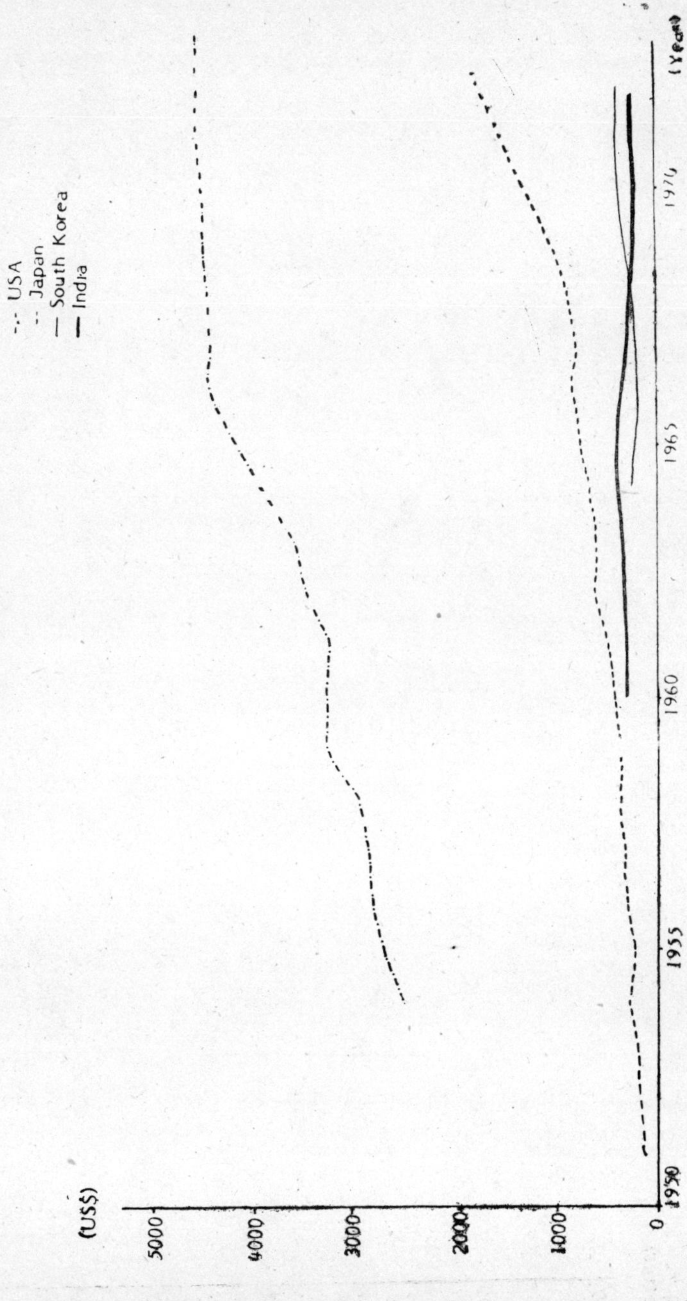

FIGURE 4.10

Cotton Fabrics: Output per Worker (O/L)

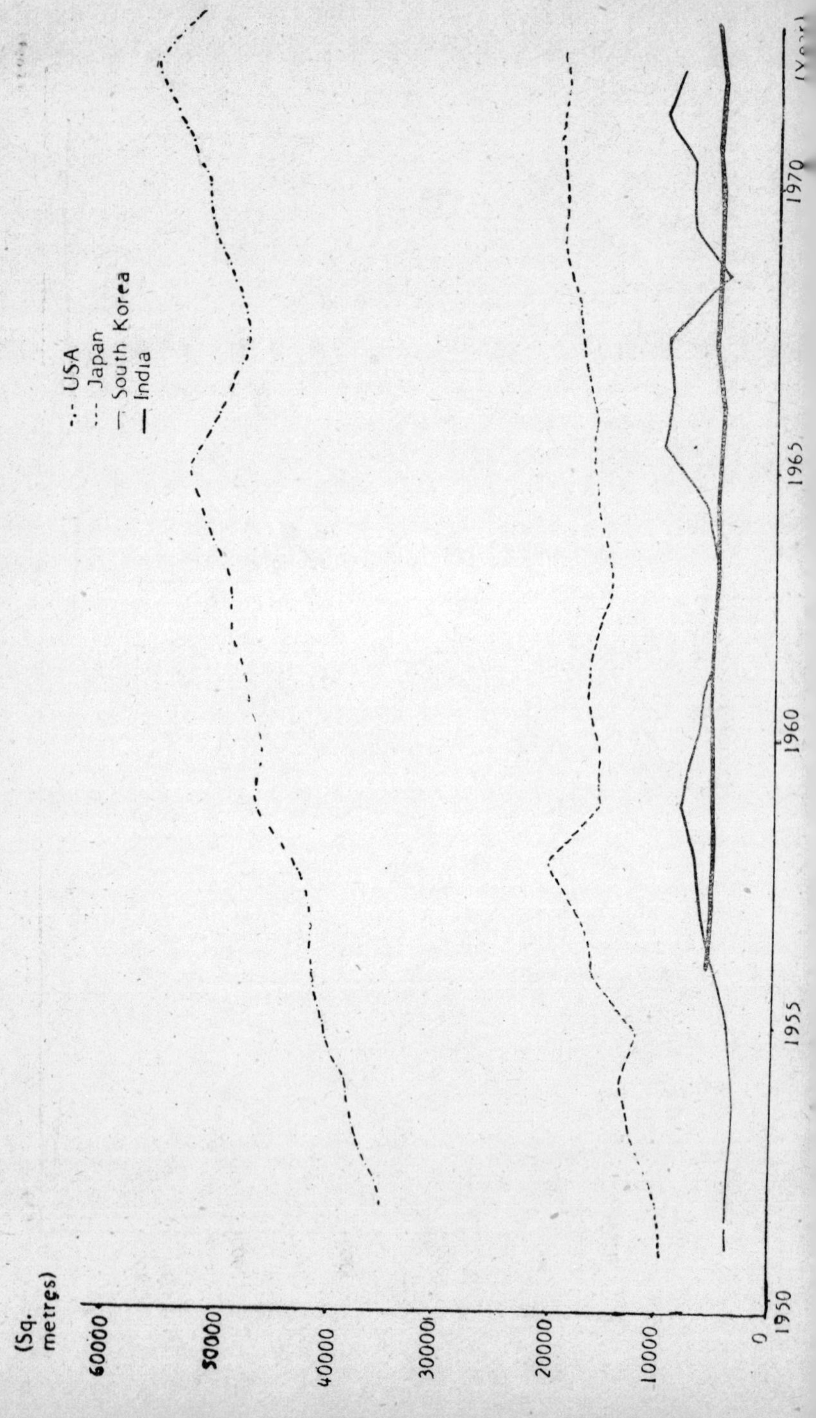

of that in South Korea. The lowest efficiency-wages in the cotton fabrics industry in South Korea since the late 1960s may reflect its comparative advantage position among the countries.

The trend in the material cost (n)[68] of cotton fabrics of Japan, India, South Korea and the U.S.A. are illustrated in Figure 4.12. The figure indicates that India, being cotton growing country enjoyed low prices of cotton yarns, particularly in the late 1950s and mid-1960s. In case of Japan, due to efficient operations in the cotton yarn producing units, maintained the low prices of cotton yarn except toward the early 1970s when these units could not overcome the rise in costs. In the U.S.A., the prices of cotton yarn remained high, despite being a cotton-growing country, reflecting higher costs in the cotton yarn manufacturing industries.

Figure 4.13 shows the trend in the output-input ratio (O/R) of the cotton fabrics industry of the four countries[69]. In all the four cases, a decline in the output-input ratio was observed. Except in South Korea, the decline in the ratio was a steady phenomenon. South Korea was unable to keep up with the other three in terms of the output-input ratio. Also, in South Korea, highest costs in terms of yarns were observed. This is due to the fact that South Korea relied on imports of cotton yarns to meet the requirement in the cotton fabrics sector to a significant extent.

Figure 4.14 presents the combined effect of the trends in the material cost and output-input ratio, namely, the efficiency-material cost. It is observed that India was successful in maintaining the efficiency-material cost at low levels especially after the late 1960s, while South Korea was at an absolute disadvantage in this respect due to the limited domestic capacity in processing of cotton yarn.

The final analysis is indicated as follows:

(i) Japan's cotton fabrics industry which entered the re-import stage of the Ganko Keitai Growth in the early 1970s had been facing a rapid increase in wages since the mid-1960s. The problem became acute when the growth in labour productivity started to level off and the efficiency-wages started to increase rapidly in

FIGURE 4.11
Cotton Fabrics: Efficiency Wages (w/O/L)

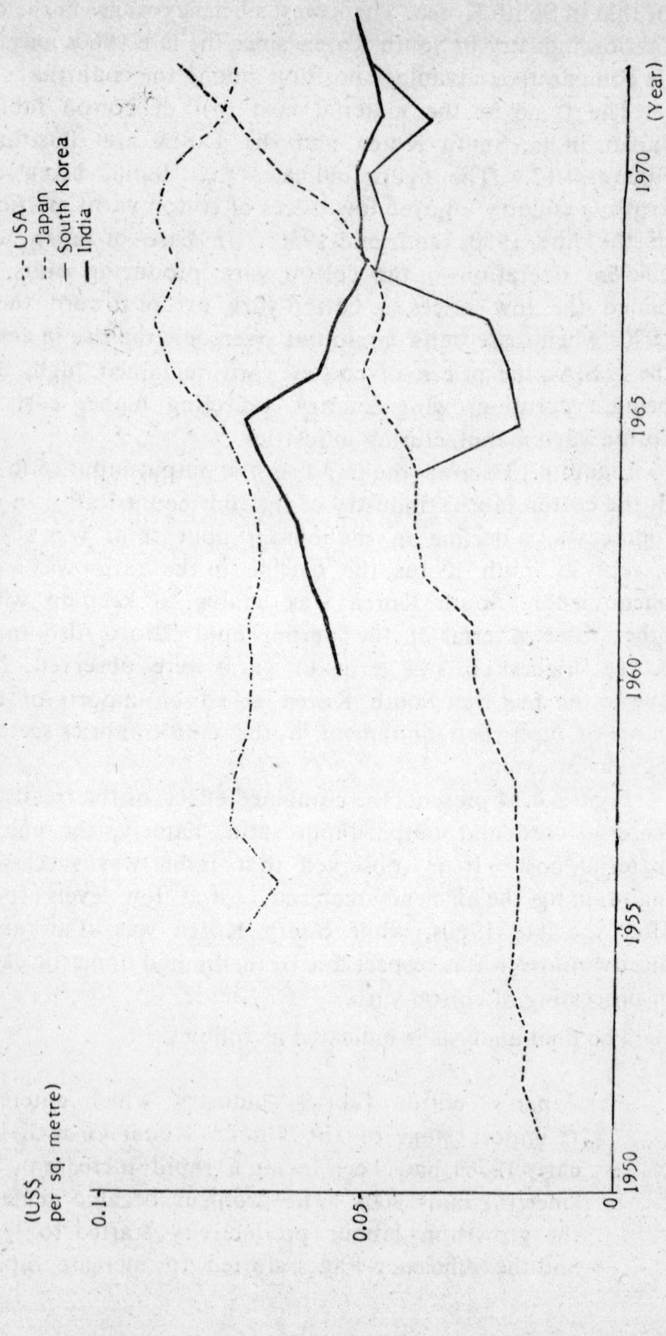

FIGURE 6.12

Cotton Fabrics: Material Cost (n)

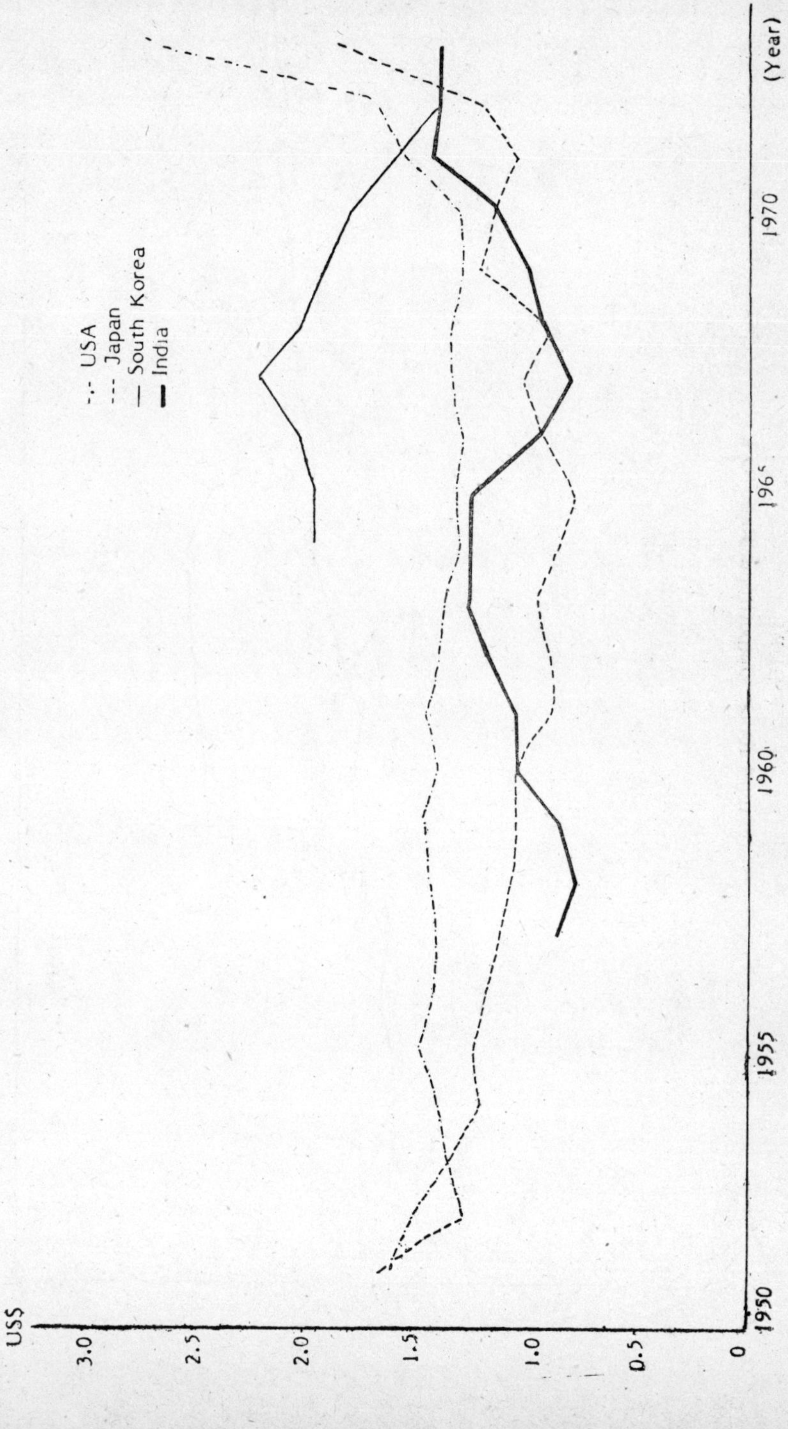

FIGURE 4.13

Cotton Fabrics: Output-Input Ratio (O/R)

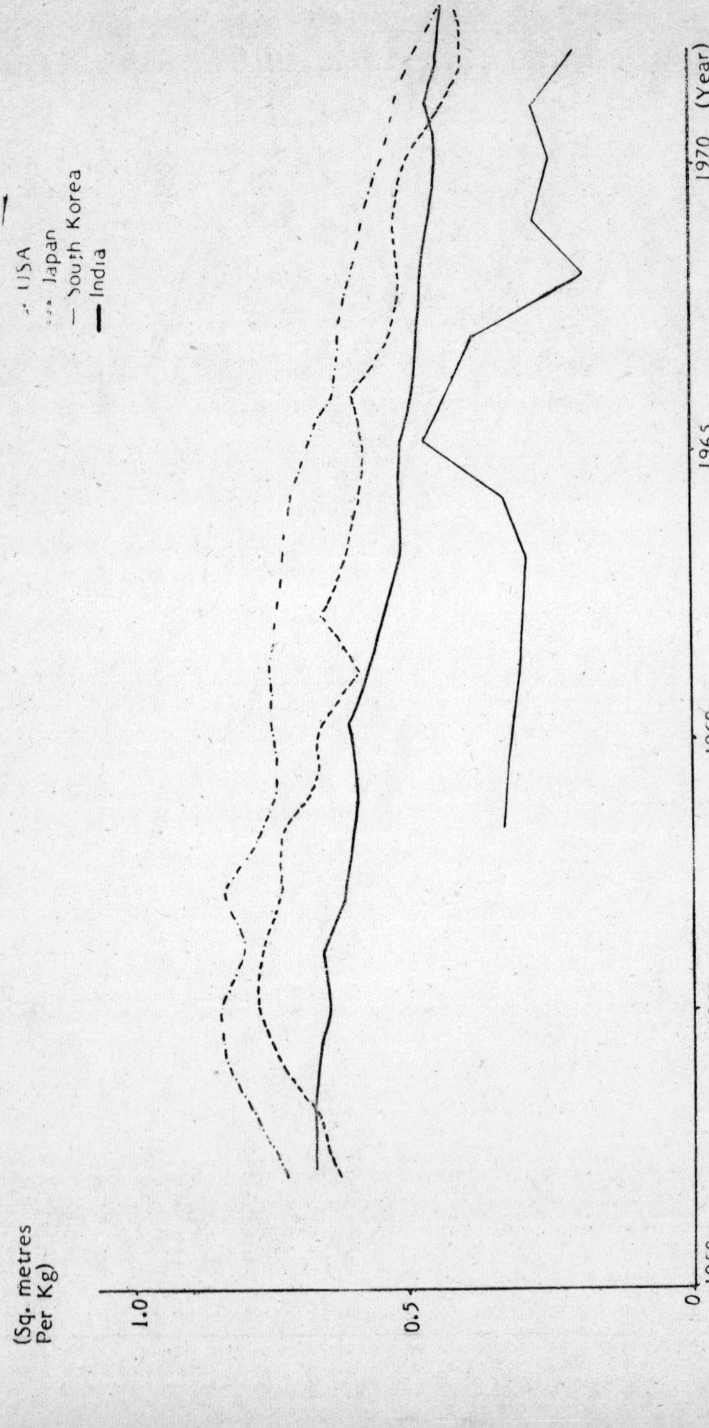

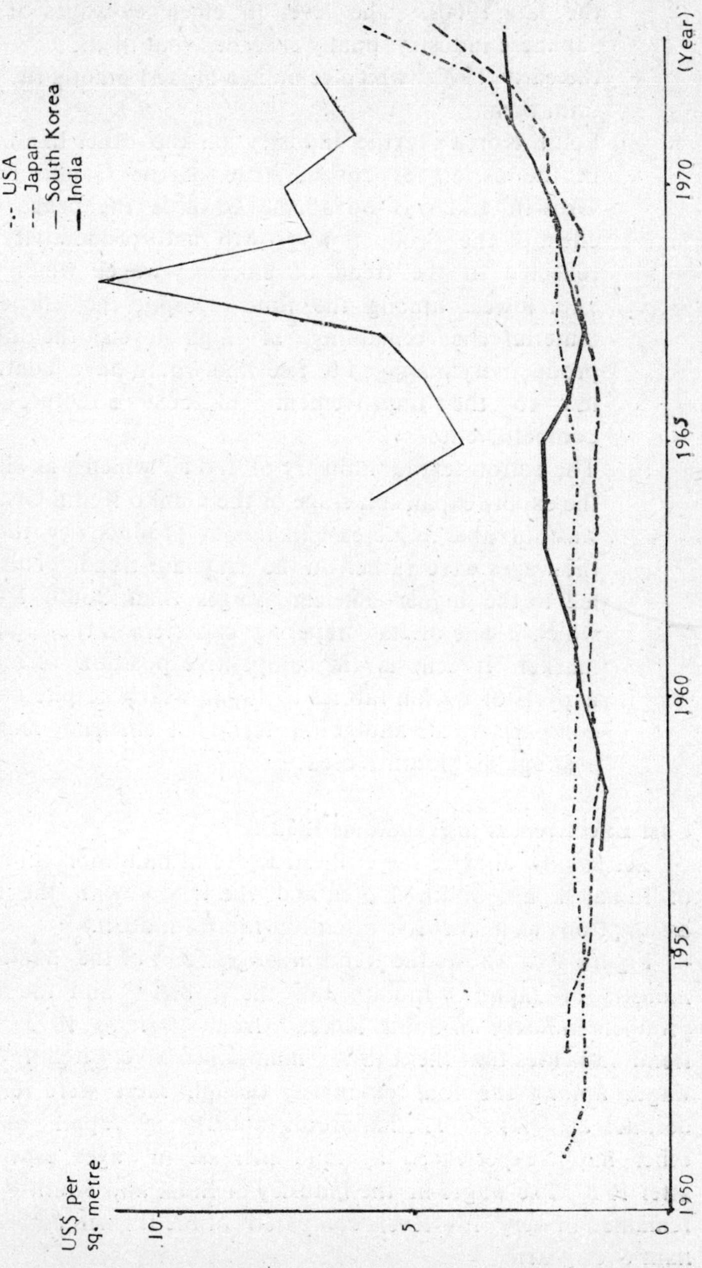

FIGURE 4.14
Cotton Fabrics: Efficiency-Material Cost (n/O/R)

the late 1960s. The level in efficiency-wages of the Japanese industry finally exceeded that of the U.S.A. in the early 1970s, which remained highest among the four until then.

(ii) South Korea's textile industry, on the other hand, was in the export expansion stage of the Ganko Keitai Growth and was advancing towards the peak. The effect of the production growth and productivity was reflected in the trend of efficiency-wages which was kept lowest among the four. Despite the efficiency-material cost remaining at high levels, the labour productivity managed to rise and would have contributed to the improvement in cost structure and competitiveness.

(iii) The cotton textile industry of India, which was also in the export expansion stage of the Ganko Keitai Growth, was not able to increase its labour productivity, though the wages were rather on the stagnant trend. This had led to the higher efficiency-wages than South Korea, which is one of its competing exporters in the Japanese market. It reflects the competitive position of India's exports of cotton fabrics to Japan which despite having comparative advantage in terms of efficiency-material cost against South Korea.

Cost Effectiveness in Handtools Industry[70]

Let us now analyse the cost structure of handtools industry of India, Japan, South Korea and the U.S.A. with the same assumptions as in the case of cotton fabrics industry.[71]

Figure 4.15 shows the trend in wages (w)[72] of the handtools industry of Japan,[73] India[74] and the U.S.A.[75] and the metal products industry of South Korea[76] from 1951 to 1973. The trend indicates that the U.S.A. maintained a very high level of wages among the four countries, though there were relative declines and falls. The handtools industry in Japan, on the other hand, experienced a rapid increase in wages especially after 1970. The wages in the industry of India and South Korea remained at very low levels compared to the former and stagnant over years.

FIGURE 4.15
Handtools: Wages (w)

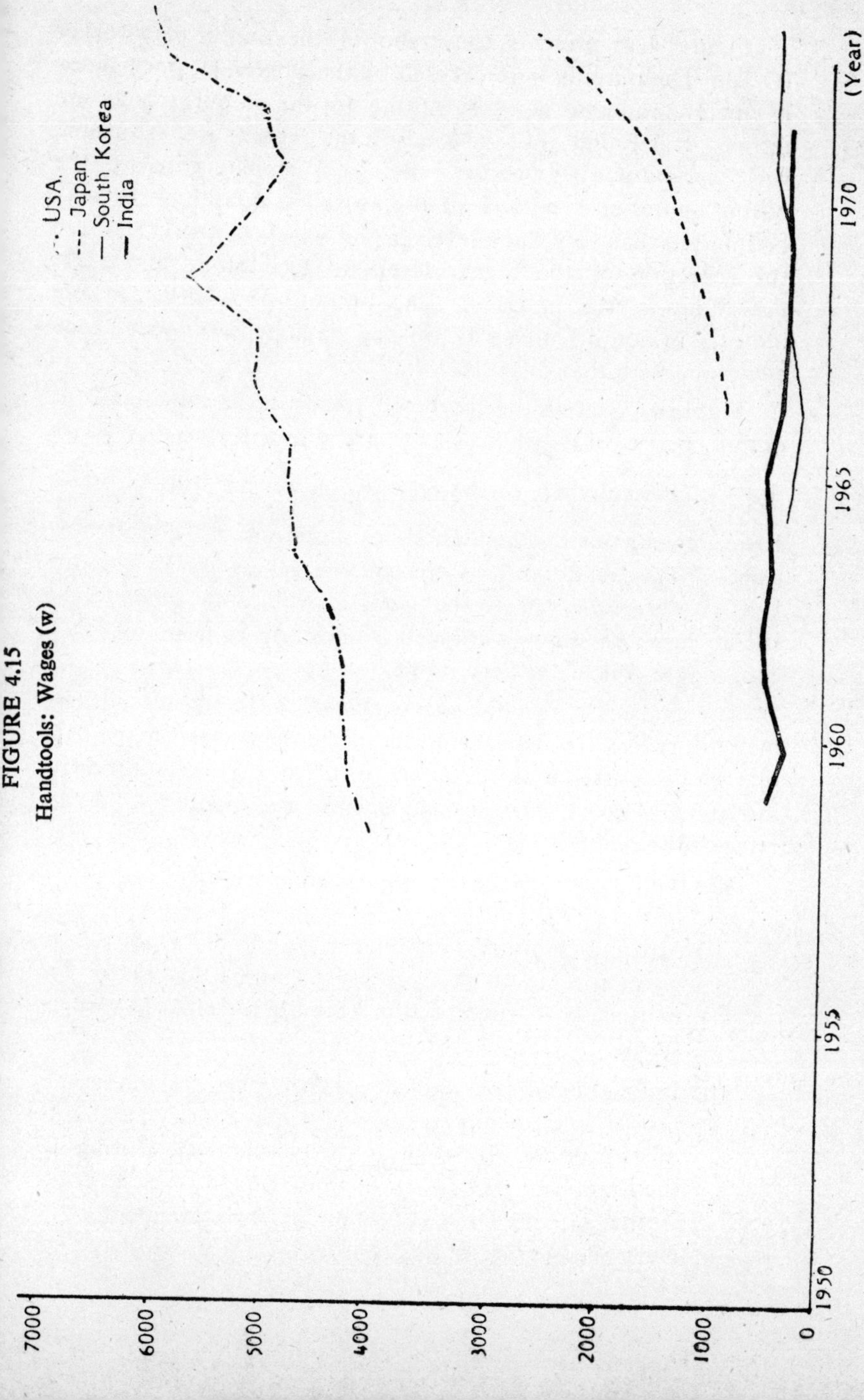

Figure 4.16 presents the trend in the output per worker (O/L). The outputs were deflated by the wholesale price index of metal products, as a substitute for the output in quantum terms. It is found that the levels in the wages are associated with the output per worker. Being in monetary terms, the output figures also reflects quality as well as quantity. It may be inferred that very high levels in the wages of the U.S.A. are the reflection of the higher levels of technology and skills prevailing in the industry. The output per worker in the industry in South Korea was low and stagnated over years, even compared with that of India.

Figure 4.17 shows the combined trends in the wages and the output per worker, that is, the trend in the efficiency wages $(\frac{W}{O/L})$. Basically due to the very low cutput per worker, South Korea emerged with the highest cost in terms of the efficiency-wages. The trends in the efficiency-wages in Japan and the U.S.A. were observed to be similar, while the trend in the Indian case also shows a competitive position in terms of efficiency-wages which was kept stable and low.

The analysis of the efficiency-wages of the handtools industry may not reflect the reality existing in the industry since the data on South Korea basically refers to that of the metal products industry. Also, it does not account for the qualitative differences in the output.

Yet the following points emerge as conclusions :

(i) Japan, a traditional exporter of handtools, made steady growth in labour productivity. Despite the sharp rise in wages, it succeeded in keeping the efficiency-wages stable.

(ii) India's handtools industry experienced rather stable growth in efficiency-wages, which may reflect the quality of its exports. It is one of the factors contributing to the lower unit realisation of India's handtools products in the Japanese market than that of its competitors as mentioned earlier in this chapter.

FIGURE 4.10

Handtools: Output per Worker (O/L)

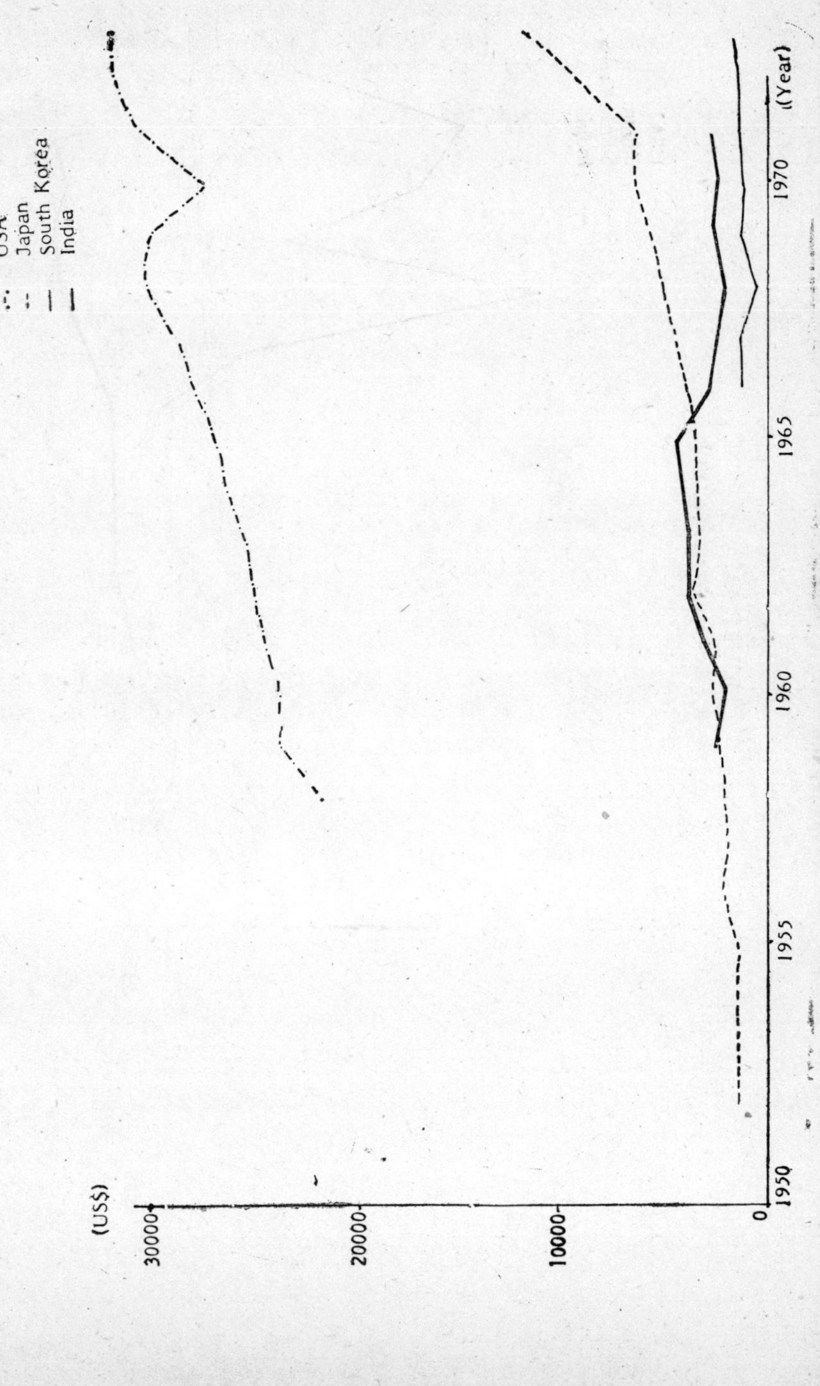

FIGURE 4.17
Handtools: Efficiency Wages (w/O/L)

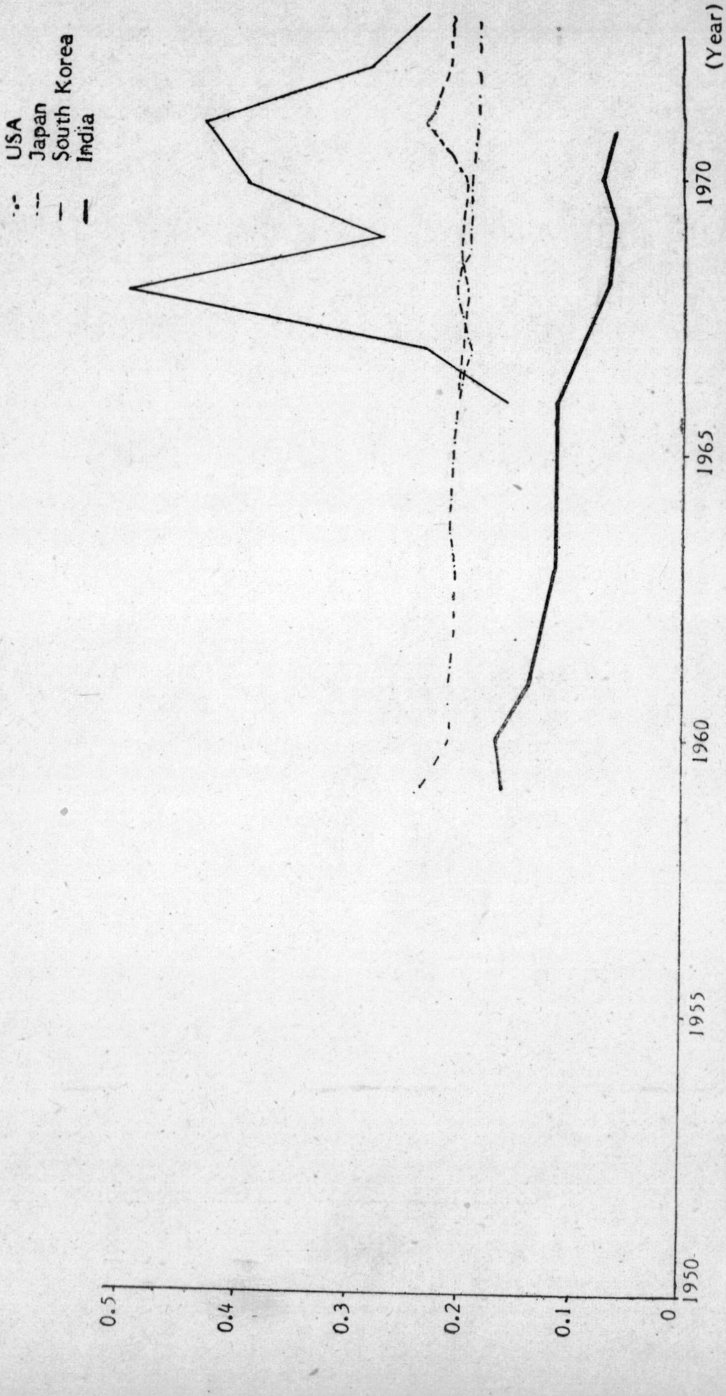

Determinants for Stimulating Trade Growth in Japan

This chapter discussed on the trend in India's exports of manufactures to Japan during 1951-73 and also analysed the causes for the slow pace of exports compared to the competitor countries.

The concept of Ganko Keitai Growth was introduced to identify the stage of industrial development of the countries. In terms of Ganko Keitai Growth, India and South Korea are found to have been at the stage of export expansion, while Japan entered the re-import stage. The gap in the levels of development that existed among them implies the possibilities for trade flow from the former to the latter with respect to the product in question.

Following the examination of the three components, namely, efficiency-wages, efficiency-material cost and efficiency-capital cost, with respect to cotton fabrics and handtools manufacturing sectors, an attempt was made to identify the factors that were responsible for the competitiveness of the industries. In case of the cotton fabrics industry, rapid increase in wages and output per worker that were noted for Japan and the U.S.A., that were accompanied by rising efficiency-wages, implying that wages outweighted output per worker in the increase. Compared to the above two, India and South Korea kept these factors at very low levels from 1951-73. Yet a certain difference were observed between them with respect to the behaviour of efficiency-wages, in which South Korea was able to keep the factor below that of India by achieving higher labour productivity.

The trend in efficiency-material cost of the cotton fabrics industry was found to be similar among them except South Korea that implies prevalence of the standard technology in this regard. On the other hand, South Korea, due to its handicap in the capacity and technology for cotton yarn production, was not able to keep the efficiency-material cost low as the others.

In case of the handtools industry, the U.S.A. and Japan, despite higher wages and labour productivity especially in the former, maintained stability in efficiency-wages factor. The efficiency-wages in India's handtools industry were stable at low levels, reflecting its technological level.

The results of analysis on the cost structure of cotton fabrics and handtools manufacturing sectors with respect to Japan, India, South Korea and the U.S.A. would indicate that it is essential to keep the efficiency factors at low levels in order to be successful in promotion of exports. Lower efficiency-wages and efficiency material-cost of an industry implies higher efficiency and competitiveness of its exports, provided that similar technology prevails. In the case of India, efficiency factors with respect to wages and material cost are directly related with the competitive position of India's manufactured exports to Japan. These two elements in the cost structure of Indian industries were not lower to competitor countries and hence manufactured exports did not maintain a lead in competitiveness in the Japanese market.

In the next chapter, the trade and industrial policies that influenced India-Japan trade from 1951 to 1973 will be examined.

REFERENCES

1. See for details, P. Jayakar, "A History Survey of Indian Textiles" in Indian Institute of Foreign Trade, ed., *Seminar on Textiles—Conclusion and Recommendations* (New Delhi, 1972), pp. 102-4.

2. United Nations, *Yearbook of Industrial Statistics 1974*, (New York, 1976), pp. 179-80.

3. The handloom industry suffered from the acute shortage of yarns when the mill sector was used to mark off the considerable portion of yarns available even in times of its shortage, such as during Second World War and soon after the partition of India. After the partition a large portion of the cotton producing areas went to Pakistan and it had caused a great fall in handloom cloth production from 1500 million yards in 1949 to 805 million yards in 1950. Realising the urgent need for an organised programme for handloom weavers, the Government of India set up the All India Handloom Board in 1952. Under the guidance of the Board, a large number of looms were organized into cooperative field which provided weavers technical help for utilising improved tools and appliances and marketing facilities. The production of handloom cloth was further stimulated when the Handloom Export Promotion Council (later incorporated to the Handloom and Handicraft Export Promotion Council) was set up for promotion of handloom exports. See for details, P. Jayakar, "A Historical Survey of Indian Textiles", *op. cit.*, p. 104.

4. Figures in this paragraph are computed from the data in Figure 4.3.

5. Central Statistical Organisation, Government of India, *Census of Indian Manufactures, 1951* (Calcutta, 1952), pp. 9, 276 and 333.

6. Central Statistical Organisation, Government of India, *Annual Survey of Industries 1970* (Calcutta, 1971), pp. 6, 52, 77.

7. Indian Institute of Foreign Trade, *Conclusions and Recommendations of a Seminar on Indian Cotton Textile Industry* (New Delhi, 1967), p. 12.

8. Office of the Textile Commissioner, Ministry of Industry, Government of India, *Indian Textile Bulletin* (Bombay), Vol. 22, No. 5, 1976, p. 3.

9. Indian Institute of Foreign Trade, *Conclusions and Recommendations of a Seminar on Indian Cotton Textile Industry, op. cit.*, p. 12.

10. R. Vishwanathan, "Raw Cotton—Problems and Prospects" in Indian Institute of Foreign Trade, ed., *Seminar on Textiles—Conclusions and Recommendations* (New Delhi, 1972), p. 34.

11. International Cotton Advisory Committee, *Cotton-World Statistics* (Washington D.C.), Vol. 29, No. 3, October 1975, p. 10.

12. Indian Institute of Foreign Trade, *Conclusions and Recommendations of Seminar on Indian Cotton Textile Industry, op. cit.*, pp. 28-29.

13. For details of the export trend of cotton textiles prior to the study period, see M. Singh, *India's Export Trends and the Prospects for Self-Sustained Growth*, (Oxford : Claredon, 1964), pp. 84-86.

14. Because of the acute shortage in supply for the domestic market, the Government cancelled a considerable number of export licences in 1951. See for details, *ibid.*, p. 86.

15. Office of the Textile Commissioner, Ministry of Commerce and Industry, Government of India, *Indian Textile Bulletin* (Bombay), Vol. 8, No. 1, April 1962, p. 10.

16. Indian Institute of Foreign Trade, *Conclusions and Recommendations of a Seminar on Indian Cotton Textile Industry, op. cit.*, pp. 20-23.

17. Table 4.2 shows that the export-output ratio of the mill sector was higher than that of all sectors in the cotton fabrics industry throughout the study period. It is also clear from the same Table that the ratio of the mill sector increased rapidly when the production expanded around the early 1960s, and vice-versa when the production declined in the late 1960s. It implies that the exports of cotton fabrics by the mill sector had been highly elastic to the level of production of the sector. Moreover, since 80 to 90 per cent of exports of the product was provided by the mill sector during the period, thus the level of production of the mill sector had been dominant in determining the overall export performance of the cotton fabrics industry.

18. International Cotton Advisory Committee, *Cotton-World Statistics* (Washington D.C.), Vol. 12, No. 1, January 1958, p. 67.

19. United Nations, *Commodity Trade Statistics 1973* (New York), Series D, Vol. 23, No. 1-43, 1975, p. 181.

20. For example, see, S. Vishwanath, "Major Commodities in India's Exports-Cotton Textiles", in Vadilal Dagli ed., *India's Foreign Trade* (Commerce Economic Studies IX) Bombay, (Vora & Co., Publishers, 1973), p. 38.

21. United Nations, *Commodity Trade Statistics, 1973, op. cit.*, p. 181.

22. Trade Development Authority of India, *Product Note on Hand Small and Cutting Tools* (New Delhi, 1978), p. 1.

23. *Ibid.*, pp. 2-3.

24. Indian Institute of Foreign Trade, *Handtools and Small Tools* (IIFT Commodity Series No. 22) (New Delhi, 1969), p. 1.

25. *Ibid.*, p. 2.

26. *Ibid.*, p. 2. However, according to an unofficial estimate by Indian Institute of Foreign Trade, the number of the cottage units decreased below 1000 by 1969. It is commented that 'with further spreading of industrialisation, the importance of the cottage sector is bound to diminish'.

27. *Ibid.*, pp. 3-4.

28. Trade Development Authority of India, *Product Note on Hand. Small and Cutting Tools, op. cit.*, p. 7.

29. Special steels as composed of high speed carbon and chrome vanadium (or chrome molybdenum), pig iron cast tools, and industrial diamonds for diamond tools. It is available in the domesticmarket, but the manufactures prefer imported materials. See, *ibid.*, pp. 8-9.

30. *Ibid.*, p. 8.

31. The 'engineering goods' indicates a category of products into which a variety of manufactures of metals are classified. See for details, Engineering Export Promotion Council, *Handbook of Export Statistics 1974-75* (Calcutta, 1975), pp. 2-4.

32. On the other hand, India had been a set importer of handtools before 1970. See Figure 4.6.

33. Trade Development Authority of India, *Product Note on Hand, Small Cutting Tools, op. cit.*, p. 8.

34. *Ibid.*, p. 9.

35. *Ibid*, pp. 22-24.

36. Engineering Export Promotion Council, *Handbook of Export Statistics, op. cit.*, pp. 140-51.

37. United Nations, *Commodity Trade Statistics 1965* (New York), Series D, Vol. 25, No. 1-30, p. 7392.

38. United Nations, *Commodity Trade Statistics 1970, op. cit.*, p. 187.

39. The study of the Trade Development Authority of India indicates that the markets of the developed countries consist of the following four major segments: (a) high professional segment for the demand of

the sophisticated engineering industry; (b) low professional grade segment for the requirements of small industries and workshops and also for the general quality requirements in the large scale units; (c) quality-conscious, do-it-yourself segment for household carpentry; and (d) price-conscious, do-it-yourself segment for households where prices are much more concerned. See for details, *ibid.*, p. 27.

40. *Ibid.*, p. 19.

41. Figures in this paragraph are quoted from W. Hunsberger, *Japan and the United States in the World Trade* (New York : Council of Foreign Relations, 1964), pp. 278-80.

42. Japan External Trade Organisation, Ministry of International Trade and Industry, Japanese Government, *Foreign Trade of Japan*, 1970 (Tokyo, 1970), p. 80.

43. Engineering Export Promotion Council, *Findings of the Market Survey Team to Japan* (Calcutta, 1978), p. 29.

44. According to the All Japan Machinist Handtool Manufacturers' Association and the Japan Small Tool Makers' Association, there were 149 manufacturers of handtools in Japan in 1978. Among the handtools manufacturers which produce small and cutting tools, the biggest five turned out 45.6 per cent out of the total value of production by the sector in the same year. These manufacturers usually have their own steel making facility for meeting their requirement of special quality steel for the production. In the other area of handtools, only four manufacturing industries are of a large scale which manufacture a wide variety of tools. See, *ibid.*, pp. 53 and 63.

45. The following analysis owes to Indian Institute of Foreign Trade, *A Study of Marketing Opportunities for Selected Engineering Goods in Japan* (New Delhi, 1970), pp. 24-31.

46. *Ibid.*, p. 31.

47. H.B. Chenery and D.B. Kessing, *The Changing Composition of Developing Country's Exports* (World Bank Staff Working Paper No. 314) (Washington D.C., 1979), p. 1.

48. According to J.M. Finger, it is possible to assume two types of the catching-up and overtaking process in international trade of the world economy. One is the process accompanied by product development and the other by price reduction. By product development as a form of competition, a country can retain old and gain new markets by offering for sale at established prices products which, in the view of buyers, are different from those on the existing list of available products. Then other countries try to catch up and overtake by means of acquiring technology for producing the products. Price reduction as a form of competition, by contrast, refers to the attempt of a country to catch up and overtake by offering items on the existing product list at prices lower than those offered by its competitors. K. Akamatsu's model may belong to the latter type of competition, since the product in question in the model is usually one on the existing product list. Under the former

category, R. Vernon's 'product cycle' may be classified. He assumes in the model the product to be technologically new as well as unfamiliar to buyers, and the competing countries as the advanced countries which are not distinguishbly different from each other in terms of their access to scientific knowledge and their capacity to comprehend scientific principles. Finger tries to define 'a technologically new product' in clearer terms. He contends that any product which satisfies the conditions as below is likely to cause the product cycle in the international trade among advanced countries:

(1) Production runs are relatively short;
(2) The producers require relatively much skilled labour. This point is obviously applicable to high rate of product turnover by industries if 'skill' is defined as 'adaptability' rather than as 'rarity of talent';
(3) They are human capital-intensive rather than physical capital-intensive. This assumes that education is designed to make one adaptable rather than rare;
(4) External economies are important. External economies refer to the use of sub-contractors and industrial service firms to avoid large investments in special purpose fixed assets as well as advertising agencies and market research services which are not directly concerned with the production process.

See J.M. Finger, "A New View of the Product Cycle Theory", *Review of World Economies* (Kiel), Vol. 3. No. 1, 1975, pp. 79-99; R. Vernon, "International Investment and International Trade in the Product Cycle', *Quarterly Journal of Economics* (Cambridge), Vol. 29, No. 2, May 1966, pp. 190-207.

49. K. Akamatsu, "A Historical Pattern of Economic Growth", *The Developing Economies* (Tokyo), Preliminary Issue No. 1, March-August 1962, pp. 3-25.

50. *Ibid.*, pp. 12-16. The model sets aside the stage before the import stage when the less advanced economy does not have the economic interaction with other economies to a considerable extent and is in the state of a closed, self-sufficient economy as its income is very low.

51. Akamatsu observed that less advanced economies, when having reached this stage, often introduced the policies for protection and encouragement of the domestic infant industries against imported goods. Also, he pointed out that the abundant availability of inputs and the sound infrastructural basis were essential for the successful transition from this stage to the next. See for details, *ibid.*, pp. 13 and 14.

52. Vernon's product cycle and Akamatsu's Ganko Keitai Growth model view the catching-up and overtaking process more or less to be a passing disequilibrium between two conventionally described long-run equilibria. The initial equilibrium, having been disturbed by a technological breakthrough, returns to the situation from which it began once the gap between technology in an innovating country and in other

countries disappears. It is a notion different from the neo-tecnhological explanation of comparative advantage, although both are concerned with the international specialization of trade. The neo-technological hypothesis of the international trade concentrates on the difference in technological level existing among the countries as comparative advantage which will determine the pattern of specialisation working, whereas the former two models concentrate on the process of change in the pattern of specialisation. For the concise explanation of "neo-technological hypothesis", see the review of the past works in this regard by B. Balassa, *A 'Stages' Approach to Comparative Advantage* (World Bank Staff Working Paper No. 256) (Washington D.C., 1977), pp. 1-5.

53. I. Yamazawa, "Industrial Growth and Foreign Trade—The Case of Japan's Steel Industry", *Hitotsubashi Journal of Economics* (Tokyo), Vol. 12, No. 2, February 1972, pp. 41-59.

54. Exogeneous changes in the price variables affect such growth mechanism. One of these changes comes from the government protection given to the industry. Tariff on import raises import price and accelerates import substitution of the industry.

55. If expressed in symbolic terms, the model consists of four behaviour equations and one equilibrium condition to determine the equilibrium values of five endogeneous variables for a given set of values of exogeneous variables in each year.

(1) Domestic demand: $D=D(Y, L)$, $D'_Y>O$, $D'_L>O$,

where Y is domestic income variable and L is demonstration effect.

(2) Import: $M=M(D,P, PM)$, $M'_D>O$, $M'_P<O$, $M'_{PM}<O$,

where P is price of the product and PM is import price of the product including tariff

(3) Export: $X=H(Z, P, PZ)$, $X'_Z>O$, $X'_P>O$, $X'_{PZ}>O$,

where Z is foreign income variable and PZ is world price of the product.

(4) Price: $P=P(S, PO, W)$, $P'_S<O$, $P'_{PO}<O$, $P'_W<O$,

where S is production,
PO is import price of materials and
W is wage rate of workers of the industry.

(5) Equilibrium condition: $D=S+M-X$.

In the equation (1), the domestic income variables determine the level of domestic demand for the product, which is represented by the total output of the industry that uses the product as input in case of capital goods and by per capita gross domestic expenditure or consumption in case of consumer goods. The level of domestic demand is also influenced by the demonstration effect of the imported product to the domestic market. The demonstration effect can be formulated as a function of the time period since the introduction of the product to the domestic market.

It is usually a function, increasing at first, then decreasing and finally reaching the static position. The time period which is necessary for the demonstration effect to reach the static position differs from commodity to commodity. The equation (2) determines the level of import by import price relative to domestic price for a given level of domestic demand. Steady reduction of domestic price relative to import price promotes import substitution, and imports decline if the price effect is more than to offset the income effect in the cost reduction. The equation (3) determines the level of export by world price of the product until the domestic price declines to the level of the world price and by the foreign income variable and domestic price relative to the world price after then. The equation (4) represents the relationship between the domestic price (cost) and the level of production of the industry. Differentiation of each equation by each variable is useful in deriving a system of log linear equations in growth rates of variables. See for details, *ibid.*, pp. 47-49.

56. Taking the example of Japan's steel industry during the period from 1900 to 1970, Yamazawa empirically finds that except for the periods during the First World War and the late 1930s, there had been a distinct negative correlation between price and the level of production. See, *ibid.*, pp. 48-49.

57. K. Akamatsu, "A Historical Pattern of Economic Growth," *op. cit.*, pp. 12-13.

58. *Ibid.*, pp. 20-21. Corresponding to this difference in definition of import substitution, D.B. Keesing indicates that there are two kinds of definition, broad and narrow, for import substitution. By a broad definition, import substitution is nearly synonymous with industrial development (The exceptions would involve the processing or the labour-intensive manufacturing for exports where the product was not first imported). By a narrow definition import substitution is only the initial production replacing imports and the subsequent expansion is a product of domestic demand growth coupled with expanding supply capacities. See for details, D.B. Keesing, *Trade Policy for Developing Countries*, *op. cit.*, p. 10.

59. Akamatsu states that an industry develops to be an export industry only after the exports exceeds the imports. Thus, the Ganko Keitai Growth model deals only with the industrial growth of an export industry or the trade growth of an industry and excludes the case of an industry of which production is mainly devoted to the domestic consumption. However, D.B. Keesing maintains that (by either a narrow or broad definition presented in the previous footnote) the amount of import substitution that takes place in an economy and how fast may depend on its success in exports and overall economic growth even more than on direct efforts to accelerate and promote import substitution. This is because total purchases including imports are limited by import capacity, which is increased by the export success. Thus, the import substitution of an industry depends on the exports of the other industries and the

overall growth of the economy. Exports are essential unless the imports for an industry are financed by the exports of the other industries, as imports cannot be usually avoided in an industry for its various requirements for production. The case of the domesitc consumption-oriented industry also can be considered in the Ganko Keitai model, if the argument as above is acceptable. See, K. Akamatsu, "A Historical Pattern of Economic Growth", *op. cit.*, p. 141; D.B. Keesing, *Trade Policy for Developing Countries. op. cit.*, pp. 11-12.

60. The products classified under the category of handtools comprises of a variety of product with various specifications from technologically low-graded products to high-graded ones. The limitations to the study arises here as it is impossible to derive the three curves in quantity terms for illustrating the Ganko Keitai Growth of the handtools industry. Earlier in this chapter, it has been pointed out that Japan's imports of handtools consisted more of those for professional use rather than for general use, whereas India's exports concentrated on those of the latter category. It would have been possible to select a few commodities among those belonging to the category of handtools which found a substantial vent in the Japanese market like drop forged handtools in the analysis. However, the trade and industrial classifications of the commodities of handtools that differ among the countries make the comparison technically difficult.

61. See for example, Tran Van Tho, *Long-term Changes in the Comparative Advantage in the Japanese Economy—A Case Study of the Cotton Industry*, an unpublished thesis submitted to Hitotsubashi University (Tokyo, 1975), pp. 48-49.

62. Before starting the analysis, the sources of the data and their limitations are to be clarified. The statistics regarding the selected organised cotton fabrics industry was compiled in the *Census of Indian Manufactures* by the Central Statistical Organization, Government of India, prior to 1959. In the *Census*, the cotton fabrics industry, together with the spinning industry, was taken in the category titled 'cotton textiles'. Since 1959, the statistics regarding all the manufacturing industries in the organised sector has been dealt in the *Annual Survey of Industries*. In the *Annual Survey*, the cotton fabrics industry was classified under Industrial Number 231-1 with a title 'cotton textiles', together with the spinning industry. Thus, the data which are taken in the analysis refers to both spinning and weaving sectors. This reflects in the organised sector are the composite ones. The classification was revised in 1973 but there was no change in this regard.

In case of Japan and South Korea, the statistics regarding the manufacturing industries is based on the Standard International Trade Classification (SITC) devised by the United Nations. The statistics regarding the cotton fabrics industry over the study period was compiled in SITC Code No. 652 with a title 'woven cotton fabrics'. SITC was revised in 1960, but there was no change in this regard. This statistics regarding the industry in the United States are compiled as in its manufacturing census similar to SITC.

63. As indicated earlier India's cotton fabrics industry consists of the handloom and the mill sectors. Since the technology employed in production is completely different from each other, each sector should be separately treated in the analysis of production cost structure. Yet as indicated earlier, a bulk of cotton textile exports from India has been constituted with those produced in the mill sector. Moreover, the intention here is to examine the performance of India's manufactured exports. Thus, only the products of the mill sector have been concerned in this analysis.

64. Calculated from the total wages of employees in a year, including those of employees other than workers of the cotton fabrics industry as defined in the footnote 62.

65. Calculated from average monthly earnings of the lowest paid operatives in cotton textile mills for a standard month of 26 working days of six major cities and two states (Bombay, Ahmedabad, Indore, Tamil Nadu, West Bengal, Kanpur, Delhi and Bhavnagar).

66. Calculated from the total wages of employees in a year including those of other than workers, of the textile industry (SITC Code No. 32).

67. Calculated from the total production of cotton fabrics (quantity) in a year divided by the number of production workers engaged in the cotton fabrics weaving.

68. The production or wholesale price per unit of cotton yarn, which is the major component of the material inputs of the cotton fabrics industry, is taken here the material cost per unit for convenience.

69. The ratio of the volume of output of cotton fabries to the volume of cotton fibers consumed by mills is to represent the output-material ratio of the cotton fabrics industry in this study.

70. The statistics regarding India's handtools industry from 1959 to 1971 is available in the *Annual Survey of Industries* in which the handtools industry is classified in Industrial Code No. 350-10 with a title 'handtools and small tools'. In case of Japan and South Korea, the statistics regarding the industry has been presented based on the Standard International Trade Classification (SITC) of the United Nations. The statistics on the handtools industry before 1959 is compiled in SITC Code No. 699-12 with a title 'handtools, tools for machines and hand implements', while the data after the revision in classifications in 1959 are found in SITC Code No. 695 with a title 'handtools, n.e.s.'. The data regarding the U.S.A.'s handtools industry is compiled as in its manufacturing census, similar to the SITC.

71. As indicated earlier, a variety of products with various classifications are classified in the categories of handtools. Since the technology employed in the production is different from product to product, it is not technically feasible to identify the material cost per unit and output-input ratio for the industry.

72. The average wages per worker in a year.

73. Calculated from the total wages of employees in a year, including other than workers of the handtools industry defined as in the footnote 70 of this chapter.

74. Calculated from the total wages of production workers in a year of the industry as defined in the footnote 70.

75. Calculated from the total wages of production workers in a year engaged in the handtool industry as defined in the footnote 70.

76. Calculated from the total wages of employees in a year including other than workers, of the metal manufactures industry (SITC Code No. 69).

5

POLICY DIRECTIONS OF INDIA AND JAPAN TOWADS TRADE GROWTH

IT can be said that growth in India's manufactured exports to Japan was the reflection of the structure and growth of India's manufacturing sector as a whole. To extend further this argument, Panchamukhi[1] refers to the particular factor in developing economies that influences the trade flow. It is asserted that the level and the commodity composition of exports and imports is closely related to the development strategy adopted by the planning authorities and that it cannot be viewed in isolation to the process of overall planning for allocation of resources. Besides gravity of the economy like national income and population, factor proportions and endowments and technology on which the traditional theories of international trade are based, Panchamukhi points out the importance of the economic institutional settings in case of determination of trade flow in developing economies, including the economic and commercial policies.[2]

Assuming the above, this chapter will investigate the policy background that have influenced the India-Japan trade from

1951 to 1973. Though there existed no specific policies meant for the promotion of India's manufactured exports to Japan, India's policies for manufactured exports to Japan are assessed in terms of the policies directed to the manufacturing export sector, especially those to the labour-intensive manufacturing[3] sector that have more implications in this context.

To conduct a complete assessment of India's trade policies and its implications to its trade with Japan, it is also necessary to examine the policies not only in the context of its domestic economy, but also to see how far India made efforts in terms of policies to respond to the incentives for exports provided by the Japanese import policies for manufactures.

India's Export Policies for Manufactures

India's trade policies during 1951-73 have basically kept the objectives of 'controls' in view since the 'Import and Export Control Act of 1947' was set out to prohibit, restrict or otherwise control imports and exports. Evolution of framework for India's trade policy has been documented in the consecutive Five Year Plans. Given the relative comfortable position of foreign exchange reserves in the Korean War boom, the First Five Year Plan was not conscious of the trade policy as an integral part of planning. However, since the Industrial Policy Resolution of 1956 was announced, a massive flow of imports began. India tried to keep the balance of trade position in equilibrium, by placing all the import activities under its control. In 1955, a comprehensive Import Trade Control Order was issued which brought almost all imports under the purview of licensing. The main objective of import licensing system was by and large to effect a right kind of import structure so as to conserve scarce foreign exchange reserves, while ensuring adequate supply of inputs to the industry and protecting the indigenous industry.

The Second Five Year Plan was pessimistic about the export growth, which originated from the following two factors. First, there was a widespread belief that India's traditional primary export such as tea and jute would be facing an unfavourable trend in the world markets in future because of their less price and income-elasticities. Secondly, it was felt that India's non-traditional exports, mainly manufactures, which constituted a tiny proportion of the country's export earnings at that time, were not able to secure sizable export markets until industrialisation was well under way.[4]

After experiencing the critical balance of payments deficit during the Second Plan period, the Third Plan reflected that 'one of the main drawbacks in the past has been that the problem of exports has not been regarded as an integral part of a country's development effort under the Five Year Plans... (Export Promotion) should be an integral part of the overall framework of economic planning.'[5] Since then, the export policy in India's planning intended to act on the commodity composition of export trade as well as the volume of exports.

Among the export items which were planned to be stepped up, the manufactured exports were given a special emphasis for promotion. Before the devaluation of Indian Rupee in 1966,[6] the basic framework of India's export system was formed, which was characterised with the schemes such as import replenishment, duty drawback and cash assistance.[7] The importance of expansion of manufactured exports was further underlined in the Export Policy Resolution of 1970. The Resolution, first of all, affirms that the export promotion is one of the important aspects of India's planning and economic growth. Among the commodities which were considered to have export potentialities, manufactured exports were identified here as the dynamic element of India's export growth.[8]

Since the export promotion policy became an integral part of India's planning and development, a series of export incentive measures have been set out. The emphasis in the export incentive scheme has been on the capital-intensive sector. The study conducted by W. Mellos and U. Lele[9] supports this argument. They maintain that India's export policy has been in favour of a rise in capital-intensive in exports. They found that an 18 per cent rise in the capital intensity was observed in India's exports between 1964 and 1969. India's export policy is partly a reflection of industrial policy. According to the above study, during the same period, out of 19 major industrial categories, the four most capital-intensive increased their proportion of investment, value added in production and employment, while the four industrial groups with the lowest capital-intensity decreased their share in each of the three measures, all of which were producers of final consumer goods.

India's Incentive Scheme for Manufactured Exports

D. Nayyar classifies the export incentives during 1951-73 into five groups[10] : (1) direct financial incentives; (2) fiscal concessions; (3) incentives implicit in import policy; (4) subsidisation related explicitly to inputs; and (5) marketing assistance[11].

The compensatory support programme for exports through cash subsidies, which was announced soon after the devaluation, is the most important among the export incentives belonging to the category of direct financial incentives.[12] About 500 items received cash assistance at the rates ranging between 3 per cent and 25 per cent of f.o.b. value in the 1960s, which were fixed separately for each product group. About 80 per cent of the items which received cash assistance were manufactures and most of them were non-traditional capital-intensive manufactures like engineering goods and chemicals, comprising 70 per cent and 19 per cent of the total of cash subsidies received in 1970-71, respectively. Over the period from 1966-67 to 1970-71, the average rates of export subsidy for all the industries worked out at 3.1 per cent of the f.o.b. value of exports. The total disbursement increased rapidly from Rs. 30.5 million in 1966-67 to Rs. 288.0 million in 1970-71.

Two types of fiscal concessions in the form of export promotion incentives were in operation. One of them relates to the payment of direct taxes, while the other relates to the payment of indirect taxes. In the former type of concession, the earnings from exports are either partially exempted from income tax, or are taxed at a concessional rate. The latter type of concession mostly takes the form of renunciation of taxes or tariffs paid on inputs used in the export output.

Among fiscal concessions provided for exports, duty drawbacks from sales tax for exports had been an important incentive to exporters. The amount of concessions through duty drawbacks accruing to export sales was estimated to be Rs. 420 million in 1973-74[13]. In practice, the exemption from sales tax on the output sold abroad has been administered based on the all-industry rates worked out by the Drawback Directorate. If an enterprise could prove that the actual duty paid exceeds the all-industry rate assessment by 25 per cent, it can choose to be considered under a brand rate which is on a firm-by-firm basis.

Incentives implicit in the import policy provides substantial encouragement to exports, since it enables exporters to purchase importable inputs at world prices as well as to sell their surplus foreign exchange in an open market at a premium. Import entitlement scheme for exporters was introduced in 1957, but the scope was limited as their objective was mainly to ease supply bottlenecks of essential industrial materials. It was in the Third Plan that the scheme acquired importance as export incentive. Under this system, exporters are allowed to retain a certain proportion of their foreign exchange earnings in the form of import licenses. There is no doubt that this policy acquired the unstated objective of giving cash subsidy to exporters.[14]

The average rates of replenishment as percentage of f.o.b. value of exports by broad product classifications ranged from 67.5 per cent for gem and jewellery to 2.3 per cent for unmanufactured tobacco in 1970-71. The total issue of import replenishment licences more than doubled from Rs. 428.7 million in 1967-68 to Rs. 947.4 million in 1970-71, and in this period, the scheme extended to approximately one-third of India's total exports.[15]

Among the support provided for inputs supplied to exporters, export credit and insurance facilities as export incentives are important in the context of India's export promotion since a bulk of its exports are constituted by primary products and traditional manufactures. Since the establishment of the Export Credit Guarantee Corporation of India in 1964, the underwriting of the risks arise in exporting was made available. The initial service the Corporation provided was the post-shipment export credit guarantee to 66.7 per cent of the total post-shipment export value. Later, the terms of guarantee were liberalised to 80 per cent. Also, insofaras advances to small merchants were concerned, the percentage of guarantee coverage under its packing credit guarantee was raised to 90 per cent.[16]

Policy Directions for Cotton Textiles' Export Growth

In the early 1960s, the industry started receive the benefits from the import entitlement scheme. In the scheme, import licenses allotted to exporters fetched them high premium in the market thereby constituting an effective subsidy. The extent of the subsidisation was limited by the restrictions on sale of the import entitlements. The exporters of cotton textiles had to surrender (i) two-thirds of their coaltar dye entitlements to dye manufacturers; (ii) four-fifths of their machinery entitlements to the manufacturers of textile machinery at fixed premium; and (iii) raw cotton entitlements to the Textile Commissioner at a fixed margin.[17]

As a result, the premium on import licenses varied considerably between the products made from different inputs. According to the study by J. Bhagwati and P. Desai, the effective subsidy for cotton textiles implicit in the import entitlement scheme in May 1965 varied between 28.3 per cent and 65.7 per cent of the f.o.b. value of exports, depending on the category of the product and the direction to which the product was exported.[18] The import entitlement scheme was withdrawn at the time of devaluation of the rupee in 1966. According to D. Nayyar,[19] the net devaluation for cotton textiles products was 14.2 per cent as against the gross devaluation rate of 57.2 per cent, taking into consideration the effect of the countervailing measures for devaluation including the abolition of the import entitlement scheme.

After the devaluation, some of the export promotion incentives withdrawn at the time of the devaluation were gradually revived. Cotton textile industry started to receive the facilities under the import replenishment scheme, but the import licenses issued to exporters of cotton textiles amounted only to 5.4 per cent in 1970-71.[20] The value of import replenishment licenses issued for exports of cotton textiles comprised 3.7 per cent out of the total value of licenses issued in 1973-74 amounting to Rs. 1512 million.[21] On the other hand, from 1968 on, the industry was given cash assistance at a flat rate of 5 per cent on the f.o.b. value for all exports of cotton textiles. The subsidy was distributed through the Indian Cotton Mills Federation and financed by a reimbursement of non-refundable taxes. The cash assistance provided for exports of cotton textiles comprised 13.5 per cent and 12.5 per cent, out of the total cash assistance of Rs. 407 million for 1970-71 and Rs. 653 million for 1971-72, respectively.[22]

In terms of export incentives by means of duty drawbacks, those provided for cotton textiles exports have been significant among other export products. In 1974-75, 28.5 per cent of the total duty drawbacks provided to the industry amounting to Rs. 601 million went to the cotton textiles industry.[23]

Wolf conducted an exercise to compute the export incentive rate, which is the ratio of value of all the incentives against export value, for cotton textiles exports in 1974-75. Against the total value of exports of US $ 399.9 million cotton textile industry was provided for cash assistance of US $ 13.8 million, import replenishment licenses of US $ 7 million with a premium of US $ 1.8 million, and duty drawbacks of US $ 21.5 million, from which the export incentive rate was worked out to be 9.3 per cent, little above the average for all exports at 5.0 per cent in 1974-75.[24]

Various problems that were pointed out in the course of the operation of the export promotion incentives for cotton textile industry in the 1960s can be summarised as follows:[25]

(1) One of the major problems in the export of cotton textiles and yarns was the very high cost of production arising out of obsolete technology generally employed in the industry. Most of the mills did not have the requisite funds for rehabilitation, since their reserves had been depleted in the past in undertaking the minimum rehabilitation programmes as well as were used to meet the ever-increasing needs of working capital due to increase in the cost. Commercial banks were reluctant to advance money to the industry, considering it to be a banking risk. Moreover, there were no specialised financial agencies for extending assistance to the textile industry. Hindustan Chambers of Commerce had suggested for rehabilitation and renovation of the industry: (i) to set up special agencies to extend financial assistance to the industry on reasonable terms; and (ii) to set aside a reasonable percentage of excise duties collected from the industry by the Government as a means of granting soft long term loans;

(2) India's cotton textile industry was facing a constraint in the supply of materials, especially raw cotton, which affected competitiveness of India's products. India's potentiality in the production of raw cotton was not properly exploited by means of utilisation of better inputs and technology. At the same time, the Cotton Stock Control Order should have been amended so as to permit the mills to stock the quantity of cotton required to fulfill the export target in addition to the normal permissible limits for the state.

(3) The Cotton Textile Export Promotion Council was set up to supervise and organise the export promotion efforts of the cotton textile manufactures and exporters. It was considered that more rigorous efforts be required by the organisation as well as exporters with respect to quantity control and marketing of the exports.

(4) Labour cost constitutes about 20 to 25 per cent of the cost of the production in the cotton textile industry. Labour cost in the industry fluctuated when the dearness allowance, an important element of the labour cost, used to be evaluated on a monthly basis.[26] The uncertainty in the wages payable from month to month was a disadvantage for long-term export contracts. It was recommended to revise dearness allowance at least on a half-year basis.

Policy Direction for Handtools Export Growth

In the pre-devaluation period, the various export incentives such as import entitlement scheme, customs and excise duty drawbacks, income tax concessions, railway freight concessions and preferential supply of raw materials were given to the handtools industry.[27] For example, 75 per cent of the f.o.b. value of handtools exports were benefited from the import entitlement scheme from 1964 until the devaluation.[28]

Despite the interruption accompanying the devaluation, most of the incentives given to the industry prior to the devaluation were revived within a few years. Instead of the import entitlement scheme, the handtools industry was given the import replenishment licenses in which 50 per cent of total f.o.b. value of handtools exports was covered.[29] Secondly, the industry was given cash subsidies, in which 15 per cent of the f.o.b. value of exports was covered in 1966-67 and 1969-70.[30] Besides, the handtools industry was provided for duty drawbacks. In 1974-75, the industry was given upto US $ 0.9 million of duty drawbacks, consisting of 1.2 per cent of the total made available to all the export sectors.[31] Thirdly, with effect from 1967, the industry was given reimbursement of the difference between the domestic and the international prices of steel used in exports.[32] Fourthly, a compulsory export obligation scheme was introduced in 1968. The handtools industry which manufactures small tools was advised to export at least 5 per cent of its total production.[33] The Engineering Export Promotion Council (EEPC) of India had made the following suggestions[34] for improvement of incentives for the handtools industry :

1. The export promotion scheme by means of cash assistance did not have adequate flexibility as its operation was not connected with the export performance. On the other hand, the schemes of import entitlement and bonus voucher were appropriate as export incentive. It is desirable, however, to allow wider transferability in the latter schemes within broad groups of the engineering industry in order to avoid delay in issuing licences owing to the lack of details and classifications about nominees, etc.;

2. Concessional freight for shipment of exports is important for the engineering industry. Concession in railway freight on all engineering goods should be given for a period of at least 5 years, within which the industry is supposed to establish export markets overseas and be in a position to bear full freight;

3. Besides the above, it is also important to make efforts in improving quality control, making market surveys and holding exhibitions and trade fairs.

Japan's Trade Liberalisation Measures

The characteristics of the strategy for economic growth and industrialisation in the post-war Japan has been : (1) that the industries which were expected to achieve high growth in future were selected for special attention from the Government; and (2) that assistance was directly given to these industries by the government;[35] and also (3) that measures to support them indirectly were taken, such as the policy to avoid ruinous competition from overseas at the infancy stage of growth of the industries so that they were able to improve competitiveness at the cost of such protections. Once an improvement in competitiveness of the industries was observed, the measures which provided protection so far were altogether withdrawn and the industries were exposed to the competition with foreign industries. These industries by then generally had developed competitiveness enough to capture domestic as well as world markets to a significant extent.

Japan's trade policies between 1951 and 1973[36] facilitated the operation of the strategy for industrialisation. For example, controls were imposed on the imports of manufactures and foreign investment.[37] A study conducted by I. Yamazawa indicates that the effective tariff rates on competitive manufactures were extremely high because of the sharp escalation of Japan's tariff schedules from the raw material through higher processing stages, especially before the Kennedy Round Reductions.[38] Another important aspect of the trade policy related with industrialisation in Japan was to encourage the imports of technology despite such controls on foreign exchange and foreign direct investment.[39] The payments made by Japanese companies to foreign companies for patent licenses, know-how and associated expenses, which provides an aggregate measure to the flow of technology, grew at an average annual rate of 31.5 per cent from 1951 to 1955 and 34.0 per cent from 1955 to 1961. The payments grew slower at 11.2 per cent from 1961 to 1964 and 15.4 per cent from 1964 to 1967, which again went up to 21.9 per cent from 1969 to 1970.[40]

However, particularly since the mid-1960s there was a significant change in the trend of Japan's trade policies, as Japan began to participate in the international economic forums like GATT and UNCTAD. To comply with the idea of the international economic cooperation, which is the guiding principle of these forums, Japan's trade policies were modified on the basis of multilateralism. In view of joining GATT, tariff schedules were restructured consistenly in the ad-valorem format in 1954. In 1960, the policy to liberalise 257 four-digit BTM items was announced. Acceptance of the GATT Charter Articles 8 and 11 led discontinuation of the policies like direct tax credits to exports, foreign exchange budgeting in 1964.

The policy for liberalisation of imports was further carried out in the face of strong trade balance and balance of payments position since the late 1960s. The number of import items subject to the quota restrictions was reduced from 118 by 1960 upto 1971. The Kennedy Round tariff reductions were implemented from 1971. Besides, Japan agreed to offer Generalised Scheme of Preferences (GSP) to the imports from developing countries from the same year, which were negotiated under the auspices of UNCTAD.

The trend toward more liberalised import policies and less export incentives since the late 1960s co-existed with Japanese growing awareness that its exports of labour-intensive products were facing keen competition in the world market, particularly in the U.S.A.,[41] where about one-third of Japan's exports were directed. Japan's share in the US imports of veneers, plywood boards (SITC 631) and perambulators, toys and sporting goods (SITC 894) declined from 27.9 per cent and 48.9 per cent in 1964 to 23.3 per cent and 37.8 per cent in 1967, respectively. On the other hand, besides these two product groups, there was a consistent rise in the share of Far East countries (excluding Mainland China) in the US imports of textile yarn fabrics and clothings (SITC 65, 85), electrical machinery and apparatus (SITC 729), of which growth in Japan's share stagnated in the same period.

Withdrawal of certain protective measures and incentives accelerated a relative decline of the light manufacturing sector compared to other sectors, which was under way since the late 1960s exposed them to competition with the industry of developing countries in the world as well as domestic markets. The share in the light industrial products in Japan's total exports decreased from 31.9 per cent in 1965 to 16.3 per cent in 1973. The extent of decline in exports was very significant in textile industry except in certain synthetic products. The export-output ratio in cotton fabrics fell from 33.5 per cent in 1965 to 10.4 per cent in 1973.[42]

At the same time erosion in the domestic market by imports was observed in these industries. In 1965 imports of textiles for final consumption was valued at US $ 15.4 million, which increased to US $ 647.5 million dollars by 1973, exceeding the value of exports of the products at US $ 435.9 million.[43] Imports of light industrial products as a whole increased in the share in total imports from 3.1 per cent to 10.8 per cent over the same period. The erosion in domestic market for the light industrial sector in Japan was accompanied by the decline in its share in value-added and employment for the entire manufacturing sector. For example, 39.6 per cent of value added in the manufacturing sector was accrued to the light industry in 1965, which declined to 32.9 per cent in 1973. There was also a decline in share of textile industry in value added from 9.6 per cent to 8.4 per cent over the period.[44]

The structural change in the industrial sector towards the early 1970s was interpreted as something inherent to the industrial growth at higher stages. There was a move to induce the change further by the Japanese Government. Industrial Structure Council, a decision-making body of the Ministry of International Trade and Industry, voiced a suggestion that domestic production of the resource-processing type heavy and chemical industrial sector should be substituted for imports, following the trend observed in textile industry since the late 1960s.[45] Pointing out the high energy consumption in the industry, it was proposed that Japan, being a resource-scarce economy, should more concentrate on the manufacturing activities of an assembling type in such international economic environment as the oil crisis of 1973.

Japan implemented GSP scheme for the imports from developing countries in 1971, which has had significant implications to India's exports to Japan. The scheme was basically suggested by UNCTAD to all the developed countries in order to promote North-South economic cooperation. Besides, the scheme for Japan was structured to incorporate the objectives of its industrial and trade policies in the 1970s. We shall examine below the structure and effects of Japan's GSP scheme with special reference to cotton fabrics and handtools imports from India.

Japan's GSP Scheme for Imports from Developing Countries

Japan's effort on the trade liberalisation until the Kennedy Round of Tariff Negotiations concentrated mainly on the relaxation of quota restrictions and the reduction of extremely high rates of tariff, which did not have a significant impact compared with that of its liberalisation efforts in the latter period. However, the trade liberalisation measures taken on those occasions were universal in effect in the sense that they applied to any country in the world. Meanwhile, the Generalised Scheme of Preferences (GSP) was recommended to be adopted by industrial countries in the UNCTAD in order to promote North-South economic cooperatian in the area of trade. Japan introduced the GSP scheme in August 1971 along with the other industrial countries.[46]

Introduction of the GSP scheme brought a more distinctive impact on India's exports to Japan than any other trade policy set out during the period, because of its specific objective and function favouring exports from developing countries against those from other developed countries. It is possible to take up the policy issues of Japan with respect to its trade with India by examining Japan's GSP scheme offered to India, in absence of integrated policy specifically meant for promoting Japan's trade with India.

The GSP scheme has the following salient features in its operations:[47]

(1) The tariff concessions were given by the scheme to agricultural products (Brussels Tariff Nomenclature (BTN) chapters 1 to 24) as well as manufactured products (BTN chapters 35 to 99). The concessions were given in the form of either further reductions of the tariff rates of the post-Kennedy Round or complete elimination of them;

(2) The list of beneficiary countries which are entitled to enjoy the preferential tariff treatment under the GSP is to be announced by the individual country which offers it;

(3) To be eligible for the GSP concessions, the exporter has to produce certificates of origin to be awarded by recognised agencies in the developing countries. These certificates are insisted to make sure that exports have been manufactured

substantially in the developing country itself;

(4) For some items, there is a system of ceiling, according to which Most Favoured Nations (MFN) rate of the post-Kennedy Round tariff rate is restored instead of the rate under the GSP scheme as soon as imports of the products covered by the scheme reaches the level of ceiling.

Besides above, the following features are incorporated in the GSP scheme of Japan:[48]

(1) In general, Japan grants preferential tariff treatments to vast majority of industrial products, that is, those under BTN chapters 35-99 with exception of 10 items including some petroleum products, apparel and clothing of leather, plywood, raw silk and silk products and leather footwear. Preferential treatment is also granted to a short list of selected agricultural and fishing products in BTN chapters 1-24;

(2) In order to provide for preference-sharing among beneficiaries, however, Japan applies 'a maximum country amount limitation' under which the preferential imports from a single beneficiary are not allowed to exceed 80 per cent of the ceiling quota, beyond which the MFN tariff rates are restored.

In the scheme of 1972, 28.1 per cent of the total dutiable imports from all the beneficiaries were eligible for GSP preferential treatment. The imports from India applicable for GSP in the same year comprised 48.6 per cent of all the dutiable imports from India. For the industrial products and raw materials under BTN chapters 25-99, the ratio of eligible to dutiable imports from India went up to 92.1 per cent.[49]

However, the imports which was actually granted preferences were much lower than expected, indicating the severe effect of ceilings and maximum country limitations in Japan's GSP scheme on India's exports. The imports which were benefited from the scheme valued at US $ 35.7 million comprised 30.6 per cent of duitable imports and 62 8 per cent of imports covered under GSP. The imports benefited from GSP, all of which happened to belong to BTN chapters 25-99, comprised 58.1 per cent of dutiable imports and 63.1 per cent of imports covered under GSP.[50]

Out of 214 items to which the ceiling was to be imposed, 94 tems were to be subject to specific maximum country limitations in the 1971 scheme. It was expected that India would be subject to maximum country limitations for 9 items namely; cokes, leather, raw fur skin of rabbits, minks, manmade fibres (continuous), carpets, handmade tapestries of coir, certain women's garments, ferro-alloys, unalloyed copper.[51]

The GSP scheme for cotton fabrics and handtools was provided for under ceilings as well as maximum country limitations.[52] The preference margin provided by Japan's GSP scheme over the MFN rate after the Kennedy Round negotiations for cotton fabrics as effective in 1973 was 5.6 per cent for a pure variety, 8.4 per cent for a variety mixed with synthetic fibres and 11.2 per cent for variety with synthetic warp and weft. The preference margin for handtools in 1973 was 6 per cent, except drills, bits, reamers and diamond tools, for which 7.2 per cent was provided.

A study by UNCTAD[53] estimated the extent of maximum country limitations which would have been imposed on major supplying beneficiaries for the scheme for 1971 based on the actual of 1970. In case of woven cotton fabrics,[54] it was estimated that the ceiling for 1971 of US $ 4731 thousand would have been exceeded by US $ 3623 thousand and that the maximum country limitation been imposed on some beneficiaries at US $ 2366 thousand by exceeding it by US $ 2826 thousand. In other words, due to the ceiling, 44.4 per cent of imports of cotton fabrics from all the beneficiaries were not able to be benefited from the GSP scheme, while 54.4 per cent of the imports from the major suppliers among beneficiaries would not utilize the scheme due to the ceiling as well as the maximum country limitations. On the other hand, it was estimated that against US $ 2321 thousand of annalised ceiling for 1971 for handtools products, imports from beneficiaries would have amounted to US $ 205 thousand, all of which would have benefited from the GSP scheme.

The picture of restrictive quotas for some items co-existing with underutilization of quotas for the other implies that distribution of quotas among GSP items was not in accordance with the export structure of beneficiary countries, owing to the methodology adopted in establishing quotas. In the GSP scheme of Japan, ceilings are established in value or quantity terms for each product group by adding to c.i.f. imports from the scheme beneficiaries in 1968 (basic amount), that is, 10 per cent of c.i.f. imports from non-beneficiaries in a year which precedes the current scheme by two years (supplementary amount).[55]

As enhancement in ceiling solely depended on the growth of imports from non-beneficiary countries, while the basic amount remained the same, there were 'closed ended' ceilings for 37 items including cotton fabrics in the 1971 scheme where eligible imports were more the respective quotas. In these cases, growth in imports from beneficiaries was very rapid since 1968 as basis year, which was not accounted for in setting out ceilings, while the growth of imports from non-beneficiaries was stagnated. For example, Japan's imports of cotton fabrics from developing economies, most of which were beneficiaries from Japan's GSP scheme, increased $ from US 3.3 million in 1968 to US $ 8.5 million in 1971,[56] which did not give any ground in enhancing the ceiling for 1971 set out at US $ 4.7 million.

On the other hand 'open-ended' ceilings were established for 177 items in 1971, some of which, including handtools, achieved the level of imports much below the ceilings. In such cases, at 1968 basis year, the imports from the beneficiaries were very insignificant, but the ceiling was set high due to large imports from non-beneficiaries. Imports of handtools, for example, from developed countries in 1968 comprised 99.6 per cent in Japan's total imports of the product.[57]

The brief analysis on Japan's GSP scheme for cotton fabrics and handtools as above reveals that the ceiling for cotton fabrics were highly restrictive compared to the export potential of developing countries including India, whereas there was much room for India to increase handtool exports to Japan under preferential treatment. The methodology adopted in establishing ceilings by Japan was with a two-fold objective to counteract the adverse impact on non-beneficiaries by introducing the GSP scheme, while encouraging exports from developing countries. In case of traditional export items where the competition among developed and developing countries was keen, the former factor worked against the latter, whereas in the non-traditional exports, the incentive factor to developing countries were found to be too excessive.

Harmonisation of Trade Policies

During 1951 to 1973, it could be observed that Japan's trade policies were used as an effective instrument for its economic growth. As the Japanese economy was highly dependent on the supply of foodstuffs and industrial inputs from abroad, the import policy was formulated to ensure the stable supply of these commodities. The import policy played another important role to protect domestic industries from harmful effects of international competition when the industries were at infant stages of development. The latter aspects of Japan's import policy was carefully integrated with its export policy. The industries improved their competitive position by making use of tariff and non-tariff protection. As soon as they achieved a certain level of competitiveness, intensive export promotion measures were introduced taking into account the existence of demand in world markets as a criterion for output expansion and technological improvement. As Japan complied with the idea of the international economic order advocated by the international economic forums like GATT and UNCTAD, major import liberalisation measures were introduced. Japan implemented the across-the-board tariff reductions on MFN rates on the basis of the results of post-Kennedy Round as well as the GSP scheme for the imports from developing countries in the early 1970s.

In view of the objective of expansion and diversification of India's exports to Japan, the extent of harmonisation in trade policies of the two countries can be assessed from various points of view. Panchamukhi has suggested one of the feasible methods of measuring it.[58] To obtain the overall effect of India's trade policies for export promotion, he works out the amount received by the exporters of manufactures and processed products for the goods exported worth one dollar (see Table 5.1). Terming it as implicit exchange rate, it is assumed that cash subsidies rate, import replenishment rate and premium on the import replenishment license are the vital factors to influence implicit

TABLE 5.1.

Relationship between Domestic Export Incentives and Preference Marign under Japan's G.S.P. Scheme for Selective Product Group

RITC Co. No.	*Items*	*Implicit exchange rates (1967-68 to 1970-71)*[1]	*Average perference margin under Japan's G.S.P. Scheme*[2]
67 & 69	Ferros manufactures	9.23 to 9.68	9.61
68	Nonferros manufactures	11.12 to 12.68	12.21
72	Electrical machinery equipments & apparatus	10.50 to 13.92	8.85
51	Chemical and chemical products	8.93 to 15.03	8.59
09	Processed foods	8.14 to 8.16	4.26
899	Handicrafts	8.94 to 9.08	9.85
12	Tobacco and tobacco manufactures	7.64 to 7.75	0.00
657	Woolen carpets, rugs and druggets	8.48 to 9.14	8.17
84	Readymade garments	7.65 to 7.95	1.66
658	Cotton textiles	7.73 to 7.95	8.17
655	Natural Silk fabrics	9.15 to 10.05	8.17
	Rank correlation co-efficient between Implicit exchange rates and G.S.P. preference margins		
	(a) Lower limit of exchange rates		+0.77
	(b) Higher limit of exchange rates		+0.66

Note : (1) Export subsidy equivalents of all export incentive scheme except duty drawbacks.

(2) Simple weighted average within a commodity group.

Source : V.R. Panchamukhi, *Trade Policies of India, op. cit.*, p. 248.

evchange rate of exports, besides duty drawback rates, which is not accounted for in this estimate.

The comparison of implicit exchange rates with preference margins offered by Japan's GSP scheme could reveal in one way whether India's export promotion policies for manufacturing industries are consistent with Japan's import policies. Panchamukhi finds in the analysis that the rank correlation coefficients between implicit exchange rates of India's export incentives and corresponding preference margins in Japan's GSP scheme are relatively high which implies a certain degree of harmonisation that existed in the policies between the two countries towards the early 1970s.

It is worth looking into the policy background underlying South Korea's trade with Japan, which induced enormous expansion of trade between the two countries. Japan's imports from South Korea increased from US $ 92.4 million to US $ 1204.7 million between 1967 and 1973. The expansion of South Korea's exports to Japan was accompanied by the increase in direct foreign investment from the latter to the former. The net inflow of direct investment from Japan to South Korea was only US $ 0.1 million in the period of 1962-66, which rose to US $ 364.6 million in 1972-76.

One of the effects of foreign investment on the host country is the economic fluctuations of the investing country transmitted to it.[59] Since the direct investment is originally meant for hedging against price fluctuations in the materials or components, the subsidiary's own sales are more or less dependent on the purchasing policy of the parent company. On the other hand, in case the subsidiary depend on the parent company for their supply of intermediate materials, it has to adjust the rate of operation according to supply of the parent company. Moreover, the way in which direct investment made is concerned with the magnitude of the effect of investment on the host country. For example, as the investment takes the form of vertical integration and provides majority capital, the economic fluctuations of the investing country are to be transmitted more intensively.

Thus the linkage through investment between an investing country and a host country induces the expansion of trade flow between them. As the business of the domestic industry in an investing country expands, the supply capacity to a host country increases and the expansion of production in its domestic industry follows it. At the same time, as the business of the investing country expands, there will be more demand for the products of the host country.

The study by C.H. Lee[60] indicates that the Japanese foreign investment to South Korea has been more oriented to its import requirements. He discovers that 61 per ccnt of Japan's direct investment to South Korea between 1962 and 1974 (on approval basis) was meant for export-oriented projects especially to the sectors such as textiles and electric and electronic equipments which were the major export items from South Korea to Japan. Also, it is found that the Japanese-type investment prefers the vertical integration in which in the same period 48 per cent of its direct investment to South Korea specified to ownership of more than 50 per cent. Such characteristics of Japan's direct investment must have intensified the effects of direct investment to host countries discussed above. It in turn implies that such characteristics of the Japanese-style investment contributed to the prompt expansion of trade flow between Japan and South Korea.

Besides the geographical proximity, Japanese direct investment was induced by the policies for direct foreign investment of South Korea which were said to include most generously legislated incentives in Asia.[61] The incentives to foreign investors under the legislation of 1960 featured a set of tax concessions including a five-year tax holiday and guaranteed for repatriation of principal and profit. In the latter years, there were two major changes in the investment environment. In 1966, the administrative procedures were simplified by creation of the 'One-Stop Service Office' in the Economic Planning Board which canalises in one place nearly all of foreign investors' dealings with the Government. Also, under the Foreign Capital Inducement Law, 1966, no legal limit was set out on the degree of foreign participation. Though it allows a foreign equity upto 50 per cent in principle, the industries which produce commodities exclusively for exports; of the projects of multinational corporations which involve the exclusive use of the confidential production and management methods or patent rights; of the industries in the high-technology area set up in particular industrial complex; and of the projects by non-resident Koreans, are exempted from application of the clause.

Evolving Policies with the Changing Environment

In this chapter the trade policies of India and Japan have been examined against the backdrop of the growth and diversification of the India-Japan trade between 1951 and 1973.

The economic policies of India and Japan had little degree of harmonisation between them even though the economies were complementary to each other. Japan has started to pave the way from early 1960s for more industrial collaborations with the developing countries, mainly by means of 'technical collaboration' and 'joint ventures'. These two mechanisms were typical of Japanese overseas investments whose fields of operation were rather of labour-intensive and technology biased investment. Most joint ventures and technical collaborations have so far been carried out in labour-intensive industries. The average size of the investment was of small scale. This pattern is in sharp contrast to similar ventures by other industrialised western countries. Some of the developing countries which are India's competitors in the Japanese market, have 'harmonized' with Japan's policies so that it can be possible for those countries to move in the areas where Japan reaches the re-import stage. Indian policies, on the other hand, were not harmonious with the Japanese policies and as a consequence no substitution of the Indian industry in place of the Japanese industry has taken place. It can be concluded that more foreign investmet and technology tranfer should have been invited from Japan for accelerating India's light industrial exports to Japan. Such investment from Japan would benefit India by the increased availability of investible resources, import substitution and export promotion via production activities and availability of new technology. It also provides several advantages such as buy-back arrangements which are extremely useful in accelerating the growth of the Indian industry for export to Japan.

REFERENCES

1. V.R. Panchamukhi, *Trade Polices of India* (New Delhi: Concept Publishing Co., 1978), pp. 17-19.

2. Among the institutional setting, the following factors are included: the product-heterogeneity, quality and brand problems, parallel black markets; and distortions and inflows of foreign aid and capital. See, *ibid.*, pp. 18-19.

3. V.R. Panchamukhi attempted to evaluate India's trade policies measures in the quantitative analysis. For the price-based policies like tariffs, export taxes and subsidies for enhancing production for trade, the magnitude and the effect of the policies is measured in terms of price-distortions, making use of the approaches such as the effective rate of protection which takes account of the implicit tariff rate both for inputs and output of a production activity and the domestic resources cost per unit of net foreign exchange earned or saved. The non-price-based policies such as incentives implicit in taxes, subsidies and industrial licensing are for enhancing domestic production in general while exchange control, import quotas and import licensing are for enhancing production for trade. Taking an example of import licensing, Panchamukhi examines the nature of the end-use structure of imports. The premium rates on import licenses are assumed to play a role of proxy for price effect of the apparently non-price-based policy. He concludes that the primary effect of the trade policies, implicit or explicit, in general, is more or less based on the structure of domestic relative prices in relation to the international prices. The major factors identified as determinants of the trade behaviour of India are: (i) technology factor; (ii) factor proportions and factor endowments; (iii) structure of input prices and product prices; (iv) trade policies and measures impiemented by the Government. It is found that the policies and the technology factor seem to have run at cross-purposes in some cases, implying that some of the former are redundant and that among the trade policies, those directed to the domestic production are more influential on trade flow than those specifically meant for export expansion. See, *Ibid.*, pp. 63-195.

4. Planning Commission, Government of India, *Second Five Year Plan, op. cit.*, 1956, p. 99.

5. Planning Commission, Government of India, *Third Five Year Plan, op. cit.*, 1961, p. 137.

6. The explicit aims of the devaluation in 1966 was "to bring domestic prices in line with external prices to restore and enhance the competitive power of exports", as well as "to provide a solution to the country's trade and payment problem." See for example, Planning Commission, Government of India, *Fourth Five Year Plan, op. cit.*, p. 96. The more crucial objective for the devaluation may have been the latter,

if the trend in the mid-1960s was taken into consideration. Despite larger utilisation of foreign aid, there was frequent recourse to borrowing from the IMF. The temporary suspension of foreign aid in 1965 put further pressure on the already strained foreign exchange position. In the same year, it happened that larger imports of foodstuffs were required. Moreover, since the devaluation was set out along with the policy package to counterveil the effect of devaluation on exports, the "net" devaluation was much smaller than the "gross" devaluation. In case of traditional exports, export duties were levied and there was negligible 'net' devaluation. On the other hand, the devaluation was neutralised largely on the non-traditional exports where the export subsidies were removed. J. Bhagwati and T.N. Srinivasan attempted to estimate the 'net' effect of devaluation of major export commodities. See for details, J. Bhagwati and T.N. Srinivasan, *Foreign Trade Regimes and Economic Development—India, op. cit.*, pp. 83-97.

7. Although, along with devaluation in 1956, the trade liberalisation measures were announced, the controls were still imposed on imports in the following years. Also, the export incentives which were eliminated at the time of devaluation, such as the budgetary tax credits and the import entitlement schemes, were revived in the later years in different forms, embodying, in practice, many of the features of the schemes prior to devaluation. See for details of the export incentives after devaluation, *ibid.*, pp. 99-110.

8. Ministry of Commerce, Government of India, *Annual Report 1972, op. cit.*, p. 105.

9. J.W. Mellos and U. Lele, "The Interaction of Growth, Strategy, Agriculture and Foreign Trade—The Case of India", in G.S. Tolley and P.A. Zadrozny, eds., *Trade, Agriculture and Development* (Cambridge: Ballinger, 1975), p. 108. The analysis by R. Bharadwaj confirms a rise in the capital intensity of exports vis-a-vis imports in 1958-59 compared to that in 1953-54. See R. Bharadwaj, *Structural Basis of India's Foreign Trade* (University Bombay Series in Monetary and International Economics No. 6) (Bombay: University of Bombay, 1962), pp. 43-57.

10. In this study, the measures which are more general in their purposes and bear indirectly on export profitability are not dealt with, because they are too far in field from the purpose of the study. Such measures including industrial licensing, foreign collaborations and other industrial policies meant for increasing production in general. The measures discussed here are only those which have been taken with a distinct purpose to promote exports.

11. D. Nayyar, *India's Exports and Export Policies in the 1960s, op. cit.*, pp. 222.

12. Figures in the following are quoted from Lok Sabha Secretariat, "Fourteenth Report of the Fifth Lok Sabha's Estimate Committee", *Ministry of Foreign Trade Export Promotion Measures* (New Delhi, 1972), pp. 227-33 and 359-60.

13. M. Wolf, *India's Exports* (World Bank: Washington D.C., 1982), p. 100.

14. For the purpose and the objectives of the import entitlement scheme, see for example, Ministry of Commerce, Government of India, *Report 1964-65* (New Delhi: 1965) pp. 14-16.

15. Lok Sabha Secretariat, *Fourteenth Report of the Fifth Lok Sabha Estimate Committee, op. cit.*, 1972, p. 356.

16. For an extensive discussion of export credit, see, S.K. Verghese, *India's Foreign Trade* (New Delhi : Allied Publishers, 1964), pp. 119-92; National Council of Applied Economic Research, *Export Strategy for India* New Delhi, 1969), pp. 52-65.

17. For details of the scheme and its operation regarding the cotton textile industry, see, J. Bhagwati and P. Desai, *India-Planning for Industrialisation, op. cit.*, pp. 417-22.

18. *Ibid.*, p. 419. The effective subsidy was relatively low for the coarse and the medium varieties of cloth and tended to be high for the fine and the superfine varieties. Within the same category the subsidy increased according to the degree of processing. For example, bleached cloth was given higher subsidy than grey.

19. D. Nayyar, *India's Exports and Export Policies in the 1960s, op. cit.*, pp. 75 and 76.

20. Lok Sabha Secretariat, *Fourteenth Report of the Fifth Lok Sabha's Estimates Committee, op. cit*, pp. 35-46.

21. M. Wolf, *India's Exports op. cit.*, p. 86.

22. *Ibid.*, pp. 84-85.

23. *Ibid.*, p. 88.

24. *Ibid.*, pp. 94-99.

25. K.D. Shah, "Cotton Textile Industry", in Hindustan Chamber of Commerce, (ed.), *Proceedings of the Seminar of Export Promotion* (Madras, 1968), pp. 146-49.

26, Dearness allowance in the cotton textile industry was determined according to the cost of living index in the previous month. The cost of the finished product changed by about 2 per cent to 2.5 per cent every year only as a result of changes in dearness allowance. See *Ibid.*, p. 147.

27. D. Nayyar, *India's Exports and Export Policies in the 1960s, op. cit.*, pp. 201 and 202.

28. R.H. Patil, "Exports of Engineering Goods—Problems and Prospects", *Reserve Bank of India Bulletin* (Bombay), Vol. 24, No. 10, October 1970, pp. 1715 and 1716.

29. *Ibid.*, pp. 1715 and 1716.

30. *Ibid.*, pp. 1715 and 1716.

31. M. Wolf, *India's Exports, op. cit.*, p. 88.

32. Reserve Bank of India, *Report on Currency and Finance 1966-67* (Bombay, 1967), p. 159.

33. Ministry of Commerce, Government of India, *Import Trade Control Policy 1968-69*, Vol. I (New Delhi, 1969), pp. 7 and 158.

34. Engineering Export Promotion Council, "Engineering Goods", in Hindustan Chamber of Commerce (ed.), *Proceedings of a Seminar on Export Promotion*, *op. cit.*, pp. 157-59.

35. Assistance was given to the key industries by the Government either explicitly or implicitly. Therefore, it is not easy to apprehend all the measures given to the industries as assistance and also to measure the extent of the benefits which the industries derived from them. However, it is worth noting the statement made by S. Okita, who took an active part in the economic decision-making of the Japanese Government, that such assistance ranged from tax concessions to underwriting their dividends obligations. See, S. Okita, *A Collection of Essays* (Japan Economic Research Paper No. 28), (Tokyo: Japan Economic Research Centre, 1975), p. 29.

36. L.B. Krause and S. Sekiguchi list up the policies which had a direct impact on Japan's foreign trade. The list of the trade policies given as below excludes that had indirect effects on trade such as policies on foreign investment and other economic and commercial policies in general which affect trade in a less conspicuous way:

(1) Formation of the Japan Export Bank, 1951, to extend long-term loans for exports (Recognised in 1951 as the Japan Export and Import Bank); (2) Formation of the Japan External Trade Organisation (JETRO) 1951, to disseminate marketing information for Japanese exporters; (3) Revision of tariff schedules, 1951; (4) Formation of the 'Link Trade System', 1952, whereby import licences were allocated based on exports performance; (5) 'Preferential Finance for the Period Proceeding Exportation', 1953 (upto 1971), to facilitate exports by easing financial terms during the production process; (6) 'Tax Credit for Export Income' 1953 (upto 1964), for exporters and export sales; (7) 'Extra Depreciation Allowance for Fixed Assets of Overseas Branches', 1953 (upto 1958), as tax concession for foreign sales facilities; (8) Establishment of the Export Conference, 1954 (upto 1969), to publish export targets; (9) Revision of the 'Law of Tariff Rates and Custom Duty', 1954, in preparation for joining GATT, to shift to ad valorem tariffs system and reduce tariff rates; (10) Formation of Japan Association for Plant Exportation, 1955, to promote exports of machinery and plants; (11) Japan started voluntary restraints on exports of cotton textiles to the U.S.A., 1957; (12) 'Extra Tax Credit for Exports', 1957 (upto 1961), an extension of item (6); (13) 'The Credit for Technology Exportation', 1959 (revised between 1964 and 1969); (14) 'Fundamental Policy to Liberalize Foreign Trade and Exchanges', 1960, to liberalise 257 four-digit BTN items in imports; (15) The Export-Import Bank to extend finance for deferred payments on softer terms, 1961; (16) The Bank of Japan to reduce the rediscount rate of export bills, 1961; (17) The reporting system of quota restrictions on imports to be switched into negative list of items from a positive list, 1962; (18) The ordinance by Ministry of International Trade and Industry (MITI), 1964, to permit firms to import technology without

approval of the Ministry; (19) Declaration of Article 11 Status, 1963, Articles 8 Status, 1964, to end direct tax credits on exports and foreign exchange budget allocation, which was partially replaced by 'Special Depreciation Allowance for Export Companies', 1964 (upto 1972); (20) 'Extra Depreciation Allowance for Exporting Companies', 1964 (upto 1972); (21) 'Special Reserve for Exploitation of Foreign Markets', 1964, (renewed in 1969); (22) 'Special Treatment of Export Promotion Expenses', 1964, to give foreign buyers tax deduction; (23) 'Special Extra Depreciation for the Exporting Countries Authorised by the Minister of MITI', 1964 (upto 1969), giving tax credits to 'export-contributing' companies; (24) Imports of completed cars liberalised, 1965; (25) JETRO began to finance for imports from developing countries, 1966; (26) Imports of technology with or without foreign management liberalised, 1968; (27) Japan began to limit exports of steel to the U.S.A., 1969; (28) Export target by the Export Conference discontinued, 1969; (29) Preferential rate of rediscount for export bills, extra depreciation allowance (items 19, 20 and 23) discontinued, 1969. Also import deposit required for import licences stopped discriminating against consumer goods and fixed to 1 per cent, which ceased to operate in next year; (30) 'Eight Items of Urgent Policy Measures to Avoid Yen Revaluation adopted, 1971, which included reduction of tariff and non-tariff barriers; (31) 'General Scheme of Preferential (GSP) Tariffs' implemented, 1971; (32) 'Accelerated Depreciation for the Companies in the Industries Related to GSP to Adjust', 1971, to permit accelerated depreciation for companies competing with developing countries; (33) Japan agreed to restrain textile export except cotton to the U.S.A., 1971; (34) Reduction of import quota restraints for 60 items completed, 1971; (35) 'International Economic Counter measures as Emergency Programme', 1972, including promotion of orderly exports and promotion of imports through enlarged quotas; (36) Creation of the Orderly Marketing Maintenance Committee in MITI, 1972. Voluntary Export Control was imposed on twenty groups of products, which was rescinded in the next year. See, L.B. Krause and S. Sekiguchi, "Japan and the World Economy", in H. Patrick and H. Rosovsky, ed., *Asia's New Gaint* (Washington D.C. : The Bookings Institution, 1940), pp. 451-58.

37. The control of foreign investment was laid down in 1950 through the law concerning foreign investment, in which foreign investment was allowed only when it helped to achieve the self-sufficiency of the Japanese economy. Foreign firms were permitted at most only 49 per cent ownership of Japanese enterprises. Over time a series of major five round of liberalisation was initiated, and by 1973 foreigners could obtain 100 per cent ownership except certain industries.

38. For example, according to his estimation, from raw cotton to clothing, the effective rate of tarifi increased rapidly, and more rapidly than the nominal rate as undergoing higher processing stages. The effective rate against the nominal rate of tariff on raw cotton, cotton yarn

cotton textiles and cotton clothing in 1967 before Kennedy Round Reductions were; none; 9.9 per cent against 5.0 per cent; 36.2 per cent against 16.0 per cent; and 48.8 per cent against 27.8 per cent, respectively. A similar trend could be found with respect to many other items. The effective rate against the nominal rate of tariff on iron ore and scrap, pig iron, steel ingot and rolled steel in the same year were: none; 24.4 per cent against 10.0 per cent; 47.0 per cent against 12.5 per cent; and 35.1 cent against 15.1 per cent, respectively. See *ibid.*, pp. 427-28.

39. K. Ohkawa and H. Rosovsky, *Japanese Economic Growth Trend and Acceleration in the Twentieth Century* (Los Angeles: Oxford University Press, 1973) pp. 93-94.

40. M. Peck and S. Tamura, "Technology" H. Patrick and H. Rosovsky, eds., *Asia's New Gaint, op. cit.*, pp. 530-32.

41. OECD, *OECD Economic Survey—Japan* (Paris: OECD, 1968), p. 18.

42. Statistics Bureau, Prime Minister's Office, Japan, *Japan Statistical Yearbook 1981* (Tokyo: Prime Minister's Office, 1981), p. 310.

43. *Ibid.*, p. 310.

44. Statistical Bureau, Prime Minister's Office, Japan, *Japan Statistical Yearbook 1967 and 1977*), (Tokyo: Prime Minister's Office, 1967 and 1977), pp. 180 and 174, respectively.

45. K. Kojima, *Harmonisation of Japanese and Australian Economic Policies* (Japan Economic Research Centre Paper No. 27 (Tokyo : Japan Economic Research Centre, 1975), pp. 24-27.

46. The countries such as Austria, Bulgaria, Czechoslovakia, Denmark, EEC, Finland, Hungary, Ireland, New Zealand, Norway, Sweden, Switzerland and the U.K. implemented the G.S.P. scheme between July 1, 1971 and April 1, 1972. The scheme introduced by the U.S.S.R. came into effect in 1965.

47. The operations of the GSP scheme during the period are explained in detail, for example, United Nations Conference on Trade and Development, *Operations and Effects on the Generalised System of Preferences* (CTD/B/C5/15) (New York : United Nations, 1974), pp. 1-30.

48. UNCTAD, *Operation and Effects of GSP* (TD/B/C.5/58) (Geneva, 1976), pp. 151-53.

49. *Ibid.*, p. 184.

50. *Ibid*, p. 195.

51. UNCTAD, *Operation and Effects of GSP* [(TD/B/C/5/15) (Geneva, 1973), pp. 155-85.

52. Japan Tariff Association, *Customs Tariff Schedule of Japan* (Tokyo : Japan Tariff Association, 1976), pp. 342 and 397.

53. UNCTAD, *Operation and Effects of GSP* (TD/B/C.5/15), *op. cit.*, pp. 155-85.

54. BTN code no. 55.09, that is, woven cotton fabrics other than Gauze (55.07) and terry towelling (55.08). Cotton fabrics other than 55.09 were also subject to the ceiling along with all the items under BTN chapter 55 except 55.09 and 55.05-2(2) (cotton yarn other than threads not

for retail sale). The same study estimated that against the annualised ceiling for 1971 for BTN chapter 55 excluding 55.09 and 55.05-2(2) at US $ 38 thousand, imports from all beneficiaries in excess of annualised ceiling was to be US $ 118 thousand, in which South Korea among other suppliers was to be subject first to the maximum country limitation of US $ 9 thousand out of the total exports of US $ 24 thousand.

55. UNCTAD, *Operation and Effects of GSP* (TD/B/C.5/58), *op. cit.*, p. 151.

56. United Nations, *Commodity Trade Statistics* (New York : United Nations, 1968 and 1971), p. 3569 and p. 2843, respectively.

57. United Nations. *Commodity Statistics* (New York : United Nations, 1968 and 1971), p. 3471 and p. 2845, respectively.

58. V.R. Panchamukhi, *Trade Policies of India*, *op. cit.*, p. 214.

59. S. Sekiguchi, *Japan's Direct Foreign Investment* (Montelair-Allanheld, Osmun and Co., 1979), pp. 70-74.

60. C.H. Lee, "United States and Japanese Direct Investment in Korea : A Comparative Study", *Hitotsubashi Journal of Economics* (Tokyo), pp. 26-41.

61. Details of legislation regarding direct foreign investment of South Korea are from L. Westphal, Y. Rhee and G. Pursell, "Korean Industrial Competence—Where It Came From" (World Bank Staff Working Paper No. 469) (Washington D.C. : World Bank, 1981), pp. 11-13.

6

EPILOGUE: TRADE GROWTH AND MANUFACTURED EXPORTS TO JAPAN AFTER 1973

THE first oil crisis in 1973 has quickened the process of the structural change in the Japanese economy, which was already under way. Japan's self-sufficiency ratio in crude oil has already been at less than one per cent. The resource endowment position has made Japan to import fuels to the extent of over 20 per cent of its total imports.

The rise in oil prices in 1973 reflected in the cost of Japan's domestic industries and caused the high rate of inflation in Japan among OECD countries. The annual percentage change in wholesale prices averaged at 3.2 per cent between 1965 and 1972 and increased up to 31.3 per cent in 1974.[1] Due to the rising costs and the world-wide depression, GNP registered a negative increase over the previous year in 1973.

The state of the Japanese economy led to the drastic implementation of development of alternative energy, resources and energy saving techniques as well as relocation of the energy-using industries such as iron and steel abroad, in order to reduce the import requirement of fuels, particularly crude oil, of the economy.

The 1973-74 Economic Survey of Japan pointed out that while other industrialised nations already worked out the pattern of international division of labour and diversified the trade structure, Japan was still engaged in 'vertical specialisation' in the trade with a high content of industrial products in exports and of raw materials in imports. In 1973, the degree of division of labour in crude steel for Japan was 2.0 per cent, much lower than that in France, Federal Republic of Germany and the U.K., which was 80.1 per cent, 67.0 per cent and 47.4 per cent, respectively.[2]

The Survey therefore advocated for increasing imports of products of the 'resource-processing' sectors in the heavy industry, including petro-chemicals, ferrous and non-ferrous metals and giving more thrust of industrial growth in the assembling industries.

The strategy to intensify division of labour induced imports of products of the resource-processing industries. The imports of ferrous and non-ferrous metals increased from US $ 4.3 billion in 1976 to US $ 10.1 billion in 1983, rising at a faster pace than the total imports. At the same time, foreign investment in these areas became prominent. In 1984, 21.8 per cent out of the total foreign investment outstanding amounting to US $ 688 billion was invested in the ferrous and non-ferrous industries, which had increased by 15.3 per cent from 1974. On the other hand, though in 1974, 43.4 per cent of the outstanding investment was invested in the mining industries, the share had gone down to 23.8 per cent by 1984.

In turn, the structural change in the Japanese economy after the oil crisis in 1973 opened up opportunities for its trade partners to expand exports in more sectors. This chapter examines the trend in India's exports of manufactures to Japan in the setting of the economic development and trade structure that emerged after 1973. The examination focuses on the degree of India's achievement in export diversification with respect to the opportunities in the Japanese market available for them.

Post-Oil Crisis and India's Comparative Advantage

Japan's import liberalisation measures which were initiated in the early 1960s stimulated many developing countries to expand and diversify exports to Japan. The economies which were producing and exporting non-manufactures switched over to exports of manufactures to a larger extent. Manufactured imports from developing countries increased from US $ 2561 million in 1975, to US $ 8667 million in 1982, to comprise 12.3 per cent of Japan's total imports from them.[3]

Japan's trade with newly industrialised countries (NICs) in Asia including South Korea and Taiwan made a steady expansion. Japan's exports to South Korea increased from US $ 2248 million to US $ 7227 million between 1974 and 1984, while Japan's imports from South Korea rose from US $ 1308 million to US $ 4213 million in the same period. As a result, the share of South Korea in Japan's total exports and imports increased from 4.0 per cent and 2.3 per cent to 4.2 per cent and 3.1 per cent, respectively.[4] Japan's exports to Taiwan expanded from US $ 1822 million to US $ 5986 million, whereas its imports from the country went up to US $ 3204 million from US $ 8120 million during the period. Consequently, the share of Taiwan in Japan's total exports and imports increased from 3.3 per cent and 1.4 per cent to 4.2 per cent and 2.3 per cent respectively.[5]

Accompanied by the increase in value of trade with Japan, these countries worked out a change in the pattern of trade with Japan, especially in their exports to Japan. Japan's imports of manufactures from South Korea comprised 63.1 per cent in 1984, over 60.4 per cent in 1974, while the share of manufactures in its imports from Taiwan increased from 43.4 per cent in 1974 to 55.2 per cent in 1984.[6]

The trend in India's trade with Japan after 1973 can be reviewed in comparison with Japan's trade with NICs. During 1974 and 1980, Japan's exports to India increased from US $ 417 million to US $ 1163 million while its imports from India increased from US $ 658 million to US $ 1132 million. However, the increase in the trade value between India and Japan failed to keep up the pace in increase of Japan's trade with the world. As a result, India's share in Japan's total exports stagnated at 0.7 per cent and in Japan's total imports fell from 1.1 per cent to 0.8 per cent over the period. It is also true that Japan's exports grew more rapidly than its imports with respect to India, which has turned India's balance of trade from a net surplus to a net deficit position since 1981 (see Table 6.1).

India achieved a very limited change in the pattern of its trade with Japan compared to NICs during the period. The manufactured exports from India to Japan fluctuated between 16 per cent and 24 per cent, without any secular trend. Textile products, which comprise a significant share in India's manufactured exports to Japan also marked fluctuations in its share in Japan's total imports between 2 per cent and 7 per cent. On the other hand, foodstuffs and raw materials continued to comprise over 70 per cent of Japan's imports from India, with iron ore and shrimps alone exceeding more than 50 per cent in their share throughout the period (see Table 6.2). Thus, there was no definite indication of diversification with respect to India's exports to Japan in the post-oil crisis period.

EXPORT TREND OF NON-MANUFACTURES

Iron ore, shrimps and raw cotton continued to feature the pattern of India's exports to Japan after 1973. In terms of value, these three non-manufactures comprised over 62 per cent during 1973-85. This indicates a very high concentration of non-manufactures in India's export structure. Among these three items, raw cotton exports from India to Japan showed a consistent decline over the period. Shrimps in a frozen or chilled form increased over years in the order of over 20 per cent of India's total exports to Japan, though a slight decline continued after 1980. As far as iron-ore exports from India to Japan is concerned, which is the largest single commodity in India's exports to Japan in terms of value, there were two cycles with peaks in 1975 and 1980, though the amplitude decreased. Despite the flactuations, iron ore is a commodity which singly comprised more than one third of the total value of India's exports to Japan throughout the period. Below we will analyse the development in India's iron ore and shrimps industries and examine the trend in their exports to Japan.

TABLE 6.1
Japan's Trade with India*
(million US $)

	Imports Value	%	Exports Value	%	Trade Balance Value
1974	658.2	1.1	594.7	1.1	—63.5
1975	657.9	1.1	471.4	0.8	−186.5
1976	801.1	1.2	375.0	0.6	—424.1
1977	800.0	1.1	503,7	0.6	—296.3
1978	793.1	1.0	730.7	0.7	—62.8
1979	1053.0	1.0	779.5	0.8	—273.5
1980	1014.3	0.7	914.8	0.7	—99.5
1981	1056.7	0.7	1197.2	0.8	140.5
1982	1122.1	0.9	1408.3	1.0	286.2
1983	1130.8	0.9	1430.7	1.0	299.9
1984	1132.4	0.8	1167.8	0.7	35.4

* Indicate India's share in Japan's trade with the world.

Source: Ministry of International Trade and Industry, Japan, *White Paper on International Trade* (Tokyo), from various issues of 1975 to 1985.

Developments in Iron Ore Industry and Export Trends

The oil crisis in 1973 made the Japanese economy reconsider its industrial structure which was highly dependent on oil imports. The policy-makers came up with the idea to shift the weightage in the industrial sector from the resource-processing type in the heavy industrial sector to more of the assembling activities, so that the domestic consumption of petroleum would be curtailed. It was suggested, that, to meet the domestic requirement of iron and steel beyond the level of the domestic production which would be bound to fall due to the shift, increase in imports with and without being associated with foreign direct investment be made necessary.[7]

Besides, there was a declining trend in the apparent consumption of steel in Japan. The apparent consumption of steel, in terms of ingot equivalent, rose from 7 million tons in 1955 to 92 million tons in 1973, which fell subsequently to 86 million tons and 79 million tons in 1980 and 1981.[8] One of the reasons for the fall in the apparent consumption of steel could be the decline in the steel intensity per unit of the national product. Japan's crude steel consumption per million US dollars of GNP at 1975 prices peaked in 1969 at about 190 tons, which fell around to 125 tons by 1979.[9]

These factors have contributed to a fall in production of crude steel from 119 million tons in 1973 to 111 million tons in 1980 and 102 million tons in 1981. Correspondingly, the imports of iron ore, which met more than 99 per cent of the domestic consumption, registered a decline towards the early 1980s.[10] Japan's imports of iron ore which peaked in 1974 at 142 million metric tons, reduced to 123 million metric tons in 1981 and 109 million metric tons in 1983.[11]

In addition, India's share in Japan's imports of iron ore stagnated over the period, which was at 12.8 per cent and 13.9 per cent in 1975 and 1983, respectively, out of the total imports amounting to 132 million metric tons and 109 metric tons in respective years. On the other hand, Australia, the largest supplier of iron ore to Japan continued to comprise a dominant share, 48.0 per cent and 45.6 per cent in the respective years. Brazil, the second largest supplier, managed to increase the share from 17.8 per cent to 21.5 per cent between the two years.[12]

The decline in imports on real terms with the share remaining at the same level reflects the absolute reduction in the quantity of iron ore exports from India to Japan. India's exports of iron ore to Japan which was at 16812 metric tons, reduced to 14653 metric tons between 1975 and 1983.[13] Thus India had to diversify the direction of iron ore exports that has heavily concentrated to Japan. When there was a fall in Japan's share in India's exports of iron ore from 72.3 per cent in 1974-75 to 63.1 per cent in 1981-82,[14] India increased exports to East European countries like Rumania and Yugoslavia, of which shares in 1974-75 were almost negligible. The directional diversification of India's exports of iron ore sustained a marginal increase of its total exports of the commodity from 22.3 million tonne to 23.7 million tonne between 1974-75 and 1981-82.[15]

There were some specific domestic constraints in India's infrastructure that stood in the way of Japan's iron ore imports from India after 1973. India's iron ore export strategy did not take into account the declining magnitude of Japanese import requirements. In addition India was not able to rationalise the cost of production nor stabilise cost of inland transport or shipping costs. It was also unable to develop port facilities with the required speed to enable buyers to employ large sized ships so that costs could be lowered with respect to ocean freight. For improving facilities construction at various ports began in 1970s almost took about ten years to make it operational. By then these were, not only smaller but became less competitive compared with international standards. For instance, the loading charge at Vizag port is currently around Rs. 26 per tonne and at Mormugoa port Rs. 26, plus a surcharge of Rs. 8 per tonne. For the same loading in other parts of the world, it is Rs. 6 to Rs. 8 per tonne.[16] Higher handling costs of iron ore at the Indian ports reflects the financial situation of port trust authorities. For example to the Vizag port, the Minerals and Metals Trading Corporation of India (MMTC) owed arrears in payment of various dues over five years. To recover the arrears besides securing 12 per cent of the investment returns, the rates for iron-ore handling was initially estimated to be Rs. 9 per tonne against the actual cost of 42 paise.[17]

Another factor that is causing the higher costs in handling at ports is due to the limitations in draft and berth facilities at the handling ports. The normal size of vessels loaded fully alongside berth No. 9 at Mormugao, is 60 thousand tonnes, against that in Australia and Brazil which can accept tonners ranging from 100 thousand to 250 thousand and 150 thousand to 270 thousand, respectively. This necessitates the additional procedure in loading at Indian ports, namely, transhipment, which costs about US $ 17 per tonne.[18]

A slack in demand for iron ore by Japanese steel mills and higher handling and transportation costs from Indian ports has made India to negotiate with the Japanese importers under keen competition and to change the strategy. The insistence on the increase in unit export price in its earlier negotiations with Japan receded to securing the reasonable export quota for negotiation for contracts for 1985-86, observing the situation in the Japanese import market of iron ore where the import price declined by

20 per cent between 1983 and 1985 due to the slack in demand.[19]

The strategy was proved to be successful by the MMTC securing the quota for 1985-86 at 10 million tons with 2 million tons added as premium for the early conclusion of the contract at the price contract a year before among major supplying countries of iron ore on the top of 8 million tons secured in the previous year.

Since 1985-86 supply of iron ore from India has been enlarged by commencement of shipment from Kudremukh. The Kudremukh project was initially designed to meet the demand of the Iranian steel industry equipped with the latest iron-ore processing facilities including the pelletisation plant, with the assistance from Iran amounting to US $ 630 million. After the interruption in the assistance owing to the Iran-Iraq War, the project was completed with imports of pelletisation equipment from Rumania under an agreement that India would pay for it in iron ore processed in the project.[20]

In the process of diversifying the market besides Rumania,[21] Japan was identified as a promising market. After a trial order of supply amounting to 1.5 million tons, it was revealed that the Japanese steel mills could save 2000 Yen per ton of pig iron by using Kudremukh ore concentrate, which has an iron content as high as 68 per cent.[22] This led to the conclusion of a long-term contract of ten years for a minimum off-take of 2.5 million tons per year. It is expected to open up possibility for India to secure a share of 20 to 23 per cent in Japan's imports of iron ore, which would amount to 27 million tonnes of exports from India in 1986-87.

Developments in Frozen Shrimp Industry and Export Trends

The Japanese import market of shrimps since the early 1970s has been characterised with steady increase in demand in the long-term which was limited by price factors in the short run due to keen competition among major supplying countries. The apparent consumption of shrimps rose from 178 thousand tons in 1977 to 217 thousand tons in 1981, while the domestic catches increased marginally from 54 thousand tons to 55 thousand tons over the same period. The excess demand over supply conditions led to an increase in imports from 127 thousand tons to 165 thousand tons between 1977 and 1981, which constituted the largest markets of shrimp imports in the world.[23]

Among the import items of shrimps by Japan, frozen shrimps account for the bulk of 97.78 per cent, amounting to 269.2 million Yen in 1981. India continued to be the largest exporter of shrimps since the early 1970s and the share expanded steadily from 20.7 per cent to 24.8 per cent in quantity terms over the period between 1977 and 1987. However, the competition with other suppliers of the commodity to Japan became very keen. Except Indonesia, other major exporters such as China, Australia, Thailand and Taiwan, which altogether comprised over 25 per cent of Japan's import market of frozen shrimps in 1981, increased their shares between 1977 and 1981.[24]

Keen competition among suppliers in the Japanese market lead to fluctuation of prices. For example, in January-July period in 1983, it was observed that some suppliers were selling, even below cost price, in order to stimulate demand under substantial inventories and liquidity problems.[25]

To increase India's exports of frozen shrimps to Japan, supply factor became the key issue particularly after 1980's. Between 1974-75 and 1981-82 India's exports of frozen shrimp increased from 35.1 thousand metric tonnes to 49.1 thousand metric tonnes. In quantity terms, Japan's share in India's exports of the commodity rather declined from 68.6 per cent to 63.2 per cent. On the other hand, its exports to the U.S.A. increased in share considerably from 17.7 per cent to 30.5 per cent over the same period.[26]

The increase in availability for exports of frozen shrimps was enabled by improvement of processing and packaging facilities for exports. The overall supply situation of shrimps had rather deteriorated. The nominal catches of shrimps by India increased from 160 thousand tons to 176 thousand tons between 1972 and 1981, a slower increase than that in the world as a whole, which led to a decline in its share in the world catches from 13.1 per cent to 10.4 per cent.[27]

The policies directed for shrimp exports have paid rich dividends between 1974 and 1985. Some of the important measures that were undertaken were the establishment of the Marine Export Promotion Development Authority (MEPDA) in 1973 and encouragement of acqua-culture against expected fall of natural production of shrimps. Other measures taken included the promotion of charters/joint ventures for development of sea-fishing. MEPDA undertook a project for extending technical assistance to farmers for commercial-scale shrimp farming. Some farmers were also encouraged in the maritime states to take up commercial scale brackish water shrimp farming. MEPDA has also set up several programmes such as Prawn Farming Training Complex in Cochin which was intended mainly for imparting training to State Government fishery officials who in turn were expected to develop the programmes in their respective states.[23]

The Indian Government also has provided cash assistance and import replenishment licences as incentives to the fishery exports. In 1979-80, for instance, cash assistance amounting to US $ 1.5 million and import replenishment licences worth US $ 32.4 million were made available to exports of fish and fish preparations out of which shrimps consisted of 46.8 per cent.[29] The cash assistance rate, that is, value of exports against cash assistance disbursed on behalf of the fishing exports worked out is found to be very significant. In 1975-76 and 1976-78, the rate was 6.1 per cent and 4.9 per cent, respectively.[30]

In addition, a new scheme for promoting export-oriented units to boost the marine exports was cleared in 1984. Under the scheme, MEPDA will participate in the equity capital of such ventures upto 26 per cent in case of indigenous enterprises and upto 11 per cent in case of foreign collaboration. The ventures which would be provided for the assistance from MEPDA through equity participation are diversification of seafood exports and promotion of exports in value-added forms.[31]

In the meantime, there were efforts to develop alternative sources for exports of marine products from India. Japan's marine products manufacturers association sent missions in the last few years to explore the possibility of exports of various fishery items from India, which was assisted by Japan External

Trade Organization (JETRO). MEPDA, as a response to their inquiry, started the investigation on the underwater resources which would be of any commercial value to the Japanese market.[32]

Besides the deposits of resources that ensures the long-run stable supply and the level of technology to undertake the primary processing according to Japanese specifications in India, the Japanese are very much concerned with the hygienity maintained in packing of the products exported. There was an instance of frozen shrimps exported by India to Japan that were found to be contaminated by cholera germs by a port quarantine authority in Japan in 1985.[33] Since the degree of hygienity of marine products affect considcrably their commercial value, the system for pre-shipment inspection of these products should be improved as one of the export promotion measures.

The above analysis reveals that there was opportunity for expanding exports of non-manufactures to Japan during the period though the long-term prospects were not appearing to be very promising. First, as in the case of iron ore, non-manufactured exports in general tend to face demand constraints in the long run. Second, in the short run, they are likely to be subject to price fluctuations as in the case of shrimps.

EXPORT TREND OF MANUFACTURES

The post-oil crisis period saw enlarged scope for developing countries to expand exports of manufactures to Japan. Diversification of the export structure by developing countries implies the industrialisation process attained in the economy. Let us examine the extent of manufactured export penetration by India in the Japanese market after 1973. We shall take the same manufactured exports studied in the previous chapter viz. cotton textiles and handtools.

Growth of Cotton Textile Industry and Export Opportunities

The performance of the organised sector of India's cotton fabrics industry was far from satisfactory. Due to the huge loss in mandays by the prolonged strikes in Bombay, production equivalent to 1427 million metres of cloth did not materialise between January 1982 and November 1983.[34] The number of sick units in the textile industry increased from 73 in 1977 to 119 in 1983.[35] The losses incurred by the National Textile Corporation alone have amounted to about Rs. 6.5 billion.[36]

The production of cotton cloth, including blended and mixed one by the mill sector declined from 4440 million metres in 1974 to 3027 million metres in 1982, and recovered to 3358 million metres in 1984 following the end of the strike in Bombay mills.[37] The peformance of the organised cotton fabrics production strikes a contrast with the decentralised sector, of which production of cotton cloth increased from 4055 million metres in 1974 to 6917 million metres in 1984.[38] The decentralised sector operated by powerlooms in particular had a remarkable growth registering an increase in production from 2000 million metres to 3470 million metres between 1979-1980 and 1984-85.[39]

Rapid growth in the powerloom sector were noted particularly since the late 1970s when the authorised powerlooms increased in number from 348 thousand to 603 thousand excluding an estimated 140 thousand illegal looms.[40] The growth in the powerloom sector is attributed to several factors. First, the powerloom sector enjoys an absolute cost advantage of about 17 per cent over the mill sector due to lower wages paid to the ununionised workers, which are said to be 50 per cent of the wages of mill operatives. Moreover, the powerloom sector, though employs similar technology as in the mill sector, remains in the small-scale sector, sometimes by means of dividing the establishment into several parts, in order to get fiscal concessions on inputs and enter the production reserves for the handloom sector.[41]

The effect of fiscal concessions on inputs that has been made use of by the powerloom sector has been most pronounced in case of synthetic fibres. For example, in the Textile Policy 1985, excise duty was imposed of Rs. 25 per kg. for polyester staple fibres and Rs. 84.5 per kg. for polyester filament yarns.[42] The powerloom sector in the small-scale industry was assigned a role to promote decentralisation of economic activities and rural employment.[43] As a means of protection, initially and use of viscose filament yarns was restricted to the decentralised sector, which was later interpreted to extend it further to the restricted use of polyester and polyamide filament by the sector.[44] As a result, the production of 100 per cent non-cotton cloth by the decentralised sector increased from 932 million metres in 1970 to 1943 million metres in 1984, comprising 99.6 per cent of the total domestic production, whereas the mill sector increased the production of cloth of the variety from 1 million metres to 7 million metres during the same period.[45]

The surge in production in the powerloom sector has been supported by the strong demand for blended cotton mixed and non-textiles which is projected to increase by 14.4 per cent and 9.3 per cent per annum by 1990, against the demand for cotton cloth which is to decline by 3.5 per cent per annum.[46] The product mix in the mill sector in which 76.5 per cent of its cloth production was cotton in 1984,[47] did not match the market structure for cloth, resulting in the loss of markets for it.

TABLE 6.3

Direction of India's Exports of Mill-made Cotton Piecegoods

(% of total)

	Japan	*U.K.*	*U.S.S.R.*	*U.S.A.*	*Asia and Africa*	*Total (million sq. metres)*
1975	0.1	18.0	17.9	9.9	32.3	332.4
1976	0.1	27.1	11.8	17.1	26.4	581.1
1977	0.9	24.5	12.4	11.4	24.7	356.5
1978	0.3	32.9	14.2	9.2	13.8	272.0
1979	0.2	32.5	15.0	6.9	8.8	384.0
1980	0.1	15.4	27.8	8.8	8.4	349.5
1981	0.1	12.3	45.2	7.3	10.4	271.7
1982	0.1	7.6	66.8	2.0	6.9	199.1
1983	0.9	16.0	55.8	1.9	3.2	272.8
1984	0.1	17.5	45.3	6.6	2.2	420.2

Source: The Cotton Textiles Export Promotion Council, *India's Exports of Cotton Textiles* (Bombay), from various issues between 1976 and 1986.

Among the markets for India's exports of cotton fabrics, the USSR has provided an increasingly large market to India. In case of mill-made cotton piecegoods, the USSR comprised a bulk in India's total exports in the 1980, when India's exports to the USA and the UK declined (see Table 6.3). The decline in the share of exports to these countries in the early 1980s is due to the factors that textile imports by then has not expanded corresponding to the growth in India's exporting capacity. Imports of cotton fabrics in the world trade declined from US \$ 7082 million in 1979 to US \$ 6415 million in 1983, that is, by 10.4 per cent. In particular exports from developed market economies, including EEC, U.S.A. and Japan declined by a faster pace, from US \$ 4277 million to US \$ 3507 million over the same period, down by 22.0 per cent.[48]

The shrinking of the developed countries markets for textiles which constitutes two-thirds of the world imports explains the growing competition among exporting countries. On the other hand, India's textile industry was not fit to match the growing competition. The renovation in the industry has been much delayed and about 63 per cent of spindles and 82 per cent of looms have been in use over 15 years. The cost for modernisation of the plant and rehabilitation was assessed to be Rs. 2.5 billion a year.[49]

In addition, it has been observed that the organised mills with inefficient management have often caused increase is prices. For example, in 1984-85 due to a record production of cotton, the wholesale price of cotton declined by 22.5 per cent, whereas the price of mill-made cotton cloth increased by 5.5 per cent.[50]

Meanwhile there was a marked increase in Japan's imports of cotton fabrics after 1973. The imports increased from 181.5 million square metres to 469.2 million square metres between 1974 and 1984. An increase in imports was accompanied by a fall in production. The production which was at 2380 million metres in 1973 declined over years to 2079 million metres in 1983. In addition, the revival of export growth of cotton fabrics in the 1980s, that was resulted from a structural change of the industry towards high-quality cloth production with electronically controlled processing,[51] reduced the overall domestic availability of cotton fabrics and induced larger imports, particularly of lower-grade fabrics.

TABLE 6.4

Direction of Japan's Imports of Cotton Fabrics
(% of total)

	India	*China*	*South Korea*	*Taiwan*	*Switzer-land*	*Total (million sq. metres)*
1974	7.7	15.5	15.8	16.8	2.6	181.5
1975	0.6	51.9	10.4	23.4	2.6	158.4
1976	2.3	49.0	10.3	22.1	2.6	142.2
1977	2.3	42.9	7.1	27.8	3.6	105.7
1978	1.7	63.0	9.9	11.6	1.7	223.6
1979	2.2	66.9	9.2	6.5	1.9	274.4
1980	2.5	73.9	8.1	3.9	1.9	224.4
1981	1.6	75.1	6.3	7.5	1.4	286.5
1982	2.6	77.4	7.2	3.3	1.1	301.1
1983	2.5	78.7	6.7	2.6	0.8	292.0
1984	4.7	82.9	4.7	—	0.6	469.2

Source: Ministry of International Trade and Industry, *White Paper on International Trade* (Tokyo), from various issues between 1975 and 1985.

Table 6.4 presents the direction of Japan's imports of cotton fabrics between 1974 and 1984. It has been noted that China, which was relatively a new entrant to the Japanese import market of cotton fabrics in the early 1970s, expanded exports progressively to 83 per cent by 1984. The success achieved by China in making inroads to the Japanese market of cotton fabrics can be explained by the cost-effectiveness of its exports. Table 6.5 presents the unit value of imports of woven cotton fabrics (grey) to the major importing countries. The Table shows that China was able to reduce the price of its cotton fabrics exports in the major markets between 1979 and 1983, while the prices of exports of the product from India rather increased during the same period. Due to the cost advantage, China succeeded in increasing the exports of cotton fabrics considerably in the early 1980s despite the unfavourable world trade environment. China's exports of cotton fabrics to the group of primarily developed economies increased from US $ 461.7 million to US $ 965.6 million with an increase in share in the total imports to the group from 8.4 per cent to 16.2 per cent between 1979 and 1984, whereas India's share registered a marginal decline from 3.4 per cent to 3.2 per cent during the same period.[52]

TABLE 6.5

Woven Cotton Fabrics (Grey) Unit Value of Imports
(US million $ per metric tonne)

	China		*India*	
	1979	*1983*	*1979*	*1983*
France	4.39	3.53	3.64	3.36
FRG	4.27	3.72	3.26	3.26
Italy	3.69	3.62	3.78	3.55
UK	4.01	3.26	3.33	3.03
USA	3.47	3.33	2.90	3.28

Source: S. Kathuria and N. Taneja, *India's Exports: The Challenge from China* (New Delhi, ICRIER, 1986), p. 50.

As reviewed previously, India's cotton fabrics industry was handicapped with a number of factors which would cause less efficiency and higher costs, which calls for immediate implementation of efficient management and modernisation, rather than export incentives, in order to expand exports of the product in a significant way.

Growth of Handtools Industry and Export Opportunities

The existing product range of India's handtools industry in the early 1980s was : grinding media, bonded abrasives, coated abrasives, engineer's steel files and rasps, forged handtools, diamond drill bits and tools, besides certain kinds of cutting tools and hard metal products. Major items in cutting tools which were in production include chases, dies, milling cutters, hacksaw blades, reamers, taps, twist drills and tools bits. Hard metal products in production were tungsten carbide tipped tools, tungsten carbide rock bits and integral chill rods.[53]

In the product range of handtools industry, India's forged handtools consists of wrenches, pliers, screw drivers, spanners and hammers, etc. is most significant in terms of production value which was at Rs. 328.4 million in 1980 and Rs. 301.3 million in 1981 in the organised sector, which is followed by bonded abrasives, coated abrasives and hard metal production and engineer's steel files and rasps (see Table 6.6).

TABLE 6.6

Production of Major Handtools Products*

(Rs. million)

	1980	*1981*
Forged handtools	328.4	301.3
Bonded abrasives	159.4	167.4
Coated abrasives	134.6	121.2
Hard metal products	129.7	156.2
Files and rasps	84.5	136.2
Diamond drill bits and tools	73.4	75.7

*Value of production in organised sector.

Source: Ministry of Industry, Government of India, *Guidelines for Industries*—Part II (New Delhi, Indian Investment Centre, 1983), pp. 56-61.

In terms of value of exports, forged handtools were by far more important than other handtools products. Exports of forged handtools in 1978-79 and 1979-80 amounted Rs. 328.8 million and Rs. 384.4 million respectively. Other items in handtools which were exported to a significant level includes files and rasps, bonded abrasives, coated abrasives, cutting tools and hard metal products (tungsten carbide tips and powder) (see Table 6.7).

Forged handtools reserved for manufacture in small scale industries[54] were relaxable for large and medium scale units if they were export-oriented. The export content of production of forged handtools by large and medium scale units were presently at 60 to 70 per cent.[55] Based on the production figures of the

TABLE 6.7

Exports of Major Handtools Products
(Rs. million)

	1978-79	*1979-80*
Forged handtools	328.8	384.4
Files and Rasps	45.2	52.9
Cutting tools*	25.8	28.1
Bonded abrasives	5.1	4.2
Coated abrasives	4.1	1.8
Tungsten tips and Powder	11.1	5.1
Total	447.3	516.6

*Includes twist drills, treading tools, hacksaw blades, tool bits, reamers and milling cutters.

**SITC 695

Source: Ministry of Industry, Government of India, *Guidelines for Industries*—Part II (New Delhi, Indian Investment Centre, 1983) pp. 56-61.

organised sector in Table 6.6, it is estimated that about 48 to 50 per cent in 1978-79 and 44 to 52 per cent in 1979-80 of the total exports of forged handtools were exported by the organised sector. This implies the significant contribution by small scale units to exports of forged handtools.

As the capacity of small scale units engaged in production of forged handtools was estimated to be around 3000 to 4000 tonnes per annum against the licensed capacity of the organised sector 15550 tonnes per annum, the performance in exports of forged handtools by the small scale sector has been very impressive. The contribution by the small scale sector to exports of handtools as a whole had increased.[56] India's total exports of handtools declined from Rs. 487.7 million in 1981-82 to Rs. 470.0 million in 1982-83, Rs. 450.0 million in 1983-84, but exports of the product by small scale units increased from Rs. 113.4 million in 1981-82 to Rs. 146.9 million in 1982-83, Rs. 150.0 million in 1983-84. As a result, the share of the small scale sector in the total exports of handtools went up from 23.3 per cent in 1981-82 to 33.3 per cent in 1983-84.

On the other hand, there has been a considerable decline in export performance of the organised handtools industry in India, particularly during the early 1980s, that led to the overall deterioration of India's exports of the product. India's exports of handtools lost shares in the world markets at the same time. For example, India's share in imports of handtools by the group mainly of developed countries[57] which provides market for about 80 per cent of India's cxports of the product declined from 1.3 per cent in 1979 to 0.7 per cent in 1983.[58]

A study prepared under the National Register of Foreign Collaboration[59] points out a number of problems existing in India's forged handtools production units which would have affected the competitiveness of exports of the product. One of the points made in the report is regarding the state of technology prevailing in the industry. The forging method prevalent in India's forged handtools production is the hot forging process. It has been observed that almost all the units under this study is unable to maintain the technology in a good condition so as to reduce the flash and rejection losses as high as 42-50 per cent of the raw material inputs. Also low efficiency is reported in the use of furnace oil required for oil fired furnace in the heat treatment which is between 7 to 9 per cent due to non-utilisation of waste heat. The hot forging process itself is behind the latest technology employed in forged handtools production in the world, namely, the cold and warm forging process which ensures better surface finish and closer tolerance.[60]

Besides the above factors which would have affected the competitiveness of exports from India, its exports of forged handtools have been less price-effective. Alloy steels need for the production of forged handtools were available indigenously, but not of comparable quality standards in comparison to imported materials. The incentives in terms of price difference between international and domestic production/import price of alloy steel for forged handtools was Rs. 1705 per ton, whereas the actual price difference was Rs. 5000-6000. Similar disparity exists for cellulose acetate which was also used for fittings to ferrous parts of forged handtools.[61] However, even after the fiscal drawbacks of excise and custom duties, the price difference is so large that the exports would not be priced competitively.

Especially, as almost all the exports of forged handtools were those of general engineering application, for which price was a more determining factor than quality.

India's exports of handtools to Japan fluctuated between US $ 0.2 million and US $ 0.7 million in the period 1974 to 1984, without any specific trend. Japan's imports of handtools increased consistently from 1975 onwards to US $ 36.0 million to US $ 103.1 million in 1982, and to US $ 1133.5 million in 1984. The U.S.A., Sweden and Federal Republic of Germany continued to comprise over 70 per cent of Japan's imports of the product except 1984, meeting its demand for specialised tools (see Table 6.8).

Imports from South Korea has been the largest among exporters of handtools belonging to the developing regions during the period. However, there have been a decline in its share in Japan's total imports of the product, implying the keen competition among exporters of developing economics. For example, Singapore's exports of handtools which was insignificant in the 1970s, expanded its share in Japan's total imports in the early 1980s. India's share of handtools exports to Japan remained small, below one per cent throughout the period, which may be also explained as inability to establish effective penetration to the Japanese market (see also Table 6.8).

Cost Structure and Productivity of Manufacturing Industries

As has been observed in the previous section, India's exports of cotton fabrics and handtools in the post-oil crisis period were facing [stiff competition to Japan, particularly from developing countries. The two export items were with labour-intensive technology. Being very standardised technology, it was widespread in the world. Thus competitiveness of the product in the labour-intensive area in international markets was largely determined by cost-effectiveness. As labour cost constitutes a considerable segment in the total cost in this product area, reduction in cost with respect to labour results in improvement of overall cost-effectiveness.

Developing economies which export labour-intensive products could make inroads into the world markets by establishing cost advantage with respect to labour. Wages paid to

TABLE 6.8

Direction of Japan's Imports of Handtools*

(% of total)

Year	*India*	*U.S.A.*	*Sweden*	*Fedral Republic of Germany*	*South Korea*	*Singapore*	*Total (million US $)*
1974	0.9	39.6	18.8	12.7	2.5	0.4	52.5
1975	0.5	43.0	18.9	11.4	2.8	n.g.	36.0
1976	0.6	42.3	20.0	11.3	2.9	n.g.	41.7
1977	0.4	37.6	23.7	10.9	2.8	n.g.	54.3
1978	0.5	38.5	21.1	10.8	2.5	n.g.	69.9
1979	0.5	37.3	20.6	12.2	3.0	n.g.	95.2
1980	0.4	38.2	22.6	10.2	3.3	0.2	109.2
1981	0.6	38.5	19.8	11.8	2.4	1.0	102.7
1982	0.7	41.9	16.1	12.1	1.9	1.5	103.1
1983	0.5	36.7	17.5	13.2	1.8	1.7	978.9
1984							1133.5

*SITC 695

Source: United Nations, *Commodity Trade Statistics* (New York), from various issues of 1974 to 1984.

labour in these economies were lower generally due to the existence of surplus labour in the low-productivity agricultural areas. The economies which could make use of low labour costs would be able to prove competitiveness in their exports of labour-intensive products.

However, it is not the case for all developing economies with surplus labour which have been successful in exporting labour-intensive products. The advantage of low labour costs is revealed only when the industry in a developing economy achieves efficiency embodied in the technology. If it fails to attain it, low productivity will offset the advantage of low labour costs, resulting in the less competitiveness in the product in the world markets, especially when the labour content is higher in the total cost structure.

Below, we will examine the trend in production and productivity of India's cotton fabrics and handtools manufacturing industries after 1973. In other words, it is attempted to analyse the productivity with respect to labour and other inputs in these manufacturing industries.

Cost-effectiveness in the Cotton Textile Manufacturing Industry

Figure 6.1 shows the trend in production[62] and export[63] of India's cotton fabrics weaving industry and the imports of cotton fabrics[64] to India after 1973. The focus of our attention is on the trend in the mill sector. As the level of production registered an absolute decline, the trend in exports has been marked by a few cycles during the period. This implies that exports of cotton fabrics have been more dependent on the trends in the world economy than on the level of domestic production. For example, in the wake of the first and second oil crises in 1973 and 1978 and the recession in the industrial economies in the early 1980s, exports of cotton fabrics from India was depressed considerably. However, the peak in 1976 at 581 million square metres of exports of mill-made cotton fabrics was never recovered or exceeded in the subsequent years of the period, indicating the general decline of export strength in the cotton fabrics industry.

It may be possible to interpret the lack in a push in exports in terms of the productivity factors of the cotton fabrics

FIGURE 6.1

Cotton Fabrics—India: Production, Exports and Imports

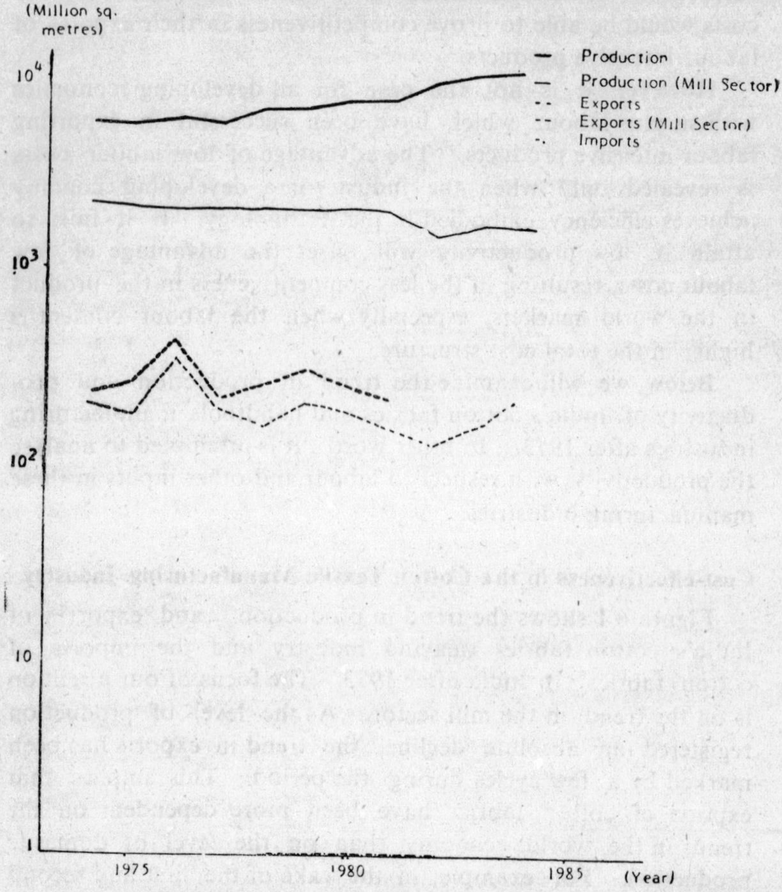

Source: Textile Commissioner, Government of India, *Indian Textile Bulletin* (Bombay) from various issues.

industry. We will analyse the trend in efficiency-wage and efficiency-material cost after 1975, as has been analysed in Chapter Four.[65]

Figure 6.2 presents the trend in wages[66] per worker in the cotton textile mills since 1974. There has been no marked change in wages paid to each worker, which would cause rise or

FIGURE 6.2

Cotton Fabrics—India: Wages (w)

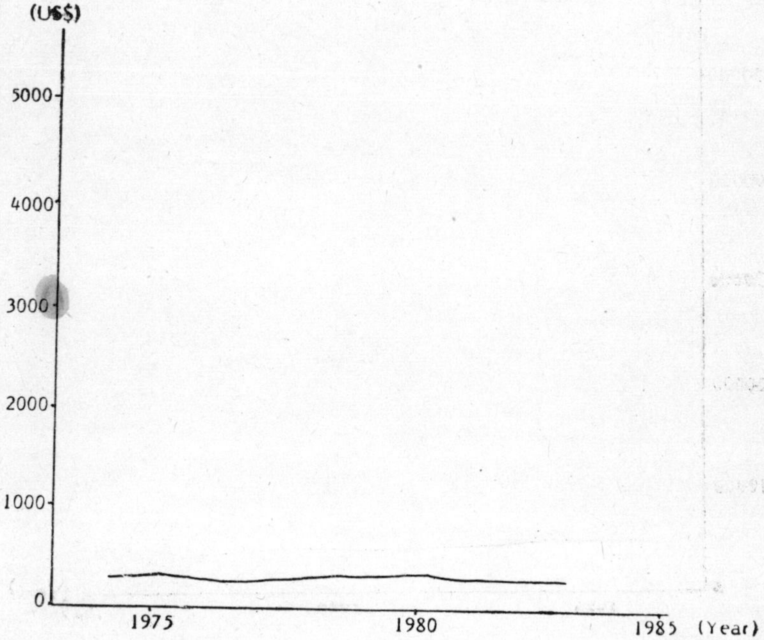

reduction in the overall cost of cotton fabrics production. On the other hand, a secular declining trend has been indicated in the case of output per worker (O/L) as in Figure 6.3.[67] The stable trend in wages and a secular decline in output worker

FIGURE 6.3

Cotton Fabrics—India: Output per Worker (O/L)

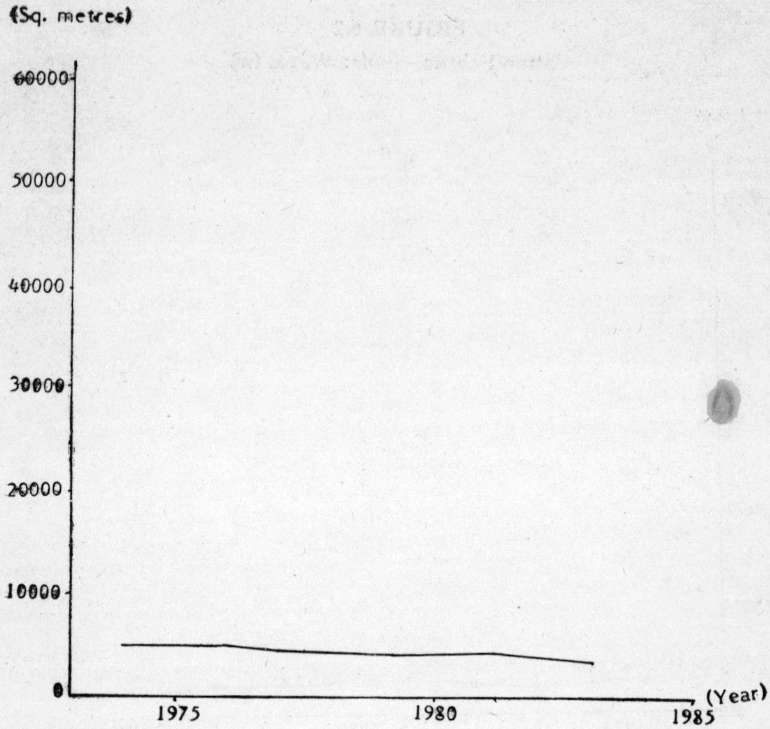

has given rise to the rapid increase in efficiency-wage (w/O/L) during the post-oil crisis period (see Figure 6.4).

FIGURE 6.4

Cotton Fabrics—India: Efficiency-Wage (w/O/L)

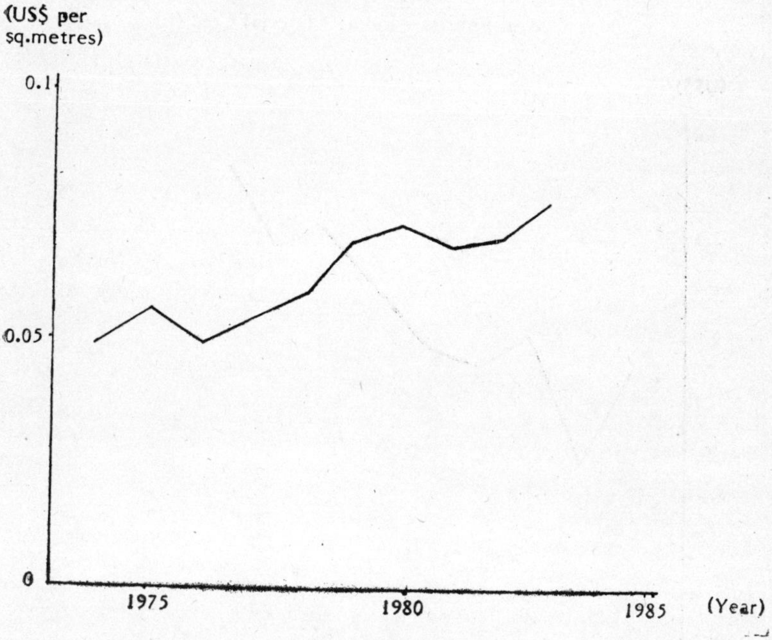

The rise in the efficiency-material cost (n/O/R) factor has been even more during the period due to the rapid increase in material cost (n) on one hand and the declining output-input ratio (O/K) on the other. Figure 6.5 shows the trend in the wholesale price of cotton yarn[68] taken as proxy of that in the material cost for the cotton fabrics weaving, which indicates that the price of cotton yarn has been on a steep increase since

FIGURE 6.5
Cotton Fabrics—India: Material Cost (n)

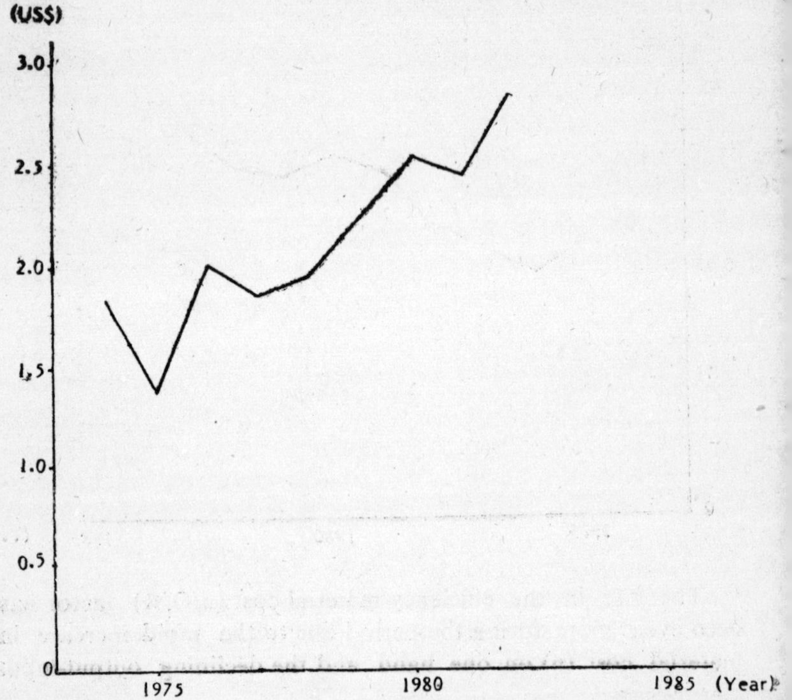

1974. On the other hand as Figure 6.6 indicates, the output-input ratio[69] was declining steadily during the period. Such

FIGURE 6.6

Cotton Fabrics—India: Output-Input Ratio (O/R)

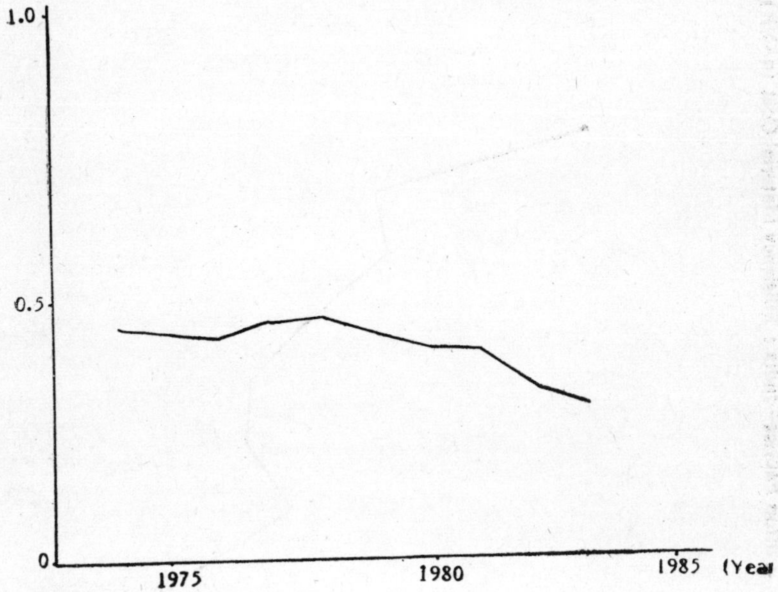

movements in material cost and output-input ratio have made a rise in efficiency-material cost factor more pronounced (see Table 6.7).

The steadily increasing trend in efficiency-wage and efficiency-material cost factors can be interpreted as the implication of the overall decline in productivity and increase in cost which have been faced in India's cotton textile industry since the 1970s. The deterioration in efficiency factors in the cotton fabrics industry certainly would have led to the decline in competitiveness of India's exports of the product during the period.

FIGURE 6.7

Cotton Fabrics—India : Efficiency Material Cost (n/O/R)

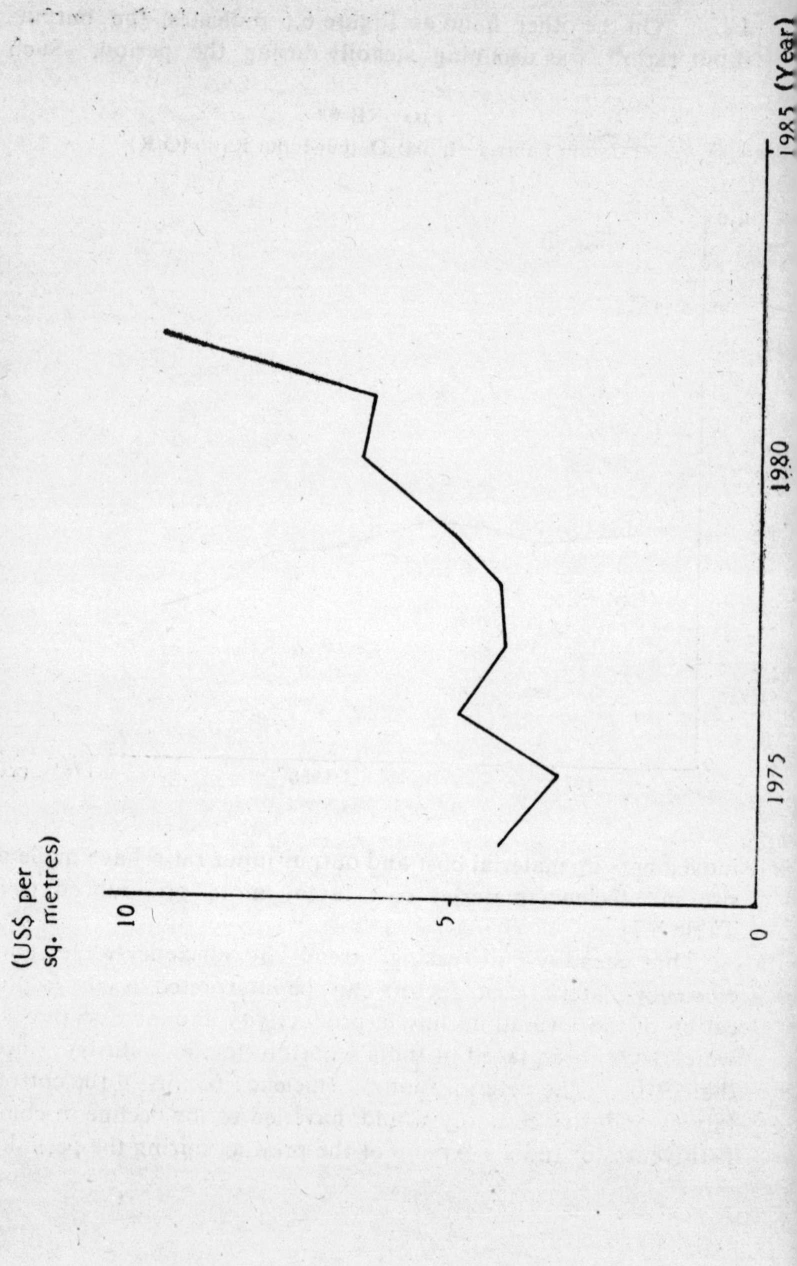

TABLE 6.9

Trend in Export Incentives

	Cash Compensatroy		*Duty Drawbacks*		*Import replenishment*	
	Value (Rs. million)	*% as of f.o.b. export value*	*Value* (Rs. million)	*% as of f.o.b. export value*	*Value* (Rs. million)	*% as of f.o.b. export value*
1974-75	599	1.8	600	1.9	1664	5.0
1975-76	1237	3.1	820	2.0	2372	5.9
1976-77	2264	4.4	1200	2.3	4155	8.1
1977-78	3103	5.7	1330	2.5	7414	13.7
1978-79	3590	6.3	1500	2.6	10967	19.1
1979-80	3441	5.4	1520	2.4	10896	17.0
1980-81	3764	5.6	1640	2.4	14220	21.2
1981-82	4524	5.8	2040	2.6	17629	22.6
1982-83	4488	5.1	1270	1.4	19635	22.2
1983-84	4299	4.6	1320	1.4	22945	23.6

Source: Ministry of Commerce, Government of India, *Report of the Commitee on Trade Policies* (New Delhi), 1984, pp. 109, 121-123.

Cost-effectiveness in the Handtools Manufacturing Industry

Production[70] and exports[71] of India's handtools manufacturing industry and imports[72] of the product to India is indicated in Figure 6.8. Although the figures in the latest years for pro-

FIGURE 6.8

Handtools—India: Production, Exports and Imports

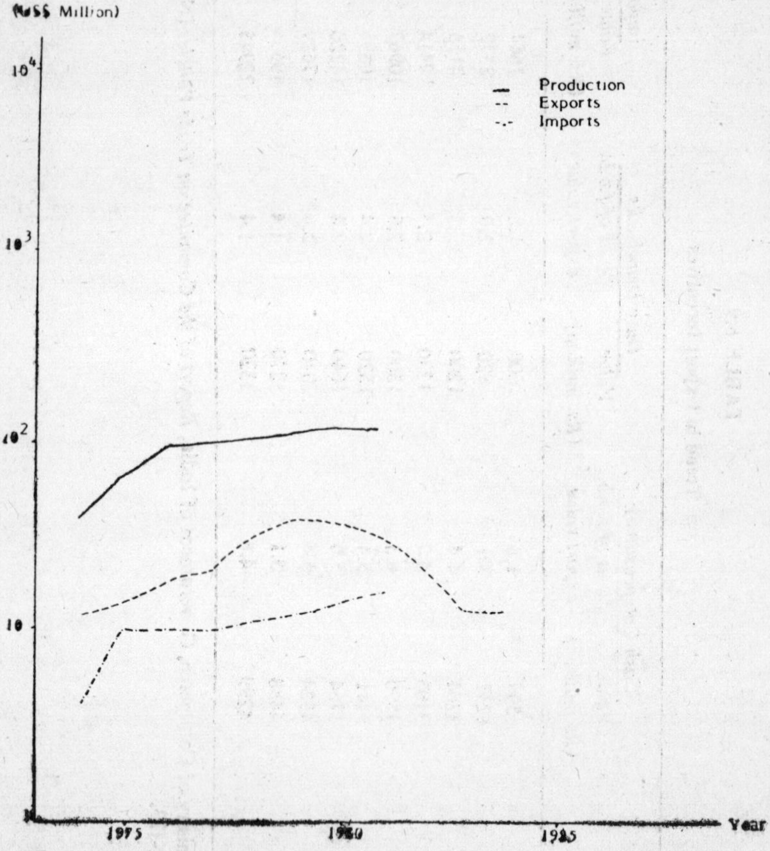

duction and imports are not available, there has been marked decline in exports of handtools from India in the early 1980, at least in terms of value, despite a consistent increase prior to 1980.

However, when we look into the efficiency factors with respect to labour in the handtools manufacturing sector, there has not been a trend in particular which would have led to the decline in exports by way of the deterioration in price competitiveness. Figure 6.9 indicates the trend in wages (w)[73] paid to

FIGURE 6.9
Handtools—India: Wages (w)

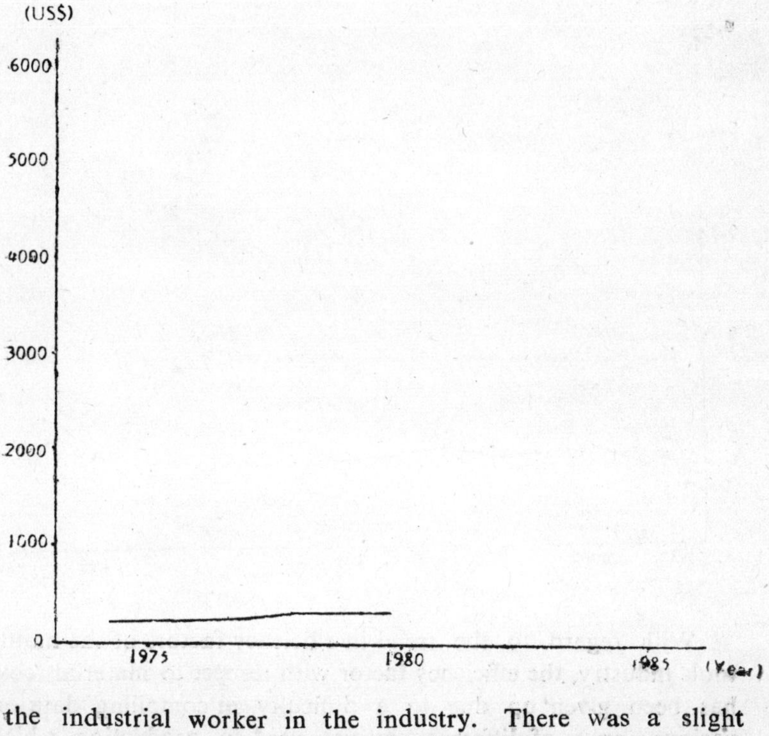

the industrial worker in the industry. There was a slight increase in wages after 1974, which would have been resulted from the change in quality and skill embodied in labour as the product range of the industry changed. There was also a slight increase in output per worker in terms of value[74] as seen in Figure 6.10. As a result, there was no explicit decline or fall in efficiency-wage in the handtools manufacturing sector. (See Figure 6.11)

FIGURE 6.10
Handtools—India: Output per Worker (O/L)

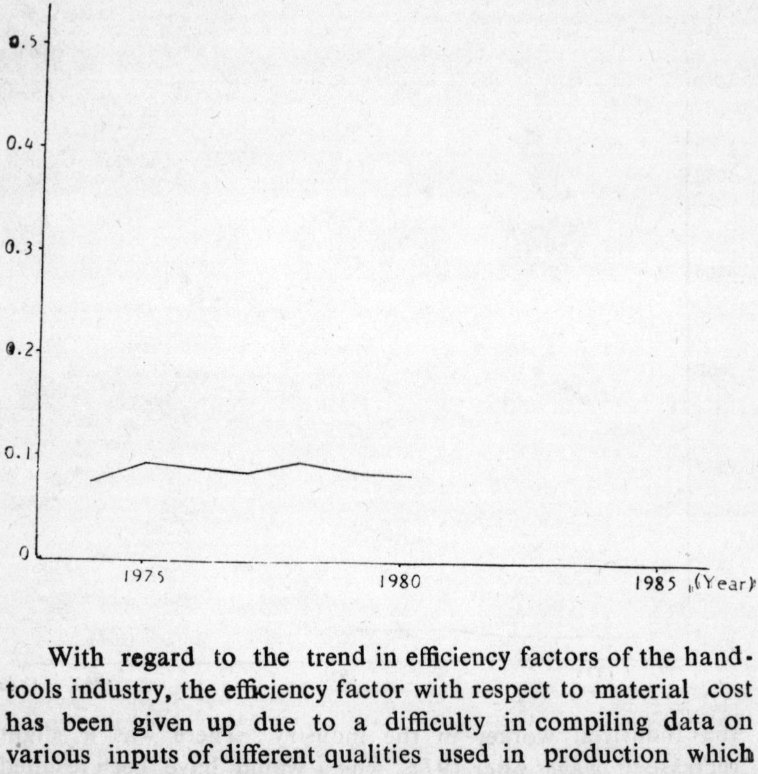

With regard to the trend in efficiency factors of the handtools industry, the efficiency factor with respect to material cost has been given up due to a difficulty in compiling data on various inputs of different qualities used in production which comes into the category of handtools. It may be seen that in the review of India's handtools manufacturing after 1973, the cost of alloy steel inputs was found to be far beyond the international standard, even after a deduction of excise and custom duties. In this light, it is important to examine the trend in efficiency-material cost after suitable adjustments in data preparation.

FIGURE 6.11

Handtools—India: Efficiency-Wage (w/O/L)

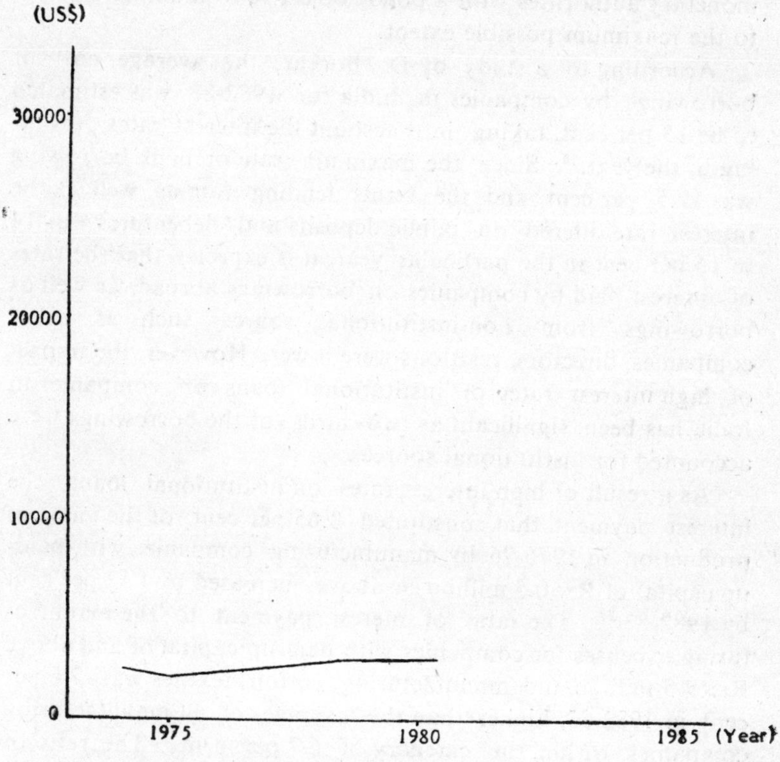

Efficiency factor with respect to Capital Cost

Besides costs on labour and other inputs, the value of production includes the cost on capital. In theory, the rate of return on capital is at least equated to the interest rate, so that lending or diverting funds for the purpose is at least as worthwhile as for other purposes. In the earlier chapter while analysing the trend in efficiency factors of manufacturing industries, namely, cotton fabrics weaving and handtools manufacturing, we had ommited the efficiency with respect to cost of capital, which is theoretically equal to the rate of interest due to the fact that the expenditure on interest payment in the total cost has been found to be very small in proportion.[75]

However, in reality the industries in India face a situation where interest rates are controlled and administered by the monetary authorities with a policy objective to mobilise savings to the maximum possible extent.

According to a study by D. Borkar, the average cost of borrowings by companies in India for 1982-83 was estimated to be 15 per cent, taking into account the interest rates prevailing in the year.[76] Since the maximum rate on bank borrowing was 19.5 per cent and the terms lending rate as well as the interest rate offered on public deposits and debentures was 14 to 15 per cent in the particular year, it is expected that the rates of interest paid by companies on borrowings abroad as well as borrowings from non-institutional sources such as other companies, directors, relations were lower. However, the impact of high interest rates of institutional loans on companies in India has been significant as two-thirds of the borrowings were accounted for institutional sources.

As a result of high interest rates on institutional loans, the interest payment that constituted 3.65 per cent of the value of production in 1975-76 by manufacturing companies with paid-up capital of Rs. 0.5 million or above, increased to 4.52 per cent by 1982-83.[77] The ratio of interest payment to the manufacturing expenses for companies with paid-up capital of and above Rs. 9.5 million and manufacturing cotton textiles was 7.6 per cent in 1982-83, higher than the average of all manufacturing companies within the category of 6.7 per cent. The ratio of interest payments to gross profits of the companies of cotton textile manufacturing was 54.8 per cent, also higher than the average of all manufacturing companies at 53.1 per cent. If we take only the companies with paid-up capital of and above Rs. 10 million, the two ratios of interest payments to manufacturing expenses and gross profits in 1984-85 was as high as 8.4 per cent and 88.2 per cent, respectively.

As interest payments have comprised a larger share in the total value of production as well as in gross profits, it is supposed that the efficiency factor with respect to capital cost would have influenced the overall productivity of industries to a greater extent. In this context, investigation on the efficiency-capital cost has become more relevant to assess the productivity and cost structure of industries in India for recent years.

Development in Policy Environment for India's Exports to Japan

There has been more positive development in the policy front related to trade between India and Japan after the first oil crisis. The development in this respect has taken place in the process of India's export promotion and Japan's economic cooperation with developing countries through trade. As a measure to step up growth in exports, India intensified the existing export incentive scheme and introduced a set of liberalisation measures in the industrial policy in order to upgrade the technological level of domestic industries for greater competitiveness.

On the other hand, Japan increased the pace of trade liberalisation in its response to the call for restructure and reform of the international economy towards freer trade after the Tokyo Round multilateral tariff negotiations concluded in 1979. In particular to developing countries, it has made the GSP scheme more comprehensive in order to promote further its declared objectives to increase export earnings of developing countries and accelerate the pace of their economic growth.

In addition, there was a trend in the India-Japan trade that had encouraged the two countries to take more advantage of the benefits to be embodied by the policies. It was that India's exports to Japan stagnated in the 1970s, while its imports from Japan recorded a rapid increase. Between 1970-71 and 1982-83, India's imports from Japan increased by 1100 per cent, while its exports to Japan increased only by 286 per cent. Due to its low export growth to Japan, India's trade deficit with Japan had widened rapidly since 1980.

Below, policies relevant to the bilateral trade between India and Japan in the post-oil crisis period are discussed with special reference to India's exports to manufactures, including cotton fabrics and handtools, to Japan.

India's Trade and Industrial Policies for Export Growth

In the 1970s, there was efforts to streamline the existing export incentive scheme as well as to introduce new instruments for export promotion through liberalisation of the industrial policies. The Committee on Import-Export Policies (P.C. Alexander Committee) constituted in 1977 set out the rationale to minimise the redundancy in the existing export incentives typically by way of cash compensation support, duty drawbacks and import replenishment scheme. The cash compensation support was to compensate fully for unrebated indirect taxes paid by exporter on inputs for export production, while the import replenishment policy to be based firmly on the actual user principle.[78] At the same time, essential inputs and capital goods for export production which are neither indigenously available nor in the restricted or banned list were allowed to be imported under open general licenses. The recommendations of the Committee were incorporated in the Import-Export Policy for 1978-79.

As Table 6.9 shows, there was a halt in the rising trend in the late 1970s in the rates of incentives through cash compensation support and duty drawback, whereas the rate of import replenishment has been on a consistent increase. The fact that the export incentive has been provided increasingly in the form of facilitating imports of critical inputs and equipments, rather than of simple subsidation, could reflect the recognition of the element of efficiency in production in the export policies. The report of the Committee on Trade Policies (Abid Hussain Committee) in 1984 points out first of all the cost of production as one of the constraints on India's export performance in recent years. The report observes that "as the technology lags have increased, the productivity differentials have widened and (that) the costs of inputs have continued to rise", which effected India's competitiveness.[79]

Subsequently, rationalisation of the trade policies was implemented on the recommendations submitted by the Hussain Committee with the Import-Export Policy 1985-1988, with the objective "to increase the degree of competition in the economy and provide ... an incentive to bring about a reduction in the cost."[80] In this context, it was recommended that non-tariff barriers on imports through licensing be replaced with OGL with a high tariff to provide an alternative protection from imports to domestic industries at the infant stage. The high tariff rates were to be de-escalated over time, so that domestic industries be given a due chance to compete with import-supplying industries above.

Incentives for exports have been provided also by liberalisation of the existing industrial policies. Industrial Policy Statement in 1980 that set a foundation of a series of liberalisation measures in the early 1980s stated as one of the policy objectives "faster promotion of export-oriented and import-substitution industries".[81] Based on this stated objective, a scheme of 100 per cent export-oriented units was introduced in 1980. The units set up under this scheme were eligible for all the entitlements available to the units in Free Trade Zones.[82] In addition, another entitlment was made available to the 100 per cent export-oriented units later to allow sales of a part of output to domestic tariff areas.[83]

The Industrial Policy Statement in 1981 underlines the importance of exports also from the point of view of optimal capacity utilisation for modern technology.[84] Though technological renovation has been found to be necessary for achieving higher productivity and improving competitiveness of Indian industries, the actual induction of advanced technology is decided on depending on the size of demand. The induction of the technology which is not expected to be fully utilised to the optimal capacity due to the limited size of domestic markets can be justified by redeeming exports for a part of output.

In this light, a set of measures have been taken to relax constraints one xpansion of production capacities. First, broadbanding of industrial licences was undertaken with respect to 25 industrial sectors. Secondly, 25 industrial sectors have been exempted from the licensing procedures under the Industries (Development and Regulation) Act, 1951. Third, a scheme of re-endorsement of capacities specified in the license without having to obtain a fresh license based on the highest level of production achieved. Further, the scheme of delicensing was extended to companies subject to monopolies or/and foreign exchange regulations for 23 sectors of a national priority or having a large export potential.[85]

Export promotion policies toward cotton fabrics and handtools industries have been restructured according to the changes in trade and industrial policies as a whole since the late 1970s. There has been a renewed awareness about the importance of the technological level of India's cotton textile industry for competitive exports, which is reflected in a step-up in support by the existing export incentives such as cash compensatory support and import replenishment licences. After an interruption in the late 1970s, cash compensatory support was resumed to exporters of cotton textiles, starting with Rs. 94.1 million in 1980-81. The amount of assistance under this scheme was subsequently stepped up to Rs. 99.5 million in 1981-82, Rs. 161.8 million in 1982-83, Rs. 391.2 million in 1983-84, respectively, despite a decline in the aggregate disbursement under the scheme.[86] The cash compensatory support rate, that is, the ratio of disbursement under the scheme to the f.o.b. value of exports for cotton textiles was worked out to be 1.1 per cent for 1980-81 and 1981-82 which went up to 1.7 per cent for 1982-83 and 3.6 per cent for 1983-84. The assistance provided under the import replenishment licences amounted to Rs. 56 million in 1974-75, which gradually increased to Rs. 233 million by 1979-80. As a result, the ratio of value of the import replenishment licences to the f.o.b. value of exports for cotton textiles rose from 1.6 per cent for 1974-75 to 3.0 per cent for 1979-80.

For the purpose of removing obsolescence of the textile industry, the Indian Government allowed imports of high technology textile machinery to a greater extent. The value of import licences issued which was at Rs. 244 million in 1979-80, increased to Rs. 525 million in 1980-81 and Rs. 539 million in 1981-82, comprising 4.7 per cent and 3.1 per cent of the total value of licences issued for imports of capital goods and heavy electrical plant.[87] The industrial policy for indigenous manufacture of textile machinery has been also liberalised.[88] Also establishing units of textiles under the 100 per cent export-oriented units scheme and Free Trade Zones has been encouraged for the first time since the initiation of these schemes.[89]

There was a two-fold approach in the industrial policy for handtools. Based on the labour-intensive nature of the traditional handtools manufacturing, a number of items of handtools, particularly forged handtools, kept as reservation for production in the small-scale sector in 1973. As an exception to this, the large and medium units could take up the area of production if they are bound with an obligation of exports for over 70 per cent of their output. The large and medium units entered collaboration with the leading manufacturers abroad so that the quality of their products would meet the international standard.[90]

However, the technology for production initially transferred to the handtools industry in India from abroad is found to be obsolete already. Take the example of forged handtools, the technology prevailing in the units in India refers to the hot forging method, was transferred from abroad. There was no efforts subsequently to improve the technology nor to transfer the latest technology in forged handtools production, namely, the cold and warm forging. In addition, transfer of technology in forged handtools has not been given priority in the policy of the Government.[91]

For handtools industry, drawbacks from excise and customs and other duties constitute an essential part of export incentives. Under the international price reimbursement scheme for handtools exports instituted in 1981, exporters of the product were compensated for the domestic and international price differential by 65-72 per cent. However, still a gap of Rs. 1705 per ton for alloy steel inputs with respect to the domestic price exists even after applying drawbacks. The industry also suffered from the shortage of immediate working capital which were estimated to be around Rs. 60 million.[92]

In sum, export incentives for cotton textiles exports have been improved considerably especially in recent years, while those directed to handtools industry need major modifications. Differences in thrusts in the export policies between the two exports could be compared with the export performance achieved by the two industries. Despite keen competition and restrictive trade practices in international market, exports of various textiles products marked a rise of 36.6 per cent in 1984-85 over the previous year in terms of export earnings,[93] while exports of handtools registered a decline of 23.3 per cent in the same year.[94]

Japan's Policies for Imports of Manufactures

Japan has taken steps since the implementation of the GSP scheme to improve the scheme in order to incorporate more of interests of its beneficiary developing exporters as well as to adjust it to changes that have taken place in the structure of the Japanese economy. First of all, the preferential tariff rates provided under the GSP scheme underwent across-the-board cut, accompanied by implementation of tariff reduction of MFN rates agreed in Tokyo Round. However, the effect of preferential tariffs in terms of the preference margin was decreased since the preferential tariffs in the pre-Tokyo Round were already low. This has shifted the emphasis of Japan's GSP scheme more on the assurance of markets for exports by developing economies under the emerging protectionism, among major importers in the world. In this light, the following modifications undertaken in the scheme have had more impact on beneficiaries.

First, the scheme which covered 96 beneficiaries initially extended to almost all the developing region with an inclusion of China in 1980. Second, the import value which was subject to ceilings have been increased from US $ 745.3 million in 1972-73 to US $ 5136.4 million, basically because of the increase in the basic quota due to the change in its reference year from 1968 to 1978.[95] Third, number of product groups subject to ceilings within BTN Chapters 25 to 99 declined from 214 in the 1971-72 scheme to 201 in 1984-85.[96]

Procedures in administering ceilings or maximum country limitations were also modified. Since 1974, a system was introduced to allow imports over and above the ceilings or maximum country limitations. For example, in the scheme for the fiscal year 1984, out of 201 product groups which were subject to the ceilings, flexible administration of ceilings and maximum country limitations were applied for 110 products and 134 products, respectively.[97]

Despite the fact that modifications and revisions of the GSP scheme were made to allow more imports from beneficiaries, competition among beneficiaries as well as with non-beneficiaries has been increased. The maximum country limitation which was decided on as half of the ceiling for each product group was scaled down as one-third of the ceiling was made the basis for it.[98] Also, the diminishing preference margin of preferential tariff rates over MFN rates contributed to the increasing competition for beneficiaries against non-beneficiaries.

The effect of these changes in Japan's GSP scheme has been illustrated in the instance of the preferential treatment to imports of cotton fabrics. After implementation of tariff cuts under the Tokyo Round agreements, the preference margin for grey pure cotton fabrics of gauze and terry towelling varieties decreased from 6.6 per cent to 4.5 per cent. The preference margin for cotton fabrics of a pure variety other than gauze and terry towelling, on the other hand, increased from 2.8 per cent to 5.6 per cent after the Tokyo Round agreements.[100]

The ceilings and maximum country limitations have been continued to be imposed on imports of cotton textile products. Although the number of ceilings within the cotton textile products (BTN Chapter 55) reduced from three to one after 1980,[101] the ceiling remained unlifted for grey and terry towelling cotton fabrics, which have been found to be one of the most binding ceilings. In the fiscal year 1983, the maximum country limitation was imposed on South Korea for imports of cotton textiles[102] after reaching 52.5 million Yen against the ceiling of 81.0 million Yen.[103] In case of the fiscal year 1984, the maximum country ceiling was imposed on all beneficiaries for the same product after their imports reached 206.5 million Yen against the ceiling of 105.2 million Yen within a month from the initiation of the scheme.[104]

On the other hand, it has been found that the ceiling for imports under GSP for handtools and cutlery (BTN Chapter 82) was never reached. Despite, the ceiling was subsequently increased due to the rapid increase in imports from non-beneficiaries which constitute supplementary quota. For example, the ceiling was set at 685.8 million Yen for 1984-85, 228.8 million Yen up from 1983-84, and was raised to 726.9 million Yen for 1985-86, although imports from beneficiaries were far below the ceiling during this period.[105]

India's exports to Japan under the GSP scheme has been insignificant compared to the size of its total imports from all the beneficiary countries. India comprised 1.3 per cent out of

Japan's total imports under the scheme in 1983.[106] India's poor performance shown in its GSP exports to Japan is in a way attributed to the incompatibility of the list of products covered by the scheme with India's export structure.[107] The products which India is supposed to have competitiveness in the Japanese markets such as shellac, seed lac, vegetable oils, ethyl alcohol and a few categories of woven fabrics are not included in the list. While the products like black and instant tea, shrimps, fruits including bananas, mangos, guavas, nicotin sulphate, bovine cattle leather, jute goods and certain categories of ready made garments need further cuts in preferential tariff rates. In case of leather goods and footwear, quantitative restrictions are found to be most binding on exports from India.

As far as India's exports of cotton fabrics and handtools are concerned, following were the constraints. India's exports of cotton textile products (BTN Chapter 55) to Japan in 1981 and 1982 amounted to Rs. 20.2 million and Rs. 9.8 million respectively.[108] The lower exports in the second year reflects the position of India's cotton textile industry which suffered a decline in production and exports. Exports of cotton textile products excluding cotton yarn and cotton fabrics other than gauze and terry towelling are subject to the ceiling in Japan's GSP scheme. Under this category, India's exports constituted 10.9 per cent and 12.0 per cent of the total value set aside by the ceiling in the respective years of 1981 and 1982. Although the figures indicate a favourable performance achieved by India with respect to its GSP exports of cotton textiles to Japan, it is yet to be comparable with South Korea which filled up to 64.9 per cent of the ceiling value in 1983.

In case of handtools, India's contribution to Japan's imports under the GSP scheme has been very small. India exported products of handtools and cutlery (BTN Chapter 82) up to 3.1 per cent and 6.1 per cent of the import value set aside as ceiling in 1981 and 1982, which was valued at Rs. 49 million and Rs. 10.8 million, respectively.[109]

As has been seen, India's exports to Japan under the GSP scheme faced various constraints, while there has been room for India to explore the possibility of expanding exports to Japan, which is the case particularly for handtools exports.

As for the GSP scheme that was introduced in 1971, has been made operational up to 1991. In the latest scheme announced by Japan, least developed of the developing countries will be getting special treatment for various agricultural and manufactured items. The Government of Japan made improvements in its GSP by introducing zero duty treatment and eliminating exclusive list. As regards quota they have promised to initiate action at GATT forum. But all these actions will be taken along with other OECD preference giving countries under GSP.

It appears in a number of products the ceilings may not affect India's exports. India's GSP quota utilization appears to be low. According to the latest figures available regarding GSP utilization, Japan imported about 1260 billion Yen worth of commodities. Under the GSP scheme, imports from India were mere 16 billion Yen whereas imports from countries like—Republic of Korea 267 billion Yen, Taiwan 62 billion Yen, China 96 billion Yen, Philippines 79 billion Yen. This largely suggests that imports under GSP have increased from these countries where Japanese investment were made.

Import needs of Japan in the next few decades are expected to increase because of certain constraints in Japanese economy. These constraints arise as a result of growing energy costs, high cost of labour, increased living standards leading to shifts in consumer preferences and pollution problem. It is expected that a planned export development of manufactures by India could enhance exports rapidly to Japan.

Japan's Trade Policy Changes in 1980s

Changes in Japan's industry and trade as witnessed during the late 60s and 70s took place under various new domestic and international conditions such as limitation of industrial resources, intensification of the environmental and industrial location problems, mounting labour and oil crisis. The changes had accentuated in the early 80s with the appreciation of the Yen.

The Japan Advisory Committee for External Economic Issues submitted a Report to the Government of Japan in April 1985 calling for reforms in five policy areas:

—Further improvements in market access.
—Sustained growth centered on domestic demand.
—Expanded overseas investment and industrial co-operation.
—Promotion of the new Round within GATT.
—Responding to the concerns of the developing countries.

Drawing upon these recommendations, Government of Japan announced an Action Programme for expanded market access in July 1985 including reduction or abolition of tariffs on over 1800 items, simplification of import procedures, acceptance of foreign generated test data, greater harmonization with international standards and other import facilitation measures. Prime Minister of Japan had also repeatedly stated that while exports have long been considered indispensable to Japan's economic health, import expansion is now even more important.

In September 1985, the Japanese Cabinet approved a plan to double Official Development Assistance (ODA) in seven years, with the understanding that the total ODA disbursements over this seven year period will top $ 40 billion. In October, a set of policy proposals was approved to stimulate the domestic demand, and in December, 1985 the Advisory Group on Economic Structural Adjustment for the Promotion of International Harmony was formed with a purpose of advising the Government on medium-term policy recommendations.

Recently, to overcome the Yen appreciation problem the Japanese have shown interest in shifting some of their production bases abroad to reap the advantages of international division of labour and make their products competitive. According to surveys made by the various Chambers of Commerce and Industries in Japan, the industries which have been affected most by high rate of Yen are textiles, ceramics, cutlery, machine tools, bicycles, precision machinery and textile machinery. India could take advantage of this shifting of the industry bases by Japan. It could be used as an effective tool to correct the trade balance which has been constantly against India.

Technology Induction Policies for Manufacturing Industries

In this chapter the trend of India's trade with Japan in the post-oil crisis period after 1973 has been examined. In the review of the trend in general, it has been noted that India's exports to Japan have not been able to expand as far as its imports from Japan and that the pattern of its exports, largely consisting of a few non-manufactures like iron ore and shrimps, has not undergone much change since the period prior to the oil crisis.

There has been efforts by India to expand exports of manufactures to Japan. The strategy was based on comparative advantage prevailing in Indian industries, that is, lower labour cost. Taking examples of India's exports of cotton fabrics and handtools to Japan, it was examined how far India was able to utilise the advantage. In case of exports of cotton fabrics, the advantage of low labour cost was found to be completely offset by low output per worker. On the other hand, a lack of competitiveness was identified with respect to exports of handtools for which the industry in the export sector, in particular, was not able to undertake technological upgradation that affected the quality of exports.

A review of India's export incentive system indicate that India has gradually developed a system of export incentives parallel to import restriction. The system is quite complicated and some of the incentives appear counter-productive. For example, the farther a plant is from a port, the larger is its transport subsidy. The incentives are also applied rather indiscriminately to all types of exports with the usual result of negative value added in some cases.

A review of the policy aspects of India's exports to Japan after 1973, reveal that India's industrial and trade policies have to be directed for shifting assistance to inputs rather than financial assistance. Also, importance of technological innovation or induction has to be recognised in the policies toward export production. While India has been able to achieve import substitution, it had not led to technological dynamism. In the next chapter, finding and conclusive remarks are presented.

REFERENCES

1. OECD, *OECD Economic Survey—Japan* (Paris, OECD, 1976), p. 19.

2. Economic Planning Agency, Japan, *Economic Survey of Japan 1972-73* (Tokyo, The Japan Times, Ltd., 1974), p. 87.

3. United Nations, *International Trade Statistics Yearbook* (New York: United Nations, 1985), pp. 1047, 1091, 1097 and 1105.

4. Japan External Trade Organisation, *White Paper on International Trade* (Tokyo, Japan External Trade Organization, 1975 and 1985), pp. 98 and 121, respectively.

5. *Ibid.*, p. 100 and p. 124, respectively.

6. *Ibid.*, pp. 98 and 100, pp. 121 and 124, respectively.

7. Economic Planning Agency, Japan, *Economic Survey of Japan 1973-74*, *op. cit.*, pp. 85-87.

8. B. Keesing, *The World Steel Industry* (EIU Special Report No. 128) (London, Economic Intelligence Unit, 1982), p. 25.

9. *Ibid.*, p. 18.

10. *Ibid.*, p. 27.

11. The Bank of Japan, *Economic Statistical Annual* (Tokyo, Bank of Japan, 1984), p. 242.

12. United Nations, *Commodity Trade Statistics* (New York, United Nations, 1977 and 1985), pp. 2408 and 3452 respectively.

13. *Ibid.*, p. 2408 and 3452, respectively.

14. Directorate General of Economic and Commercial Intelligence, *Monthly Statistics of Foreign Trade of India-March* (Calcutta, 1977 and 1985), pp. 249 and 287, respectively.

15. *Ibid.*, pp. 249 and 287, respectively.

16. V.D. Chowgule, "Need for a Realistic Policy and Reducing Loading Cost", *Economic Times* (New Delhi), December 5, 1984, p. 3.

17. Economic Times, "Vizag Outer Harbour Rates Hiked,' (New Delhi), October 22, 1985, p. 1.

18. S. Mangekar, "Mormugao Too Costly For Japan," in *Economic Times*, January 12, 1985, p. 1.

19. *Japan Economic Journal*, "Iron Ore Prices Left Unchanged", (Tokyo), February 1985, p. 5.

20. *Financial Express*, "Big Japanese Order for Kudremukh", (New Delhi), February, 1986, p. 1.

21. To facilitate exports of larger proportions of production from Kudremukh, the Indian Government set out a policy to allow the facility of 100 per cent export oriented units to the iron ore extraction industry in 1985.

22. *Financial Express*, "Big Japanese Order for Kundremukh", *op. cit.*, p. 1.

23. International Trade Centre, *Shrimps, op. cit.*, p. 192.

24. *Ibid.*, p. 194.

25. Quoted in *ibid.*, p. 261.

26. Directorate General of Commercial Intelligence and Statistics, *Monthly Statistics of Foreign Trade of India* (Calcutta, March 1975 and March 1982), p. 48 and p, 54, respectively.

27. International Trade Centre, *op. cit.*, p. 10.

28. N. Joshi, "Marine Products Exports Need Push", in *Economic Times* (New Delhi), August 17, 1985, p. 5.

29. M. Wolf, *India's Exports* (Washington D.C., The World Bank, 1982), pp. 84-25, 81-89.

30. *Ibid.*, pp. 86-87.

31. *Economic Times*, "Contaminated Shrimps Export to Japan" (New Delhi), February 20, 1985, p. 1.

32, *The Asahi Shimbun*, "India's Marine Exports to Japan" (Tokyo), September 1984, p. 6.

33, *Economic Times*, Contaminated Shrimps Exports to Japan", *op. cit*, p. 1.

34. Government of India, *Economic Survey 1984-84* (New Delhi, Government of India), p. 28.

35. K. Khanna, "Textiles in Flatspin", in *Times of India* (New Delhi), p. 5.

36. B. Kakatkar, "New Textile Policy", in *Economic Times* (New Delhi), p. 3.

37. Indian Cotton Mills Federation, *Handbook of Statistics on Cotton Textile Industry* (Bombay, Indian Cotton Mills Federation, 1986), p. 33.

38. *Ibid.*, p. 33.

39. K. Khanna, *op. cit.*, p. 5.

40. P. Jha, "Effects of Textile Policy", in *Times of India* (New Delhi), December 1985, p. 5.

41. K. Khanna, *op. cit.*, p. 5.

42. H. Rao, "Anomalies in Excise Structure" in *Economic Times* (New Delhi), October 1, 1985, p. 1.

43. The Ashoka Mehta Committee in 1964 sanctify the existence of powerloom sector by recommending fiscal concessions to it.

44. C. Radhakrishnan, "New Textile Policy", in *Financial Express* (New Delhi), July 22, 1985, p. 4.

45. Indian Cotton Mills Federation, *Handbook of Statistics on Cotton Textile Industry, op. cit.*, p. 33.

46. *Times of India*, "Steps for Modernising Textile Industry Urged" (New Delhi), December 1985, p. 6.

47. In the 1985 Textile Policy, measures have been taken to give incentives to the mill sector to increase production and change in the product mix. Such measures include : (1) removal of curbs on creation of new loomage capacities by composite and spinning mills : (2) removal of curbs on manufacture of synthetic fabrics by the organised mills;

(3) imposition of access for rehabilitation of unemployed workers of closed mills; (4) extension of soft loans to mills, including Rs. 3.02 billion to the National Textile Corporation; and (5) reduction of duties of certain inputs like polyester staple fibres.

48. United Nations, *International Trade Statistics Yearbook*, Vol. II (New York, United Nations, 1985), pp. 488 and 489. Figures on cotton fabrics imports here stand for SITC 6521 plus SITC 6522.

49. *Financial Express*, "Textile Exports", May 3, 1985, p. 5.

50. A. Joshi, "New Textile Policy", in *Financial Express*, April 1, 1986, p. 4.

51. Japan's exports of cotton fabrics was depressed at US $ 195 million at the time of the first oil crisis, second-lowest in the post-war period. However, by exporting more of high quality cloth, it managed to increase exports in the late 1970s and recorded the all-time high export value at US $ 64.4 million in 1983, despite the declining trend of the world trade in this commodity.

52. S. Kathuria, and N. Taneja, *India's Exports: The Challenge from China* (New Delhi, ICRIER, 1986), pp. 98 and 99.

53. Ministry of Industry, Government of India, *Guidelines for Industries*, Part II (New Delhi, Indian Investment Centre, 1985), pp. 56-61.

54. As per notification S.O. 98(E)/IDRA/293/74/1 dated 16 February 1973, the following items of handtools were reserved for small scale sector: pliers, screw drivers, spanners, hammers, wrenches, chisels, pincers, handtools for black smithy, carpentry hand forging, foundry, etc.

55. *Ibid.*, p. 57.

56. A circular by the Engineering Export Promotion Council, 1985.

57. Imports figure on handtools here refer to SITC 6953 and 6954. The group constituting of 22 countries including, EEC, USA and Japan had imports of these products valued at US $3702.6 million and $ 3635.8 million in 1979 and 1983, respectively, which was approximately equivalent to 70 per cent of total import by market economies.

58. S. Kathuria and N. Taneja, *op.cit.*, pp. 68 and 69.

59. Ministry of Science and Technology, Government of India, *Technology in Indian Handtools Industry* (draft) (New Delhi, October 1985), pp. 5-12.

60. *Ibid.*, p. 6.

51. *Ibid.*, p. 7.

62. Indian Cotton Mills Federation, *Yearbook of Statistics on Cotton Textile Industries* (Bombay, 1986), p. 33.

63. *Ibid.*, p. 73.

64. Directorate General of Commercial Intelligence and Statistics, *Monthly Bulletin of Foreign Trade of India* (Calcutta), from various issues of 1975 to 1982.

65. See Chapter Four, p. 97.

66. Based on the average of minimum monthly earnings of the

lowest-paid operative in the cotton textile mills in Bombay, Ahmedabad, Indore, Tamil Nadu, West Bengal, Delhi, Bhavanagar and Kanpur for a standard month of 26 working days, which has been deflated by wholesale price index of mill-made cloth, from Office of Economic Adviser, Ministry of Industry, Government of India, *Revised Index Number of Wholesale Price in India* (New Delhi), from various issues of 1975 to 1985; Indian Cotton Mills Federation, *Indian Cotton Mills Federation Journal* (Bombay), August 1986, p. 67.

67. Derived from the statistics on output of mill-made cotton fabrics and labour engaged in composite mills of cotton textiles, which may be an underestimate of output worker in cotton fabrics weaving. *Ibid.*, pp. 33 and 68.

68. Wholesale price of cotton yarn of 20 counts. Textile Commissioner, Government of India, *Indian Textile Bulletin* (Bombay), from various issues of 1975-83.

69. Proxy of the output-input ratio for the cotton fabrics weaving has been taken as the ratio of output of cotton fabrics in the mill sector to the cotton fibres consumed by mills. The data on mill consumption of cotton fibres are from International Cotton Advisory Council, *Cotton World Statistics* Washington D.C., March 1983, p. 124.

70. The value of production in the handtools manufacturing sector are derived based on the actual figures in Ministry of Industry, Government of India, *Annual Reports* (New Delhi, Government of India, 1977, 1978, 1979 and 1980), which has been extended forward and backward using the production index published by Central Statistical Organisation, Government of India, in *Monthly Statistics of the Production of Selected Industries of India* (Calcutta), from issues of 1975, 1976, 1981 and 1982.

71. Engineering Export Promotion Council *Handbook of Export Statistics* (Calcutta), from various issues of 1976 to 1981.

72. Directorate General of Commercial Intelligence and Statistics, *Monthly Statistics of Foreign Trade of India. op. cit.*, from various issues of 1975 to 1982.

73. Wages paid to the worker engaged in the manufacture of handtools and general hardware (National Industrial Classification (1970) No. 343), taken as proxy from Central Statistical Organisation, Government of India, *Annual Survey of Industries* (Calcutta), from various issues of 1974-75 to 1980-81, which has been deflated by wholesale price index of metal products, from Office of the Economic Adviser, Ministry of Industry, Government of India, *Revised Index Number of Wholesale Price in India*, *op. cit.*, from various issues of 1975 to 1984.

74. Output value in the manufacture of handtools and general hardware deflated by the wholesale price index of metal products, which has been divided by number of labour engaged in the same manufacture.

75. See pp. 149-51.

76. D. Borkar, "Interest Burden on Industry", in *Economic Times*, April 5, 1986, p. 5.

77. *Ibid.*, p. 3. The following figures in this paragraph are also quoted from the same study.

78. Ministry of Commerce, Government of India, *Report of the Committee on Trade Policies* (New Delhi, 1984), p. 25.

79. *Ibid.*, pp. 15-16.

80. *Ibid.*, p. 82.

81. Ministry of Industry, Government of India, "Industrial Policy Statement, July 23, 1980", in *Guidelines for Industries*—Part I (New Delhi, Indian Investment Centre, 1982), pp. 41-52.

82. Entitlements available to 100 per cent export-oriented units and units in Free Trade Zones over other domestic units are : (1) duty free import of capital goods, components and raw materials under OGL. (2) tax holiday/investment allowance for the former units, investment allowance for the latter units; (3) exemption of excise duty and other levies for output and (4) exemption of excise duty, sales tax, etc. for inputs supplied locally to the units.

83. In case of units in Free Trade Zones, 25 per cent of rejects are allowed to be sold to domestic tariff areas against valid import licences, while in case of 100 per cent export-oriented units, 5 per cent of rejects are allowed to be sold unconditionally.

84. *Ibid.*, pp. 41-52.

85. See for details, Indian Investment Centre, *Liberalisation in Industrial Policy* (New Delhi, 1986), pp. 4-23.

86. Ministry of Commerce, Government of India, *Report of the Committee on Trade Policies* (New Delhi, 1984), p. 111.

87. *Ibid.*, p. 122.

88. For example, manufacture of industrial sewing machines have been exempted from licensing subject to certain conditions. See for detail, Indian Investment Centre, *Liberalisation in Industrial Policy*, *op. cit.* p. 5.

89. The first 100 per cent export-oriented unit for manufacture of grey cotton fabrics, a 70 million-rupees fully computerised project, was signed in 1985. The project was undertaken by a non-resident Indian in collaboration with a Hungarian company, which includes a buy-back agreement. See for details, *Times of India*, "100 per cent Textile Export Unit To Be Set Up", (New Delhi), p. 3.

90. For example, Gedore Tools, Hindustan Everest Tools and Taparia Tools among largest exporters of handtools in India, initially obtained the technology transfer from abroad. See for details, Engineering Export Promotion Council, *Hand Tool Industry Problems and Prospects* (New Delhi, 1985), p. 1.

91. An illustrative list of industries for which foreign collaboration may be considered was published by the Indian Investment Centre, includes bonded abrasives, cutting tools and tungusten carbide tipped tools among the product range of handtools. See for details, Indian Investment Centre, *Economic News Digest* (New Delhi), August 1982, p. 3.

92. Engineering Export Promotion Council, *Hand Tool Industry Problems and Prospects*, *op. cit.*, p. 8.

93. Press Information Bureau, Government of India, *Encouraging Trends in Export of Textiles* (New Delhi, July 1986), p. 1.

94. Engineering Export Promotion Council, *Hand Tool Industry : Problems and Prospects*, *op. cit.*, p. 4.

95. UNCTAD, *Operation and Effects of Generalized Scheme of Preferences—Scheme for Japan* (TD/B/GSP/Japan/5) (Geneva, 1984), p. 3.

96. UNCTAD, *Operation and Effects of Generalized Scheme of Preferences—Scheme for Japan* (TD/B/C.5/Japan/10) (Geneva, 1985), p.2.

97. *Ibid.*, p. 3.

98. *Ibid.*, p. 4.

99. Japan Tariff Association, *Tariff Schedules of Japan* (Tokyo, Japan Tariff Association, 1986), p. 89.

100. *Ibid.*, p, 91.

101. UNCTAD, *Operation and Effects of Generalized Scheme of Preference—Scheme for Japan* (TD/B/GSP/Japan/5), *op. cit.*, p. 16.

102. The ceiling which existed separately for cotton yarn (55.05-2(2)) and cotton fabrics other than gauze and terry towelling (55.09) were lifted after 1980. However, the ceiling remained to be imposed for all the other items of BTN Chapter 55.

103. UNCTAD, *Operation and Effects of Generalized Scheme of Preferences—Scheme for Japan* (TD/B/C-5/Japan/8) (Geneva, 1985), p. 2.

104. UNCTAD, *Operation and Effects of Generalized Scheme of Preferences—Scheme for Japan* (TD/B/C.5/Japan/10), *op. cit.*, p. 9.

105. *Ibid.*, p. 3.

106. Federation of Indian Chambers of Commerce and Industry, *Report—Eighteenth Joint Meeting of the Business Cooperation Committees of India and Japan* (New Delhi, 1986), p. 23.

107. *Ibid.*, p. 24.

108. From a data file of Trade Development Authority of India, New Delhi.

109. *Ibid.*

7

JAPAN'S TECHNOLOGY TRANSFER AND INVESTMENT IN INDIA'S INDUSTRIAL AND FOREIGN TRADE DEVELOPMENT

INDIA'S export constraints to Japan emanate from the fact that considerations of increasing exports on an enduring basis have not received adequate attention since the evolution of India's economic and industrial policies. In the field of industrial development and foreign investment, import substitution has had the leading role. These policies have, no doubt, resulted in considerable expansion and diversification of the industrial base, but in the process consideration of cost and comparative efficiency have often been given inadequate attention. For achieving a high rate of growth in exports and sustaining them over a long period, India's basic economic policies need to be reviewed and changed, where necessary, to encourage not merely growth but growth with efficiency.

In this chapter, we shall first summarise the findings of the study from the previous chapters to identify the constraints that affected enhancement of trade-growth with Japan. Subsequently to assist in strengthening India's production base for manufactured exports, technology transfer and investments from Japan are suggested. To frame a suitable scenario of trading in commodities and technologies between the two countries, it is imperative to examine the major changes in India's industrial policies in 1980s and the role of foreign investment in India's industrial development in addition to India's foreign investment policy, trends in India-Japan industrial collaboration and the influence of yen on Japanese investments in India.

Principal Findings

The result of the analysis in this study can be summarised as follows :

—India's trade with Japan has been characterised with the former exporting non-manufactures to the latter while importing manufactures from it. A major part of India's non-manufactured exports to Japan consisted of iron ore, frozen shrimps, raw cotton and vegetable oil cakes. Iron ore, the most important export item to Japan by India during 1950s to 1980s, constituted half to one-third of India's exports to Japan. India's exports of iron ore, however, has faced with increasing competition from other countries in the Japanese market such of Australia and Brazil, both of which offer competitive prices due to their efficient loading and handling transportation systems. In addition, the price of iron-ore has also been falling. In the most recent concluded agreement between MMTC and Japanese steel mills, the level of exports by India in 1986 would be maintained with an assurance that Japan might import an additional 1.5 million tonnes in 1987, with a five per cent cut in price.[1] On the other hand, it is found that India's exports of shrimps is likely to be under supply constraints in the long run. Imports of shrimps from India has been stagnating at the level of $225 million since 1983 and further exports dependent upon development of deep sea-fishing as well as prawn culture.[2] Short-term price fluctuations also has created obstruction to the steady growth of exports.

- From the point of view of stabilization of export earnings in the long run and industrialization through exports, it is suggested to diversify the export structure by stepping up exports of manufactures.
- Japan's expanding market for manufactures also had provided opportunities for India's exports. However it was observed that India's exports of manufactures such as cotton fabrics and handtools, despite the comparative advantage in cost that Indian industries have with respect to labour, was not able to improve its export competitiveness due to low output per worker offsetting it. India's manufacturing industries should not rely solely on low wages, but rather should raise productivity to enhance industry's competitiveness. Also, in case of cotton fabrics exports, India's cost advantage in raw materials have not been reflected in its competitiveness due to low output-input ratio.
- Japan's imports of manufactures steadily expanded following implementation of import liberalisation measures in the 1960s and the GSP in the 1970s. In particular, the GSP scheme provided an enlarged market for developing countries to export manufactures to Japan. Those countries among NICs such as South Korea and Taiwan subsequently took this opportunity to expand manufactured exports to Japan, by raising productivity and advantage in low labour cost.
- Technology transfer from Japan is useful for increasing exports of manufactures from India, as it could raise the standard of technology used by Indian industries. Another benefit India could have derived by technology transfer would have been the transfer of modern equipment and buy-back agreements, which would have brought about a greater opportunity for two-way trade expansion with the technology-transferring country.
- India's industrial collaborations with Japan in the field of manufacturing industries such as cotton textiles and handtools have been very insignificant. As of June 1985, there were only three cases of technology transfer to India in the field of handtools production, while there have been no cases of collaboration in cotton fabrics weaving.[3] The

greater industrial cooperation with Japan in these fields by means of technology transfer and investment would help India to expand and diversify exports to Japan.

Widening India's Production Base for Manufactured Exports

Competitiveness of India's exports is in a significant way influenced by the cost structure of export industries. Improvement in competitiveness by reduction in cost can be realised by reducing factor prices such as wages and prices of raw materials and fuels and by increasing productivity with respect to various inputs such as output per worker and output-input ratio.

Although factor prices are determined by the factor endowment position or the socio-economic structure and so on, realisation of productivity is achieved only by technology and economies of scale. In general, the more sophisticated the technology is, the larger economies of scale is required for commercial viability. In this connection, it is imperative for Indian industries to explore the possibility of utilising demand in the domestic economy when adequate demand to sustain the capital capacity is not expected to be obtained in the markets abroad and vice-versa when introduction of new technology is considered. In case of India's manufactured exports, the possibility of incorporating domestic demand for market for its products is larger.

Thus the strategy to improve competitiveness of exports should be integrated with that for the overall industrial growth. It is found that India's export incentive scheme has been more oriented to maintaining profitability of exports through subsidies for example, rather than to improvement of productivity. The thrust of export promotion policies should be more toward technological upgradation of the industries by means of technology transfer and application of research on the existing technology.

Moreover India's technological needs and imports of foreign technology for its industries need to be carefully assessed. Import of technology per se is not a sufficient condition to the technological advancement of an industry. Of critical importance is the ability to build the capacity and the infrastructure to absorb and further develop imported technology, Innovation, indeed, is the key and this is where India has not developed adequately. Technology imports have been by and large confined to absorption and adaption of the technology to suit the needs of the domestic market. Rarely have the firms gone in for further innovation and advancement of the imported technology. Repetitive technology has become a trend rather than an exception. At the same time, such imports have failed to stimulate exports as Indian exports have been unable to match the technology offered by other countries on the global market. The Fourth Survey on foreign collaborations in Indian industry conducted by the RBI[4] has found that such companies have become a drain on the country's foreign exchange with their total export earnings being much less than their imports.

It is perhaps, with these factors in mind that Government of India in 1982 made R & D activities obligatory for firms entering into foreign collaborations which involve payments in excess of Rs. 20 million. But it is doubtful whether the policy will show the desired results. What will play a crucial role is the gradual removal of controls on domestic front which can unleash competitive forces in the country.[5] Liberal imports of technology in a licence permit regime can only lead to foreign exchange losses. Another factor of importance is the restriction on the terms that Indian firms are allowed to offer for technology imports and the duration of collaboration agreements. Despite the discretion which authorities have in permitting departures from the norms, Indian firms are unable at times to get the best technological package surely because of their inability to offer terms acceptable to the suppliers. Greater flexibility in this respect may bring about an improvement in the quality of technology imports and save foreign exchange in the long run.

Major Industrial Policy Changes in 1980s

From the review of industrial policy between 1949 and 1980, it can be observed that the successive policy statements, enunciating Government policies in the field of industrialization, were strong on statements of goals or objectives but were not effective with regard to the operating strategy, and there was, virtually, no regular mechanism for the appraisal of policies.[6] There was also a certain amount of reluctance to make major changes in policies. As a result over years, the gap between objectives and achievements, between what was intended and what actually happened and between what the particular policy instruments were supposed to achieve, and what, in fact, they achieved continued to widen. The trend in India's industrial policies before 1980 could be summed up in the words of Bhagwati and Desai. . . . "Indian planning for industrialisation suffered from excessive attention to targets down to product level and a wasteful physical approach to setting and implementation thereof, alongwith a generally inefficient framework of policies designed to regulate the growth of industrialisation. India did not plan too much; in certain important ways it just planned inadequately. Physical, cost-benefit ignoring and choice-negligent planning, combined with detailed regulation of such inefficiently-determined targets really proved to be a negation of national planning."[7]

The policy changes in recent years have emanated from two basic considerations. In the first place Government of India appreciated that export competitiveness was really a production problem and what is needed is to provide the necessary inputs which could help increase production, and export could be carried on without, in any way, affecting the domestic market.

Secondly, the Government of India appreciated that export operation cannot be carried on for long unless export is an economic proposition to the exporting industry. Arising out of these two motivations a series of steps were taken aimed at increase in production on the one hand and compensation to exporting industries for various disabilities caused because of imposition of taxes, octrois and disparities in the rate of interest etc. The policy decisions calculated to increase production include:

— automatic expansion of capacity by 25% in five years for a range of industries. This expansion was in addition to the normal permissible expansion by 25% of the approved capacity.

- treating export production outside the licensed capacity.
- extending free-trade zone facility to 100 per cent export oriented units.
- Liberalisation in import policy with the object of expanding production.
- Removal of certain restraints on the MRTP units by treating export production outside the limit,
- Raising the limit of investment of small scale industries from Rs. 1 million to Rs. 2 million and ancillary units from Rs. 1.5 million to Rs. 2.5 million.
- Liberalisation of procedure for import of technology by export oriented units,

As regards schemes aimed at compensating the exporter for various disabilities of taxes, levies and disparities in interest rates, the following schemes have been introduced:

- Cash Compensatory Support by way of refund of sales tax, octrois and other disadvantages.
- Refund of import and excise duties by way of duty draw back.
- Reimbursement of difference between domestic and international prices of pig iron and steel.
- Duty free import of raw materials going into production of items for export.
- Export finance at concessional rate of interest.
- Relift under section 80 HHC of Income Tax Act.

The Government of India has created two very important high level committees—viz., Cabinet Committee on Exports headed by the Prime Minister himself and an Empowered Committee on exports headed by Cabinet Secretary. These Committees take high level decisions to promote export. During 1987 some unprecedented decisions have been taken to make export more competitive and remunerative. Some of the important decisions are as follows:

- Import of Capital goods which are not indigenously available would be allowed at low rates of duties for thrust industries with high export potential. These proposals would be considered on a case basis.

- International Price Reimbursement Scheme for steel has been extented to cover alloy steel and aluminium. Schemes are being worked out for other materials which account for significant part of the cost of the production. It has been decided that consumable and process accessories would also be treated in the similar manner as raw material for supply at international price if they form a high percentage of cost structure.
- Scheme has been announced by the financial institutions for providing interest rebate of 20% on all new term loans for units which export more than 25% of their output. This scheme has come into effect from December 1, 1986.
- A decision in principle has been taken to allow exporters to use 5-10 per cent of their foreign exchange earnings for prescribed promotional activities.
- It has been decided in principle to allow exporters to pay agency commission abroad based on the prevailing international trade practice for specific products in specific countries.
- It has been decided in principle to provide debt equity ratio of 4 : 1 for export oriented units as against 1.5 : 1.

There may still be some areas requiring improvement but by and large the existing policy framework should provide sufficient inducement for industries to increase production and improve the quality of their products.

After having examined India's industrial policy changes in 1980s, let us examine the role of Japanese investment in strengthening India's industrial production and export base.

Technology Transfer and Foreign Investment as Catalyst for Trade Development

There is a considerable controversy about the relative costs and benefits of foreign investment to developing countries. The principal argument in its favour is that the package of capital and technological and managerial resources generally increases and real domestic income of the host country by more than the profits returned to the investor. This increase is manifested in higher tax revenues, higher labour incomes or lower prices. Moreover, since profits are earned only when the investment earns a positive return, part of the risk is borne by the foreign investor. Nevertheless, the association of foreign investment with some degree of overseas managerial control and generally with large foreign companies, can have wide-ranging effects on the economy of the host developing country. Concern that some of the activities of the enterprise might have adverse consequences for a country's development prospects may lead to the adoption of restrictive policies toward foreign investment. This concern has been reinforced by dissatisfaction with some of the results of earlier investments.

In assessing the overall effects of foreign investment, however, it is relevant that many of the principal benefits and costs can be substantially affected by the economic policies of the host country. If these are inappropriate, the investment will also be inappropriate and of less benefit to the economy. The foreign investors themselves can also help to ensure that the foreign investment process is naturally beneficial by co-operating with a host country's chosen development strategy and showing willingness, where necessary, to consider alternative arrangements, such as joint ventures and minority equity participation.

While foreign technology can play an effective part in the development process, effective utilisation of technologies acquired from abroad rests significantly with the host country. Where the need to import technology is established, every effort should be made to ensure that it is of the appropriate level, consistent with requirements and resources. The technology import should be so planned by the host country as to have effective transfer of basic knowledge (know-how) and to facilitate further advancement.

Technology transfer do result in increased outflow of foreign exchange on account of payment of royalties, technical fee etc. and rise in imports of machinery and components. In short run, it implies increased dependence on imports with consequent implications for balance of payments. The outflow of foreign exchange is reversed only when industrial development resulting from technology transfer enables the country to enlarge the industrial base through backward and forward linkages and enhances the country's export capabilities. These expectations can materialise only when foreign technology is fully assimilated and adapted to meet the requirements of industry in the host country,

There are major differences among countries in the degree to which foreign investment can be substituted for other forms of foreign capital inflow. The differences in substitutability are the result both of variation in economic structure that affect countries' attractiveness to investors and differences in the underlying micro-economic causes of the need for capital inflow. Continued with small internal markets, few natural resources, a relatively underdeveloped infrastructure and limited possibilities for manufactured exports may not be able to attract substantial foreign investment, even with liberal regulations and generous incentives. Such countries are also not able to borrow significantly on commercial terms and must rely primarily on concessional borrowing. Consequently the possibilities for substitution between overseas commercial borrowing and foreign investment mainly concern countries that are longer, better endowed with natural resources or that have more developed industrial sector.

Trade Linked Investment

One of the effects of foreign investment on the host country is the transmission of business fluctuations of the investing country. The transmission of fluctuations are more intense if the foreign investment is in the form of vertical integration, rather than horizontal integration, which is found to be preferred by Japanese companies. K. Kojima finds in his study on Japan's foreign investment in the ten countries of Asia and Pacific developing region, that changes in the industrial structure of host countries induced by Japanese investment are crucial link between foreign investment and other effects imparted by it including trade structure and flow between Japan and its investee countries during the period between 1972 and 1982.[8] He first identified the positive correlation between the amount of foreign investment by Japan into the sample countries and its pattern of the sectoral allocation. Then another correlation was established between the pattern of Japanese foreign investment and the structure of domestic output in the investee countries. Finally, the structure of domestic output in countries receiving Japanese investment was also correlated with their trade structure and flows with Japan. By virtue of the induction process, he reached a conclusion regarding the positive correlation between the level and the pattern of Japan's foreign investment and those of trade structure and level of its investee countries.

The above analysis clearly indicates the strong correlation existing between Japan's foreign investment and trade. Industrial collaboration with Japan in the form of technology transfer and investment if directed in the industries where Japan is losing comparative advantage could enhance trade flow between India and Japan.

Foreign Investment Policy of India

Foreign investment in India dates back to the years of the East India Company. Initially, it came in the form of loans to Government, railway companies, public utilities companies engaged in the plantation of tea and coffee and the agro-based industries like cotton and jute, which processed raw material for export. During this period, there was no conscious efforts to provide economic and financial infrastructure necessary for industrialisation and, therefore, foreign investors had hardly any incentive to invest in manufacturing industries in India except for creating a raw-material base.

After the First World War boom, India granted protection to nascent industries. The high profitability of industries thus attracted more and more foreign capital. The inflow of British capital which was only \$ 15 million in 1913-14, increased to a level of \$ 29 million in 1921 and \$ 36 million in 1922. Between the two World Wars, the investment flowed into a number of consumer industries like cigarettes, matches, rubber, tyres, paints, chemical industries, paper, cement, textile, leather, sugar etc. During the Second World War, the Government encouraged the setting up of new industries in India both to replace imports and to support war efforts. It was during this period that the foreign investment had diversified and channelled into light engineering industries as well as general purpose workshops, chemical industry and oil sector with defence orientation.

By 1948, the foreign private investment in India was estimated to be around Rs. 2.5 billion. Of which 21 per cent was in the manufacturing industries, 16 per cent in plantation, 4 per cent in mining, 27 per cent in trading and 14 per cent in banking. Within the manufacturing sector, more than 50 per cent of the foreign capital was invested in jute, cotton and rubber industries and around 10 per cent in iron and steel and other hardware industries.

India's foreign investment policy was for the first time enunciated on 6 April, 1949. The guiding principles of the policy were even today continue to be:

—All undertakings—Indian or foreign—had to conform to the general requirements of the Government's industrial policy;

—Foreign enterprises would be treated on par with Indian enterprises.

—Foreign enterprises would have freedom for remittance of profits and repatriation of capital, subject to foreign exchange considerations.

—If foreign enterprises were compulsorily acquired, compensation would be paid on a fair and equitable basis; and

—As a rule, the major interest, ownership and effective control of an undertaking should be in Indian hands.

The above policy was to govern the entry of fresh foreign investment into India in future, but it was silent on regulation of existing foreign private investment in Indian industry. It was only in 1973 that legislative measures were taken to cope up with the problem posed by the existing foreign owned companies. This was done by amending the Foreign Exchange Regulation Act (FERA), in 1973 which regulated the entry and channelised the growth of existing foreign investment into the country. Until then, the foreign companies continued to grow, expand and diversify their activities in their own way, until they were required to induct fresh foreign capital, which required Government clearance.

In 1980s special incentives and concessions have been granted to the industrial units that export major part of the production. The normal limit of 40 per cent foreign equity is not applicable to export-oriented units. A higher percentage of foreign equity is permissible in units that export a minimum of 60 per cent of their total output. The higher the export, the higher will be the permissible percentage of foreign equity. In wholly export-oriented units, foreign equity up to 100 per cent is allowed.

Units set up in the 6 Free Trade Zones of the country are also given special consideration in the matter of foreign collaboration. Foreign entrepreneurs can set up fully owned units in these zones. While the Santa Cruz Electronics Export Processing Zone (SEEPZ) is meant exclusively for electronics industries, the other Zones, i.e., in Madras, Cochin, Noida, Falta and Kandla, are open to all types of industrial units. The units in these Zones enjoy a number of tax and other concessions. India has announced complete tax exemption in respect of the income derived by the units established in the Free Trade Zones for a period of 5 years from the initial assessment year. As a further incentive India has now allowed units in these Zones to sell up to 25% of their output in the domestic tariff area to valid import licence holders.

In the case of 100 per cent units, it can be set up anywhere in India. They enjoy all the facilities provided to the units located in the free trade zones except that they are not allowed an initial 5 year tax holiday. In turn, they have been allowed a number of other incentives admissible to other exporting units. For streamlining the units working and dealing with various organisations and Government agencies, such units have been issued Green Cards. A Green Card holder unit gets an overriding priority in the allotment of various inputs and facilities.

Various incentives have been provided to other categories of exporting units. The exporting units are provided with REP licences, cash compensatory support, air freight subsidy, duty drawbacks, advance licences, foreign collaboration facility, market development assistance, and deduction on export turnover.

India-Japan Industrial Collaboration

India was one of the first countries in which Japan invested in the post-war period. In the 1950s there was Japanese investment in India for fishing trawlers, sheet glass making, manufacture of refrigeration facilities and fountain pens. In the 1960s Japanese investment in India was directed to import substitution manufacturing industries such as rayon, wire-ropes, bicyle chains, wall tiles, electric motors, transformers and bearings. In the 1970s when Japan's current account of international balance of payments moved firmly into surplus, there was a rapid increase in Japanese investment world-wide. However, this strong growth was not reflected in Japanese investment in India. Investment in a small measure flowed to industries undertaking manufacture of dry cell batteries, agricultural tillers, hydraulic pumps and valves. Even though this investment did not represent much in absolute amounts, they still made no small contribution to the Indian economy.

In early 1980s Japanese investment in India has seemingly broken with past pattern. In 1982, M/s. Suzuki, one of the largest manufactures of passenger cars in the world, collaborated with M/s. Maruti Udyog Ltd. of India in the public sector for the manufacturers of passenger cars in India with equity participation and transfer of technology. The joint company is manufacturing passenger cars micro-buses, pick-up vans, jeep etc.[9] Another encouraging feature is the spurt in approved collaborations with Japanese automakers. Almost all the leading Japanese auto-manufacturers have already tied-up with Indian leading industrialists for collaboration in automotive industry. The attractiveness of the Indian investment market also prompted Japanese auto-ancillary manufacturers for collaboration with India.

Industrial collaborations between India and Japan started in 1950s with a solitary approval for collaboration with Japan in 1951, the number of collaborations increased to 15 (8.2% of the total approvals) in 1970, 34 (65%) in 1980, 108 (10.5%) in 1985 and reached 111 (11.6%) collaborations in 1986. Cumulative collaborations approved with all foreign countries between 1957 to 1986 were 10,617 cases and out of which 970 (9.1%) cases were approved with Japan. Table 7.1 shows the trends in India's collaboration and investment approvals with major industrialised countries.

Japan had also participated in India's 100% export-oriented scheme (EOU) as well as in the free trade zones. In the 100% EOU scheme the items cover like; disc type ceramic capacitors and feed through type ceramic, opthalmic lens, skip jack fish with processing of marine products, xylited polyalcohols, colour TV receiver, domestic and industrial sewing machines, needles, etc. Between 1981 and 1986 there were 18 units set up by Japan. Similarly there have been some units set up with Japanese collaborations in the Free Trade Zones.

When we compare Japan's transfer of technology and investment in India with other countries, India occupies a very small position representing only 0.1 per cent of that in the whole of Asia. About 55.8 per cent of Japanese technology from medium and large firms were exported to developing countries. According to a study by Shoji Ito,[10] ESCAP developing countries were the most important among them, their share being nearly 40 per cent, in spite of the fact that Japanese exports to North America had increased in 1980-81, ESCAP countries, particularly eastern and south eastern countries occupy a larger share of Japan's technology exports.

Taiwan's and South Korea's dependence upon Japan's technology especially high-technology collaborations with Japan were about 65 per cent of Taiwan's total collaborations in 1962-82 and 55 per cent of South Korea's in 952-83. India's share was 0.8 per cent in terms of the number of agreements. Japan's share in Indian technology imports was 6.5 per cent in 1980, 8.6 per cent in 1982 and 11.6 per cent in 1986 in terms of number of new agreements.

A detailed summary of Japanese technology export to India and other Asian developing countries are shown in Table 7.2. Japan's technology export to India by industry is indicated in Table 7.3. These figures explain the number of cases of technology transfer and investment actually made by Japanese

Japanese companies in various industries in India between 1973 and 1984 fiscal years.

The passive attitude of Japanese companies towards investing in India reflect:[11] first, that the Indian market is a minor one for the Japanese firms and that most of them have no base of their own in India; second, that the companies do not consider India as an attractive market for their technology exports; and third, they rely on General Trading Companies as intermediaries. The constraints that Japan feels are:[12] (1) restriction on foreign equity ratio (2) restriction on the repatriation of royalties (3) high tax rate on royalties and (4) bureaucratic and procedural delays which affect every stage of management including time consuming procedure for remittances to foreign countries or insurance of working visas for foreigners (6) problem steming from deficiencies in infrastructures such as supply of electricity or water, communication, road and transport (6) plans of hasty indigenisation of the products together with immediate ancillary industries.

Based on the technology transfer trends in 1980s to India, Japan also feels that the whole process of transfer to the Indian industries was not smooth thus causing difficulties and unique situations.[13] It is attributed to the perception gap between Japanese and Indian industrialists on the nature of technology transfer and the process of transfer. Moreover the software part of production has become increasingly important in modern manufacturing and it is important for India to emphasies on the software part of technology as it assists in the smooth transfer of technology by assimilating into Indian conditions. The adjustment or assimilation has to be seriously pursued by Indian entrepreneurs and engineers so that the process of indigenisation programmed could be achieved.[14]

There are some cases of technology transfer from Japan where it has proved successful. They may be considered worthy of emulation in future collaboration efforts. According to a Report of the Japan Committee[15] of the India-Japan Study Committee, the following conditions should be satisfied for successful Indo-Japanese collaborations:

—Since technology transfer between companies is

implemented on commercial basis, any technical collaboration should bring profits to both the partners concerned;

—Technology is transferred through a long period of human contact, in the course of which both parties should try to understand each other's circumstances and ideas, deepening mutual trust; and

—Most importantly, technology transfer should certainly lead to technical improvement on the part of the recipient. It would be ideal if the recipient could learn how to properly maintain the transferred technology, and in particular, how to modify and improve the technology at its own initiative according to changes in socio-economic conditions and needs in India.

While acquisition of Japanese technology has benefited Indian economy in a number of ways, such as broadening the industrial base, rise in output and improvement in quality, in a number of cases the results have not been commensurate with the expectations. According to a Report of the India Committee[16] of the India-Japan Study Committee, some of the problems faced by Indian collaborators are rigid approach of Japanese collaborators, inadequate guidance in implementing the projects, high prices for components, strong preference for Japanese machinery and component, casual attitude towards training, indifference towards programmes of indigenisation, export and research and development and restrictions of diffusion of technology. According to the India Committee of the India-Japan Study Committee,[17] Indian companies need assistance in:

—accelerating indigenisation process making companies self-reliant to the maximum possible extents;

—increasing productivity particularly at shop floor level by inducting the proven Japanese methods;

—enhancing the effectiveness of training programmes for Indian technicians, whether in India or Japan;

—assimilating technology through more detailed guidance and technical documentation;

—developing ancillaries for making intermediates and components;
—exporting to Japan and elsewhere including markets not permitted under the agreement;
—keeping Indian companies informed of latest developments in respective fields;
—setting up Research and Development facilities.

Perspective of Trading in Technologies and Commodities

There has been considerable thinking of how the Japanese policies are going to shape with the developing countries. A closer answer to this question can be seen in the Japan's Economic Planning Agency's "Long-term Outlook Committee's Report" entitled *Japan in the year 2000* and subtitled "Preparing Japan for an Age of Internationalisation, Aging Society and Maturity."[18]

The Report pointed out that economic relations with developing countries will become increasingly closer and increasingly inter-dependent as Japan develops. Although this was not so important when Japan was a minor factor in the world economy, it is imperative that Japan harmonises its policies now that Japan has come to have a major impact on the rest of the international community. Able to export massive amount of manufactured products in the past, Japanese companies must now join with companies in developing countries to share in the profits, promote joint technological development and expand employment opportunity everywhere.

The Report also mentions of Japan's concern of population aging. In 1960 only 5 per cent of the population was 65 years old or older. In 1985 it was 10 per cent and by the year 2000 it is expected to be over 15 per cent. While many other industrialised countries currently have aged population ratios of 13 per cent to 14 per cent, Japan is expected to overtake these countries and to have the highest aged population ratio in the world by the start of 21st Century. Moreover the Japanese population centre is aging about 3 times as fast in the United States and Europe and this has major implications for the Japanese economy and society.

The third major long-term issue for Japan is that of industrial restructuring based on the influence of the strong Yen. Some people predict a shift to more science and technology intensive industry, others the onset on the information society and still others a greater role for the service sector. In *Japan in the Year 2000* it was predicted that the three economic sectors employment percentages would go from 10 per cent primary, 35 per cent secondary and 55 per cent teritiary in 1980 to 5 per cent, 33 per cent and 62 per cent respectively by the year 2000 as the percentage of labour force employed in production drops and the percentage in service sector takes up the slack.

It is expected that the Japanese economy will strive further for energy conservation to contain the growth in its import of energy resources, which was commenced after first oil crisis. The strategy for energy conservation requires the more efficient use of energy in the economy as well as relocation of energy using industries abroad. This has had an inevitable consequence to the structure of the Japanese economy, in which the emphasis on resource allocation and growth has been shifted to assembling industries and the technology-intensive sector.

At the same time, as a surplus continued to be recorded in its trade balance in 1980s, Japan has been required to take more initiative in expanding imports in the international economy. Integrating above two trends in the Japanese economy, it is more likely that Japan would further expand imports, particularly of products with lower technological sophistication.

The strategy called as 'international division of labour' to transform the Japanese economy more based on the knowledge-intensive sector presupposes the involvement of catching-up countries to specialise in the operations at the other end of the technological development. It is up to the catching-up developing economies to apprehend implications of the structural change in the Japanese economy and respond to the policies and incentives set out in this regard.

The trend in the Japanese economy in the late 1980s suggests that Japan has already started to move vigorously to expand trade and investment cooperation with the developing world.

Keidanren (Japan Federation of Economic Organisations) has also issued a set of proposals, on February 19, 1987 to the Government of Japan to internationalise Japanese economy and in support of free trade regime.[19] It also recommended for expansion of imports and the promotion of overseas investment and of technology exchange.

With the massive trade surpluses, Japan has been also faced with international pressure to play an international role commensurate with the increased size of its economy. To demonstrate both at home and overseas its intention to fulfil its true obligation, Japan announced on May 27, 1987 emergency economic measures[20] by vigorously expanding the economy centering on domestic demand and to rectify its external imbalances and thus to formulate more harmonious external economic relations. These measures are to facilitate transformation of Japan's economic structure into one led by domestic demand, as well as improving quality of Japanese life. One of the most significant pillars of the package is further expansion of imports and improvement of market access. Under this package, there are measures to specially import manufactured goods. To support its import expansion and improvement of market access programme, a special and extraordinary budgetary provision has been made in the supplementary budget to realise the additional import of foreign manufactured goods through the Government procurement totalling about $1 billion. The Government of Japan is also making efforts to have the private sector import more manufactured goods, with timely follow-up activities.

In view of the mounting debts and depressed commodity prices of the developing countries, Japan plans at a positive contribution to the international community, to enhance the flow of capital and technology needed by these countries and also the necessary budgetary provisions are being made for these measures.

Japan also is seeking to promote financial flows to the developing countries, especially those in debts, by recycling more than $ 20 billion in new and completely united funds over the next three years by way of making contributions to the

Multilateral Development Banks and mobilising the resources of Export-Import Bank of Japan, Overseas Economic Cooperation Fund and the private sector.

To further promote the technology transfer from Japan to the developing countries, technical cooperation like despatching of experts is being enhanced markedly drawing upon private sector resources as well. International Research and Development Cooperation is also being expanded to utilise research institutions both in Japan and overseas.

While making efforts to move up the targets in the third medium term ODA expansion programme, Japan plans at least to advance the original seven year doubling target by two years and make ODA disbursements in 1990 more than double $ 7.6 billion.

Comparing with the decades of 1950s, 1960s and 1970s, the 1980s witnessed a larger inflow of Japanese technology transfer and investment into India particularly into some sophisticated areas. The industries that benefits will be able to upgrade its production efficiency and international competitiveness and also assist in shifting the pattern of trade. Industrial collaboration that were approved with Japan since 1980s in the manufacturing industries were: light commercial vehicles and passenger cars, mini 4 wheel tractors; auto ancillaries such as engine valves, tie-rod ends, auto-electrical, shock absorbers, piston rings, control cables for automobiles, pistons, clutch assemblies for 2-wheelers; communication equipment; electronic components such as: ceramic capacitors, polyester film capacitors, hard ferrites, electrolytic capacitors, carbon film resisters, watch crystals, colour T.V. picture tubes, quartz timing movements, cement variable resistors, T.V. deflection components, magnetic heads; machine tools such as metal cutting and grinding machines, automatic heat strapping machine, radial drilling machine, semi-automatic clamping machine; electrical equipments such as: moulded case circuit breakers, special types of cables, miniature button type batteries for watches, electric motors; steel forgings/forged rolls, steel castings, industrial machinery such as: chemical plant and equipment accessories, procalcinator, tunnel and shuttle kilns for ceramic industry;

electronic equipment such as : mini computer based acquisition system, high power amplifier systems, digital electronic watches, water meters, rotary heremetic compressors, etc.

The non-engineering collaborations with Japan include: hydroquinone and by-products; clay-refractories graphite stoppers, basic refractories, etc.; hydrogen peroxide; chloromethanes; mica paper based on mechanical disintegration process; 18 per cent hydro flurosilic acid; caustic soda; acrylamide and polyacrylemide; fish meal, fish oil etc.; glass wool; spun silk yarn; plain sheet glass; kitazin; KWM viscose staples fibre; natural rubber latex contraceptives; L. Cyatine and amino acid powder; refractories for sliding gate system, magnesia-graphite bricks etc.; cyazoccrylete adhesives, anearobic adhesives etc.; madrine made glass beeds, oil well cement; compound glue, etc.

Some of the areas in which India is keen and where Japanese could transfer technology, *inter alia*, include digital microwave, UHF; digital MUX; computer systems in the range of supermini-midi and main frame; computer peripherals such as laser printer, optical disc storage, microfische reader/printer etc.; distributed digital control systems; micro-packaging technology, auto ancillaries, particularly pistons and carburetors; selected industrial machinery, particularly in the fields of metallurgical machinery, machine tools and machinery for the electronics industry; optics and optical instruments like cameras, optical glass blanks etc.; electro-mechanical and electronic products—like, two-way communication equipments including portable telephones etc.; high technology electronic components and sub-assemblies—like multi-layer capacitors, multi-layer PCB's, semi-conductor devices, consumer electronic components, video tapes etc.; automation systems including robotics.

The study on the trend of India's trade with Japan in the post-war period has shown that there existed a larger scope for bilateral trade-growth between the two countries than actually achieved. Assuming the state of technological and economic development in India in the 1980s, a further shift in the pattern of the pattern of the industrial production and the structure of the economy could bring about a corresponding change in India's pattern of trade with Japan.

Japan's trade policy in the 1980s is likely to be largely influenced by the factors such as the structural change of the economy with more weightage poised towards more capital-intensive and knowledge-intensive sector. Also, expansion of the volume of trade, accumulation of foreign exchange reserves would exert more pressure on the domestic economy for positive use of import policies for betterment of the quality of living. And there would be a further change in the import structures from raw materials to manufactures, particularly to labour-intensive products.

To facilitate overseas investment, the Japanese Government has also started taking various measures in such areas as finance, taxation and information services to offset the heavy burdens and enormous risks entailed in investing in overseas market. Overseas investment by Japanese companies has been further liberalised. Such investment, however, fulfils an important role by helping to create cmployment opportunities and raise technological standards in host countries. It is also a key to solving Japan's balance of payment imbalance.

From late 1980s Japan offers enormous potential in India's international trade and its imports of manufactures[21] particularly is expected to rise faster. The size of Japan's GNP in 1986, was twice the size as that of the Federal Republic of Germany and approximately three times as large as that of UK or France. With the liberalisation of India's economic and fiscal policies, prospects for more technology transfer and investment have become brighter. Japan has become encouraged in India's liberalisation of economic policies to 1980s and it is showing increasing interest and also becoming more confident of technology transfer and investment in India. When technology transfer and investment flow increase on a larger scale to Indian manufacturing industries, a new trading scenario would emerge based on a new set of commodities and technologies enabling India to enhance trade growth with Japan and bring down the trade gap between the two countries in the coming years.

Thus the main problem for India and Japan moving into the

21 century seems to be how the horizontal division of labour can promote industrial dynamism in both the countries. With India's developing industrial and rich labour resources along with the increasing purchasing power and with Japan's capital and technological strengths, the potential is obvious. If India and Japan continuously make efforts and pool their strengths together, they can make economic cooperation mutually beneficial and also may accomplish their endeavour to scale new heights by the 21st century.

REFERENCES

1. "Japan sees scope for direct investment", *Business Standard* (Calcutta), 4 April 1987, p. 1.

2. *Ibid.*

3. Japanese textile firms are keen on having tie-ups with Indian mills to manufacture cotton fabrics and export not only to Japan but also to Europe. A Japanese team consisting of representatives from textile mills and trading houses that visited India in May 1987, also claimed that they have developed a very high quality fabrics from Indian cotton. They are not only prepared for technology transfer to India but also ready for financial investment. See "Japanese Companies keen on tie-ups", *Economic Times* (New Delhi), 1 May 1987.

4. See Reserve Bank of India, *Foreign Collaboration in Indian Industry—Fourth Survey Report*, 1985, Bombay.

5. The Planning Commission Government of India, has prepared a discussion paper on India's new industrial policy for the 'Eight Five Year Plan' where it suggests that the licensing system be retained only for MRTP and FERA companies and for projects involving of more than Rs. 500 million. See for details, Text of Planning Commission's note on 'New Industrial Policy' in *Economic Times* (New Delhi), 6 May 1987 p. 8.

6. For a comprehensive discussion on India's industrial policy and developments since 1947, see Marathe, S.S., *Regulation and Development—India's Policy Experience of Controls over Industry* (New Delhi : Sagar Publications, 1986).

7. Jagdish Bhagwati and Padma Desai, *Indian Planning for Industralisaition : Industralisation and Trade Policies Since 1951* (London and New York : Oxford University Press, 1970), p. 494.

8. K. Kojima, "The Allocation of Japanese Direct Foreign Investment and Evolution in Asia", in *Hitotsubashi Journal of Economics* (Tokyo), Vol. 26, No. 2, December 1985, pp. 113-116.

9. Also a beginning has already been made in exports. Recently, a consignment of cars in semi-knocked down condition was despatched to Bangladesh and an order for the vans from Nepal was supplied. Negotiations are under-way with many East European and West Asian countries. Maruti vehicles were recently displayed in a trade fair at Hungary where it aroused considerable interest. Earlier the Hungarian purchasing agency Mogurt had indicated a possibility of purchasing up to 5000 cars a year. Maruti cars will soon be at display in several other countries also.

10. Shoji Ito, "Technology Transfer from Japanese firms to India", *Economic and Political Weekly, Special Number*, Vol. XX, Nos. 45, 46 and 47 (Bombay), 1985, p. 2033.

11. *Ibid.*, pp. 2035-2042.

12. Takumi Hosaki, "Liberalisation—a Welcome Step", in *Economic Times* (New Delhi), April 29, 1987, p. 11.

13. Shinsuke Horiuchi, "Transfer of Technology", in *Japan Economic Report* (New Delhi), Spring 1985, pp. 10-11. See also Shoji Ito, *op. cit.*, 1.

14. There has been considerable debate on problems of indigenisation in a major Indo-Japanese industrial collaboration. Japanese, however, are doubtful about India's capability to indigenise at the required pace owing to India's domestic constraints. For a discussion on this subject, see T. Hamaguchi, "Prospects for Self-Reliance and Indigenisation in Automobiic Industry—Case of Maruti-Suzuki Project", in *Economic and Political Weekly*, Vol. XX, No. 35, August 1985, pp. M-115-122.

15. "Process and Problems of Technology Transfer between Japanese and Indian Firms", The Japan Committee, The India-Japan Study Committee (Tokyo), January 1987, p. 1.

16. "A Review of Specific Aspects of Cooperation in Trade and Technology between India and Japan", The India Committee, The India-Japan Study Committee, (New Delhi), March 1987, p. 61.

17. *Ibid.*, p. 68.

18. Saburo Okita, "Japan-India Relations for the Twenty-first Century", a paper presented at the Indo-Japan Seminar, (New Delhi), 10-12 March 1986.

19. Japan *Economic Report*, *op. cit.*, p. 7.

20. "Emergency Economic Measures", in *News from Japan*, Embassy of Japan (New Delhi), Press Release No. 12, May 29, 1987.

21. See a list of the manufactures though nominal in 1987, has good potential for export to Japan, "A Review of Specific Aspects of Cooperation in Trade and Technology between India and Japan", *op. cit.*, p. 62.

SELECTED BIBLIOGRAPHY

Reports and Documents

Brook, E.M., Grilli, E.R. and Waelbrook, etc., *Commodity Price Stabilization and the Developing Countries—The Problem of Choice* (World Bank Staff Working Paper No. 262), (Washington D.C.), 1977.

Chenery, H.B. and Keasing, D.B., *The Changing Composition of Developing Countries Exports* (World Bank Staff Working Paper No. 314), (Washington D.C.), 1979.

Cotton Textile Export Promotion Council, *Preliminary Memorandum on the Long Term Strategy and Plan for Export of Cotton Textiles During 1980s* (Bombay), 1980.

Economic Planning Agency (formerly, Economic Stabilisation Board, or Economic Counsel Board), Japanese Government, *Economic Survey of Japan* (Tokyo), from various issues of 1950 to 1975.

Engineering Export Promotion Council, *Findings of the Market Survey Team to Japan* (Calcutta), 1978.

Federation of Indian Chambers of Commerce and Industry, *Report on Business Cooperation Committee of India and Japan* (New Delhi), from various issues of 1968 to 1982.

Federation of Indian Export Organisations, '*100% Export-Oriented units*', (New Delhi), February 1987.

India Committee, *The India-Japan Study Committee*, (New Delhi), A Review of Specific Aspects of Cooperation in Trade and Technology between India and Japan', 1987.

Indian Institute of Foreign Trade, *Conclusions and Recommendations of a Seminar on Indian Cotton Textile Industry* (New Delhi), 1967.

—————————, *Handtools and Small Tools* (Commodity Series No. 22), (New Delhi), 1969.

—————————, *India's Export Potential of Marine Products* (Vols. I-V), (New Delhi), 1970.

—————————, *A Study of Market Opportunities for Selected Engineering Goods in Japan* (New Delhi), 1970.

—————————, *Seminar on Textiles—Conclusions and Recommendations*, (New Delhi), 1970.

International Trade Centre, UNCTAD/GATT, *Shrimps* (Geneva), 1983.

Japan Chambers of Commerce and Industry, *Economic Picture of Japan* (Tokyo), from various issues of 1960 to 1982.

—————————, *Japanese Agenda for the 11th Joint Meeting of Japan-India Business Cooperation Committee* (Tokyo), 1978.

Japan Committee, *The India-Japan Study Committee*, (Tokyo), 'Process and Problems of Technology Transfer between Japanese and Indian Firms', January 1987.

Japan External Trade Organization, Ministry of International Trade and Industry, Japanese Government, *Access to Japan's Import Market—Frozen Shrimp* (Tokyo), 1980.

Joseph, A., *Indo-Japan Collaboration in Third Countries*, a paper presented to the India-Japan Study Committee, Planning Commission, Government of India (New Delhi), 1980.

—————, *A Comparative Study of Japanese Foreign Investments in South East Asia and India*, a paper prepared for the International Economic Division, Planning Commission, Government of India (New Delhi), 1981.

———————, *Economic Perspectives of India and Japan*, a paper *prepared for the India-Japan Study Committee*, Planning Commission, Government of India (New Delhi), 1981.

Katano, H., Saito, M. and Ogawa, B., *Technology Transfer in Japanese Joint Venture in Thailand—A Case Study of Textile Industry*, a paper presented to the Economic Cooperation *Center for Asian and Pacific Region* (Bangkok), 1976.

Kojima, K., *Harmonization of Japanese and Australian Economic Policies* (Japan Economic Research Centre Paper No. 27), (Tokyo), 1975.

Marine Products Export Development Authority, *A Note Prepared for the India-Japan Business Cooperation Meeting in New Delhi, 1980*, (Cochin), 1980.

Ministry of Agriculture and Irrigation, Government of India, *Report of the National Commission on Agriculture* (Vol. VIII), (New Delhi), 1976.

Ministry of Commerce, Government of India, *Report of the Committee on Import-Export Policies and Procedures* (Alexander Committee Report) (New Delhi), 1978.

—————————————, *Report of the Committee on Trade Policies* (Abid Hussain Committee Report (New Delhi), 1984.

Ministry of Foreign Trade, Government of India, *Report of the Working Group on Cotton Textiles* (New Delhi), 1973.

Ministry of Industry, Government of India, *Guidelines for Industries* (New Delhi), 1982.

Ministry of Science and Technology, Government of India, *Technology in Indian Handtools Industry* (Draft) (New Delhi), 1985.

National Council of Applied Economic Research, *System Study for Iron Ore Exports* (New Delhi), 1969.

Reserve Bank of India, *Foreign Collaboration in Indian Industry-Fourth Survey Report* (Bombay), 1985.

Trade Development Authority of India, *Product Note on Hand. Small and Cutting Tools* (New Delhi), 1978.

—————————————, *Study on Japan* (New Delhi), 1978.

Tran Van Tho, Industrial *Growth of the Japanese Cotton Spinn-*

ing Industry, a thesis submitted to Hitotsubashi University, (Tokyo), 1975.

United NationsConference on Trade and Development, *Operation and Effects on the Generalised System on Preferences* (Geneva), various issues.

World Bank, *World Development Report* (Washington D.C.), from various issues of 1978 to 1985.

Statistical References

Bank of Japan, *Price Indices Annual, 1975* (Tokyo), 1975.

Bureau of Statistics, Office of the Prime Minister, Japanese Government, *Japan Statistical Yearbook* (Tokyo), from various issues of 1951 to 1984.

Bureau of Mines, Ministry of Steel and Mines (formerly Ministry of Steel, Mines and Fuel), Government of India, *Indian Mineral Yearbook* (Nagpur), from various issues of 1958 to 1984.

Central Statistical Organisation, Ministry of Planning (formerly, under Ministry of Commerce and Industry, or Department of Statistics), Government of India, *Annual Survey of Industries* (formerly, *Census of Indian Manufactures*), (Calcutta), from various issues of 1951 to 1981.

Department of Commercial Intelligence and Statistics, Government of India, *Monthly Statistics of Foreign Trade of India* (Calcutta), from various March issues of 1957 to 1982.

Economic Planning Board, Korean Government, *Economic Statistics Yearbook* (Seoul), from various issues of 1960 to 1974.

Engineering Export Promotion Council, *Handbook of Export Statistics* (Calcutta), from various issues of 1975 to 1985.

International Cotton Advisory Committee, *Cotton-World Statistics* (Washington D.C.), from various issues of 1951 to 1984.

Japan External Trade Organization, Ministry of International Trade and Industry, Japanese Government, *White Paper on International Trade* (formerly, *Foreign Trade of Japan*), (Tokyo), from various issues of 1962 to 1983.

Ministry of International Trade and Industry, Japanese Government, *Census of Manufactures—Report by Industries* (Tokyo), from various issues of 1966 to 1975.

United Nations, *Commodity Trade Statistics* (New York), from various issues of 1951 to 1983.

———————, *Yearbook of International Trade* (New York), from various issues of 1951 to 1985.

———————, *Growth of the World Industries* (formerly, *Yearbook of Industrial Statistics*), (New York), from various issues of 1951 to 1985.

World Bank, *World Tables* (Baltimore and London : The Johns Hopkins University Press), from various issues of 1976, 1980 and 1983.

Books

Bhagwati, J.N., *Trade Balance of Payments Growth* (Amsterdam: North Holland), 1971.

Bhagwati, J.N., Desai, P. and Panchamukhi, V.R., *India's Industrialisation and Trade Policies* (Paris: Organisation for Economic Cooperation and Development), 1970.

Bhagwati, J.N. and Srinivasan, T.N., *Foreign Trade Regimes and Economic Development/India*, (New Delhi: Macmillan), 1975.

Chakravarthy, S., *Reflection on the Growth Process in the Indian Economy* (Hyderabad: Administrative Staff College of India), 1974.

Cline R. William, *'Export of Manufactures from Developing Countries'*, (Washington D.C. Brooking Institutions), 1984.

Cohen, J.B., *Japan's Economy in War and Reconstruction* (London: University of Minnesota Press), 1949.

Desai, P., *Import Substitution in the Indian Economy 1951-63* (Delhi: Hindustan Publishing Co.), 1972

Frank, I., *The Japanese Economy in International Perspective* (Baltimore: Johns Hopkins University Press), 1975.

Findlay, R., *Trade and Specialisation* (London: Cox and Wyman), 1971.

Grubel, H.B. and Lloyd, P.J., *Intra-Industry Trade—The Theory and Measurement of International Trade in Differential Products* (London: Macmillan), 1975.

Halder, A., *India's Export Pattern—Analysis on Potential Diversification* (Calcutta: Minerva), 1976.

Holleman, L., *Japan's Dependence on the World Economy—The Approach Toward Economic Liberalisation* (Princeton: Princeton University Press), 1967.

Johnson, H.G., (ed.), *Trade Strategy for Rich and Poor Nations* (London: George Allen and Unwin), 1971.

Kahn, H, and Pepper, T., *The Japanese Challenge—The Success and Failures of Economic Success* (London: Harper and Row), 1978.

Ken, B., *The Structure and Operation of the Japanese Economy* (Sidney: John Wiley), 1970.

Kravis, I.B. and Lipsey, H.E., *Price Competitiveness in World Trade* (New York: National Bureau of Economic Research), 1971.

Kreinin, M.E., *International Economics—A Policy Approach* (New York: Harcourt Brau Jovanovich Inc.), 1979.

Kruegar, A.O., *The Benefits and Costs of Import Substitution in India—A Microeconomic Study* (New Delhi: United States Agency for International Trade and Development) (Mimeographed), 1970.

Kunio, Y., *Japanese Economic Development* (Tokyo: Oxford University Press), 1979.

Lakdawala, D.T., Bhagwati, J., and Bharadwaj, R. (eds.), *Readings in the Theory of International Trade and Commercial Policy* (Bombay: Lalwani Publishing House), 1975.

Little, I., Scitovsky, T. and Scott, M., *Industry and Trade in Some Developing Countries—A Comparative Study* (London: Oxford University Press), 1970.

Lloyd Reynolds, *Economic Growth in Third World Countries 1850-1980*, (New Haven : Yale University Press) 1985.

Maizels, A., *Exports and Economic Growth of Developing Countries* (London: Cambridge University Press), 1968.

Marathe S.S., *Regulation ar d Development-India's Policy Experience of Controls over Industry* (New Delhi : Sage Publications) 1986.

Mehta, S.D., *The Indian Cotton Textile Industry—An Economic Analysis* (Bombay: The Textile Association, India), 1953.

Michaely, M., *Concentration in International Trade* (Amsterdam: North-Holland Publishing Co.), 1962.

Minami, R., *The Turning Point in Economic Development: Japan's Experience* (Tokyo: Kinokuniya), 1973.

Murray, T., *Trade Preferences for Developing Countries* (London: Macmillan), 1977.

Nayyar, D., *India's Exports and Export Policies in the 1960s* (London: Cambridge University Press), 1976.

Okita, S., *Japan in the World Economy* (Tokyo: The Japan Foundation), 1975.

————, *Developing Economics and the Japanese Experience* (New Delhi: Indian Council for Cultural Relations), 1979.

Patrick, H. and Rosovsky, H. (eds.), *Asia's New Giant* (Washington D.C.: The Brookings Institution), 1976.

Panchamukhi, V.R., *Trade Policies of India* (Delhi: Concept Publishing House), 1978.

Patrick, H. (ed.), *Japanese Industrialisation and Its Social Consequences* (Berkeley: University of California Press), 1976.

Sekiguchi, S., *Japanese Direct Foreign Investment* (Montelair: Osun and Co. Publishers), 1979.

Shinohara, M., *Structural Changes in Japan's Economic Development* (Tokyo: Kinokuniya), 1970.

Singh, M., *India's Export Trends* (Oxford: Clarendon Press), 1964.

Sung, J.K., *Stages of Industrial Development of Asia* (Philadelphia: University of Pennsylvania), 1966.

Uri, P. (ed), *Trade and Investment Policies for the Seventies New Challenges for the Atlantic Area and Japan* (New York: Praeger Publishers), 1971.

Verghese, S.K., *India's Foreign Trade—Organisational and Financial Aspects* (New Delhi: Allied Publishers), 1964.

Wolf, M., *India's Exports* (Washington D.C.: The World Bank), 1982.

Articles

Akamatsu, K., 'A Historical Pattern of Economic Growth', *The Developing Economics* (Tokyo), Preliminary Issue No. 1, March-August 1962.

Arora, D.S., 'Export Opportunities for Handtools and Cutting Tools', *Foreign Trade Review* (New Delhi), Vol. 16, No. 4, January-March 1982.

Bagchi, A., 'Export-led Growth and Import Substituting Industrialisation', *Economic and Political Weekly* (Bombay), Vol. 12, Nos. 6, 7 and 8, February 1977.

Chenery, H.B., 'Comparative Advantage and Development Policy', *American Economic Review* (Wisconsin), Vol. 51, No. 1, March 1961.

Chenery, H.B., and Bruno, M., 'Transitional Growth and World Industrialisation', in B. Chlin (ed.), *The International Allocation of Economic Activity* (London: Macmillan), 1977.

Chidambaram, K., 'Marine Products Export Prospects', *Foreign Trade Review* (New Delhi), Vol. 9, No. 1, April-June 1974.

Chopra, V.S., 'Pattern of India's Exports to Japan', *All India Congress Committee Economic Review* (New Delhi), No. 7, October 1968.

Chowgule, V.D., 'Japanese Market for Iron Ore', *Commerce* (Bombay), No. 23, No. 316, December 1971.

Da Costa, G.C., and Sheth, R.N., 'External and Domestic Constraints on Indian Exports—An Econometric Study', in J.C. Sandesara (ed.), *Indian Economy—Performance and Prospects* (Bombay: University of Bombay), 1974.

Eastern Economist, 'Attracting Japanese Investments' (New Delhi), Vol. 69, No. 19, November 1977.

Economist, 'Tomorrow's Leaders—A Survey of Japanese Technology' (London), 10-25 June 1982.

Engineering Export Promotion Council, 'Engineering Goods' in Hindustan Chamber of Commerce (ed), *Proceedings of a Seminar on Export Promotion* (Madras), 1968.

Finger, J.M., 'A New View of the Product Cycle Theory', *Review of World Economies* (Kiel), Vol. 3, No. 1, 1975.

Guha, A., 'India's Foreign Economic Policy—A Theoretical Framework', *International Studies* (Bombay), Vol. 9, No. 4, April 1968.

Gulati, I.S., 'Export Promotion Schemes', *The Developing Economies* (Tokyo), Vol. 5, 1967.

Hamaguchi T., 'Prospects for Self-Reliance and Indigenisation' in Automobile Industry-Case of Maruti-Suzuki Project, *Economic and Political Weekly*, Vol. XX, No. 35, August 1985.

Hesari, B.R., 'Import Intensity of Consumption in India', *Indian Economic Review* (New Delhi), Vol. 2, No. 2, October 1967.

Hicks, J.R., 'Technology and the Theory of International Trade', in R. Vernon (ed.), *The Technology Factors in International Trade* (New York: National Bureau of Economic Research), 1970.

Horiuchi Shinsuke, "*Transfer of Technology*" Japan Economic Report, Embassy of Japan, New Delhi, Spring 1985.

Hosaki Takumi, "*Liberalisation—A Welcome Step*", Economic Times, New Delhi, April 29, 1987.

Ito Shoji, *Technology Transfer from Japanese firms to India*", Economic and Political Weekly, Special Number, Vol. XX, Nos. 45, 46 and 47 (Bombay), 1985.

Joshi, V., 'India's Export Incentive System', in United Nations Industrial Development Organization (ed.), *Industry and Development No. 2* (New York: United Nations), 1978.

Kelkar, V.L., 'Evaluation of India's Trade Policies', *Economic and Political Weekly* (Bombay), Vol. 12, No. 25, June 1977.

Kojima K., "*The Allocation of Japanese Direct Foreign Investment and Evolution in Asia*", Hitotsubashi Journal of Economics, Tokyo, Vol. 26 No. 2, December 1985.

Lal, D., 'Foreign Exchange Constraint on Economic Development: A Geometric Note', *Indian Economic Journal* (Bombay), Vol. 18, No. 1, July-September 1970.

Lal, D., 'Industry and Trade', in R. Thaper (ed.), *Indian Economic Thinking—A Seminar Compilation* (New Delhi: The Allied Publishers), 1979.

Lee, C H., 'United States and Japanese Direct Investment in Korea—A Comparative Study', *Hitotsubashi Journal of Economics* (Tokyo), Vol. 20, No. 2, February 19 0.

Lewis, W.A., 'Exports and Economic Growth', *Indian Cotton Mill's Federation Journal* (Bombay), Vol. 10, No. 6, October 1976.

MacDougall, G.D.A., 'India's Balance of Payments', in P.N. Rosenstein-Rodan (ed.), *Pricing and Fiscal Policies* (London: George Allen and Unwin), 1964.

Mellos, J.W., and Lele, U., 'The Interaction of Growth Strategy, Agriculture and Foreign Trade—The Case of India', in G.S. Tolley and P.A. Zadrozny (eds.), *Trade, Agriculture and Development* (Cambridge: Ballinger), 1975.

Mitra, P.K., 'Import Substitution and Export Promotion as Means of Industrialisation', *Economic Internationale* (Geneva), Vol. 27, Nos. 3 and 4, August-November 1974.

Najundaiya, B., and Raipuria, K.M., 'Export for Survival—Focus on New Strategy through 2000 A.D.', *Foreign Trade Review* (New Delhi), Vol. 11, No. 2, July-September 1976.

Nayyar, D., 'An Analysis of the Stagnation in India's Cotton Textile Exports during Sixties', *Oxford Bulletin of Economics and Statistics* (Oxford), Vol. 55, No. 1, February 1973.

Okita Saburo, "*Japan-India Relations for the Twenty-first Century*", a paper presented at the Indo-Japan Seminar, India International Centre, New Delhi, March 1916.

————, 'Perspective of Indo-Japanese Relations', *Commerce* (Bombay), Vol. 123, No. 3161, December, 1971.

————, 'Linkage in Industrialisation—A Survey of Selected Developing Countries in Asia', *Journal of Development Planning* (New York), No. 8, 1975.

Panchamukhi, V.R., 'A Quantitative Analysis of Trade Policies in India', in J.C. Sandesara (ed.), *Indian Economy—Performance and Prospects* (Bombay : University of Bombay), 1974.

Shah, K.D., 'Cotton Textile Industry,' in Hindustan Chamber of Commerce (ed.), *Proceeding of the Seminar on Export Promotion* (Madras), 1968.

Singh, M., 'International Trade and Payments—A Trend Report', in Indian Council of Social Science Research, *A Survey of Research in Economics* (New Delhi : Indian Council of Social Science Research), 1975.

Srinivasan, T.N., 'The Foreign Trade Sector in Planning Models', in C.R. Blitzer and L. Taylor (eds.), *Economy-wide Models and Development Planning* (London : Oxford University Press), 1975.

Vernon, R., 'International Investment and International Trade in the Product Cycle', *Quarterly Journal of Economics* (Massachusetts), Vol. 29, No. 2, May 1966.

Vishwanath, S., 'Major Commodities in India's Exports—Cotton Textiies', *Commerce* (Bombay), Vol. 123, No. 3161, Demember 1971.

Yamazawa, I., 'Intensity Analysis of World Trade Flow', *Hitotsubashi Journal of Economics* (Tokyo), Vol. 12, No. 2, February 1972.

————————, 'Industrial Growth and Foreign Trade', *Hitotsubashi Journal of Economics* (Tokyo), Vol. 12, No. 2, February 1972.

————————, 'Trade Policy and Change in Japan's Trade Structure with Special Reference to Labour-Intensive Manufactures', '*The Developing Economies* (Tokyo), Vol. 13, No. 4, December 1975.

INDEX

Abid Hussain Committee 190
Africa 73
Akamatsu, K. 8, 84, 87, 90, 119f, 120f, 122f
Alexander Committee 190
Annual Survey of Industries 11
Ashok Mehta Committee 201f
Asahi Shinbun 201f
Australia 47, 49, 50-1, 53, 60, 159, 160, 162
auto-ancillary 219
automobile industry 230f

Bailadila 46-7
Balassa, B. 26f
balance of payments 2, 13-4, 16, 20, 24, 136, 214, 228
Belikera 48
Bellery Hospet 48
Bhagwati, J. 131
Bhagwati, J. and Desai, P. 149f, 211, 229f
Bharadwaj, R. 148f
Borkar, D. 188, 204f
Brook, E.M. 25f
Brazil 50-1, 53, 159-60
business cycle 16, 52
Business standard 229
Burma 54

Cabinet Committee on Exports 212
Capital Cost 188-9, 212
—goods 6, 20, 22, 24, 85-6, 90
—intensity 128-9
cash assistance 22, 128-9, 163
—compensatory support 190, 192, 212
—subsides 129, 133
catching up 78, 80, 86, 88
Centrally Planned Economies 73, 77
Chenery H.B 12f, 119f
China 47, 56, 81-2, 136, 162, 168-9, 194, 197
Chidambaram, K. 66f, 68f, 177
Chowgule, V.D. 65f, 200f
Cline, William R. 12f
commercial borrowings 23
commercial loands 2
Comparative advantage 5-6, 8, 16, 18, 20, 24, 28, 105, 110, 199, 206, 208
comparative efficiency 206
—cost 188-9, 212
—benefit 211

—effectiveness 175, 184
cost of production 87, 100, 132, 213
—structure 97, 100, 102, 173
cotton fabrics 70, 72-3, 80, 84, 90, 91, 97, 100, 102, 137, 140, 141, 164, 167-9, 171, 191, 208
Cotton Stock Control Order 133, 175, 180, 187, 191, 195-6, 199, 208
Cotton Textile Industry 70-74, 78-80, 131-3, 164-9, 181, 196
CSO 117, 203f

DCSSI 75, 201f
debt servicing 1, 2, 21, 23
devaluation of rupee 52, 72, 131
developing coutries 6, 11-2, 14, 16, 18-9, 25, 53, 69, 198
developed countries 12
Desai, P. 131, 211
DGCIS 202f-3f
DGTD 74-5
diminishing return to scale 8
diversification of export 19, 25, 62, 69
DIY Market 82, 87
domestic consumption 57
domestic tariff area 23
domestic production 85
Drawback Directorate 130
Dungan 48, 85, 129
duty drawbacks 22, 128-9, 132-4, 144, 190, 218

economies of scale 5, 8, 25, 209
economic fluctuations 144
—growth 6, 13 4, 20, 25
—Planning Agency 200f
—and Political Weekly 230f
—Survey of Japan 155
—Times 12f, 200f
—Survey of Japan 155
efficiency capital 9, 100, 189
—material 9-10, 100, 102, 105, 110, 179, 181, 186
—wages 9-10, 100, 102, 110, 112, 186
Emergency Economic Measures2 25 230f
Empowered Committee on Export 212
engineering export 22, 76
—Industry 81
—Export Promotion Council of India 11, 75, 118-9, 134, 150, 202f, 204f-5f
energy conservation 224
engine of growth 13
energy serving techniques 154
ESCAP countries 220
—Credit Guarantee Corporation 130
—Credit Gurantee and Insurance facilities 130
export concentration 69
Export expansion stage 8-9, 85-6, 91
—growth 10
—Import Bank of Japan 226
—Import policies 23
—incentive 22, 129
export policy 128, 142
—Policy Resolution 21-2, 178
—production 22, 199, 212
—promotion 2, 5, 8, 132
—oriented 145, 170, 191-2, 212-13, 218, 220
—output ratio 50, 72, 76, 136
Exporting Units 218
External debts 2

FAO 11, 17-8, 60, 65f-6f
factor accumulation 14
FERA 217
FICCI 68f, 205f
Financial Express 200f, 202f
Finger, J.M. 245
fiscal concessions 129, 165
Five Year Plan 6, 20
Five year tax holiday 145
foreign assistance 1, 2, 21

foreign capital inducement law 145
—exchange 6, 77, 136, 210, 213-4, 228
—exchange constraints 20
—collaborations 61, 163, 210
—exchange reserve 1-2, 20 53, 214
—investment 135, 144, 155, 213-4, 215-6
—trade 24
—technology 53, 77, 130, 135-6, 214-5
Fourth Five Year Plan 21, 147f
forged handtools 172, 193
free trade 13, 225
—Trade Zones 22-3, 191-2, 212, 218, 202, 204f, 212, 218, 220

Gandhi, J.C. 65f
Ganko keitai growth 8-9, 70, 84-97, 85, 87, 90-1, 97
GATT 18, 68f, 135, 142, 150f, 197
GDP growth 2, 23, 52
gems and jewellery 22
Grilli, E.R. 26f
GSP 136-42, 144, 189, 194-98, 208
Green Cards 218

Haldia 47-8
Hamaguchi, T. 230f
Handbook of Export Statistics 11
Handtool Industry 11, 74-78, 81-4, 88, 169-75, 184-9, 192-3, 208
Handtool manufacturing 185, 187
Heavy and Chemical Industry 79
Hindustan Chambers of Commerce 132, 149f
Hong Kong 80
Horiuchi, Shinsuke 230f
horizontal and vertical diversification 18-9
horizontal trade 20, 62
Hosaki, Takumi 230f
Hunsberger W. 119f

IIFT 67f, 117f, 119f
income elasticities 127
import entitlement scheme 127, 131, 133-4
Import-Export Policy 190
—licences 131
—liberalisation 57, 80, 90
—policy 131
—stage85
—substitution 8-9, 85-7, 90-1
—replenishment 22, 75, 128-9, 130-3. 142, 163, 190
India's balance of trade 157
Indian Bureau of Mines 11
Indian Investment Centre 202, 204f 205f
—Cotton Mills Federation 131, 202
India's foreign trade 28
—handtool industries 169
India-Japan Study Committee 221-2, 230f
Indian Textile Bulletin 11, 117f, 203f
Indonesia 60, 162
indigenisation 222
industrial collaboration 146, 207-8, 216, 218-9, 226
Industrial Policy Statement 2, 22, 127, 129, 191
industrial structure 3, 137
Industries (Development & Regulation) Act 191
inflationary pressures 16
infrastructure 18, 53, 61f, 209, 216
International Cotton Advisory Committee 117f, 203f
International Commodity Agreements 18
International division of labour 6, 155, 198, 224
—Monetary Fund 16, 23, 25f, 148f
—Price Reimbursement Scheme 213
International trade 13, 21
intensity of trade 29
Investment and technology transfer 7
Iron and Steel Industry 22, 44, 52

iron-ore 11, 34, 44-53, 62, 157, 161, 169
Ito, Shoji 220, 230f

Japan's Advisory Committee for External Economic Issues 197
Japan's economic growth 6
Japan Economic Research Centre 150f
Japan Economic Journal 200f
Japan Economic Report 230f
Japan's direct investment 145
—Economic Planning Agency 223
—foreign trade 3, 28-9
—import structure 69
—import liberalisation 60, 70, 156
———policy 57
—marine products 163
—self-sufficiency ratio 154
—steel mills 160, 207
—trade policies 135, 142, 197, 228
—Tariff Schedules 135
Japanese overseas investments 146
Japanese technology transfer and investment 11-2, 206, 216, 224
TETRO 57, 59, 66f, 118f, 150f-51f, 164, 200f, 219-23
Jha, P. 201
Johnson, H.G. 18f
Joint venture 146, 214
Josh, N. 201f-2f

Kakatkar, B, 201f
Karwar 48
Kathuria, S. and Taneja N. 202f
Kenya 73
Keidanren 225
Kerala 56
Keesing, B. 26f, 119f, 122f, 200f
Kennedy Round Reductions 135, 136
———round negotiations 138, 140, 151f
Khanna, K. 200f
Kiriburu 48
knowledge-intensive technology 3
Kojima, K. 152f 215, 229f
Krause, L.B. and Sekiguchi 5, 150
Kudremukh 161, 200f

labour-intensive export orientation policies 25
———industries 18, 146
———industrialization 25
———products 136, 173, 175
labour productivity 10, 105, 110, 112, 228
—intensive sector 19
Lee, C.H. 145, 153f
light manufactures 7, 79
Llyod, Reynolds 27f
Lok Sabha Estimate Committee 148f-9f
locomotive industry 6, 11
Long Term Outlook Committee 223

Madras Port 48
Maharashtra 57
Malaysia 47-8, 60, 160
Mangekar, S. 200f
manufactured exports 5, 12, 19-20, 24
manufacturing sector 7
Marathe, S.S. 229f
Marine Product Export Promotion Council 59-60, 163-4
Maruti Udyog 219 230f
material input-cost 9-10, 70
Mellos, J.W. and Lele 128, 148f
Mexico 56, 60
MFN 139-40, 142, 194-5
millsecor 70-1
mineral resource 50-1
Ministry of International Trade and Industry 11, 137, 150f-51f
Ministry of Commerce, Govt. of India 149f 204f
Ministry of Science and Technology, Govt. of India 202f
—of Steel and Mines 11
MMTC 51-2, 65f, 160-1, 207

Mormugao 48, 160
MRTP 212
multi-national corporations 146
Myrdal, G. 13, 25

National Commission on Agriculture 59
National Textile Corporation 165
—Register of Foreign Collaboration 172
natural resourses 19
Nayyar, D. 63f-4, 129, 131, 148f, 149f, 229
NCAER 50, 51, 63f-5f
NIDC 71
Nigeria 73
newly industrialised countries 8, 156, 157, 208
non-engineering collaboration 227
non-manufactures 5, 14, 16, 18, 28, 29, 34, 41, 44, 61, 62, 164, 199
non-manufactured exports 11, 21, 28, 164
North-South economic-coperation 137-8

ODA 198, 226
OECD 10, 52, 65, 152f, 154, 197
OECF 226
OGL 22, 190, 200f
Ohkawa K. 152
Oil crisis 10, 154, 157, 158
Okita, S. 12f, 150f, 230f
One stop service 145
output capital ratio 10, 100
output-input ratio 9-10, 100, 102, 105, 181, 208, 209

Pakistan 73
Panchamukhi V.R. 126, 142, 144, 147f, 153f
Patil, R.H. 149f
Patrick H. and Rosovsky H. 151f
patent rights 145
Paradip 47, 48
Peck, M. and Tamura, S. 152f
Peru 47
Philippines 48, 197
Planning Commission 20, 147, 229f
pollution problem 197
Prebisch, R. 13
price elasticity 16
price fluctuations 164
productivity differentials 11
production efficiency 8-9, 10, 97, 226
production expansion 8-9
production technology 8
powerlooms and handtools 70, 165
Pursell, G. 153f

R and D. 22, 210, 223
Radha Krishnan, C 201f
Rao, H. 201f
raw cotton 34, 44, 71, 133, 157
raw materials 9, 19, 44, 157, 209, 212-13, 216
re-import stage 8, 9, 24, 85, 86, 91, 97, 105, 146
Report by the National Commission on Agriculture 59. 66f
REP Licences 210
Resource Processing Industries 155, 158
royalties 214, 221
Rumania 51, 159, 161

Second Five Year Plan 1, 3, 20, 127 147f
Second World War 13, 18, 171
Sekiguchi, S. 153f
self-reliance 21
SEEPZ 218
Seventh Five Year Plan 2, 23
Shah, K.D. 149f
shrimps 11, 34, 45, 53-62, 157, 161-64, 199, 207
SITC 10, 136
small scale industry 170, 212
small scale sector 22, 75, 165, 193
Sondhi Committee 27f

South-east Asian countries 7
South Korea 10, 24, 29, 38, 41, 61, 69, 78, 80, 81, 91, 100, 102, 105, 110-12, 115, 123f-4, 127, 153, 195, 144-45, 156, 173, 196, 208, 242
Structural Adjustment for the promotion of International Harmony 198
structural change 18, 68, 78, 137, 154-5, 224
Singer, H.W. 13
Singapore 173
SISI 75
Sri Lanka 54, 60, 73
Suzuki 219, 230f
Sweden 81, 173
Switzerland 81
Singh, M.1 17f

Taiwan 24, 38, 41, 61, 69, 78, 80, 81, 156, 162, 197, 208, 220
Technical Development Fund 22
technology intensive sector 224
technical know-how 59
technical fee 214
technology transfer 193, 208-9, 213-5, 222, 228
terms of trade 14, 18
Textile Policy 165
Thailand 56, 162
Tho, Tran Van 123f
Third Five Year Plan 20, 128, 147f
Times of India 201f-4f
Tokyo round 189, 194-5
transitional growth 8
TDA 118f, 205f

U.K. 3, 38, 70-3, 78, 81, 155, 167, 220, 228
U.N. 62f-3f, 116f, 118f, 124f, 153f, 200f, 202f
Unemployment problem 16
UNCTAD 18, 68f, 135-6, 137-8, 140, 142, 153f, 205f
UNIDO 52
UNESC 18
U.S.A. 3, 10, 38, 54, 73, 78, 81, 91-7, 100-5, 110-2, 115, 124f, 136, 151f, 153f, 162-7, 173, 223
U.S.S.R. 3, 167

value added 21, 52, 71
Varma, M.L. 67f
Verghese, S.K. 149f
Vernon, R. 120f
vertical diversification 18
vertical specialization 120
Visakapatnam 48, 49
Vizagport 160

Waelbroock, J. 25f
wages 9-10, 18, 110, 165, 173, 177, 185
wage cost 10
West Germany 78, 155, 173, 228
Westphal, L. 153f
White Paper on International Trade 11
Wolf, M. 26r, 149f, 201f
World Bank 2, 23, 153f
World Bank Report 1-2
World economy 7, 18, 62, 151f, 223
World trade 2
World War II 10, 216

Yamazawa I. 26f, 28, 62f, 87, 121f-22f, 135
Yearbook of fishery statistics 11
Yen app reciation 12, 151f, 197-8
Yugoslavia 159
Zanzibar 73